GET REAL:

ON EVANGELISM IN THE LATE MODERN WORLD

Edward Rommen

Get Real: On Evangelism in the Late Modern World

Copyright 2010 By Edward Rommen

Published by William Carey Library
1605 E. Elizabeth Street
Pasadena, CA 91104 | www.missionbooks.org

Naomi Bradley McSwain, editorial manager
Johanna Deming and Rose Lee-Norman, assistant editors
Hugh Pindur, graphic design

William Carey Library is a ministry of the
U.S. Center for World Mission
www.uscwm.org

PRINTED IN THE UNITED STATES

14 13 12 11 10 5 4 3 2 1 BP   2010500BP

Library of Congress Cataloging-in-Publication Data

Rommen, Edward, 1947-
  Get real : on evangelism in the late modern world / Edward Rommen.
     p. cm.
  Includes bibliographical references.
  ISBN 978-0-87808-463-0
  1. Missions. I. Title.
  BV2061.3.R66 2009
  266.001--dc22
                              2009036492

GET REAL:

ON EVANGELISM IN THE LATE MODERN WORLD

Edward Rommen

WILLIAM CAREY
LIBRARY

Acknowledgements

Writing a book is never the work of one person and I would like to acknowledge a number of the people who have made the project possible. My wife, Ainee, patiently encouraged me throughout the course of writing. My son, Timothy Rommen, read every line of my manuscript and provided invaluable and, above all, honest critique. My son-in-law, Bryan Hickman, also read the manuscript and provided valuable feedback. Students at Duke Divinity School worked through these ideas in a seminar, challenging, correcting, and encouraging. The Academic Dean of Duke Divinity School, Laceye Warner, took the time to read the manuscript and write a foreword. Carole Baker, research associate at Duke, proofread and edited the manuscript. My friends at William Carey Library, Johanna Deming and Naomi Bradley McSwain, patiently guided me through the process of publishing the book. Without their help this project would never have been finished. So I thank them all for their encouragement and abiding friendship.

CONTENTS

Foreword

In this ground-breaking book, Fr. Edward Rommen, Ph.D., wisely connects the richness of the Gospel and its embodiments in Christian tradition to contemporary Christianity with an able assessment of opportunities and challenges confronted within the current landscape of late modernity. The study and practice of evangelism, particularly related to serious theological reflection, can be filled with difficult polemics often limited to shallow exchanges and resulting in less than helpful guides. Additionally, a significant number of scholarly projects addressing evangelism ultimately are unable to offer any proposal or guidance for its practice. However, the readers of this latest book from Fr. Rommen will find another richly textured study, building on previous works, drawing from biblical and theological foundations for the understanding and practice of evangelism.

The contemporary climate of mainline denominational decline and general malaise in North America clamors for techniques to reverse these trends, preferably swiftly and simply. While an increasing number of practitioners flood the market with guide books encouraging the latest technique (a possibly more lucrative occupation than that of the theologian, pastor, or priest), rarely do these afford a biblically, theologically and historically robust—or *real*—understanding or practice of evangelism.

Such resources are not without value, and indeed sometimes what they offer may be better than simply ignoring the biblical commission. Quick-fix remedies may ease the symptomatic sting of decline, but ultimately these will not address the deeper problems working within society and challenging Christian communities and institutions. Deep biblical foundations for evangelism and the construction of a coherent theology that takes seriously the complexities of the contemporary context for this ecclesial practice are desperately needed, and what Fr. Rommen provides in this book.

Much of the difficulty faced by contemporary American mainline congregations related to evangelism/mission needs to be addressed through careful study and rediscovery of biblical and theological foundations with attentiveness to historical perspectives in order to inform practices of local Christian communities across the contemporary international landscape. However, as an academic area of study as part of theological education within a university context, in spite of increased attention given to evangelism in broader ecclesial conversations, and the borrowing of evangelistic language among corporate cultures, evangelism is, ironically, unattractive. In this book, Rommen elegantly locates the study and practice of evangelism within the theological landscape, while at the same time critically reflecting upon the relevance of the Gospel in a post-Christian setting. He accomplishes this by drawing from a wide-range of sources, most not typically engaged in studies on evangelism such as the theology and wisdom of Eastern Orthodox Christianity.

So often studies related to evangelism too narrowly and too thinly address the dynamics of the contemporary situation turning too quickly to a defensive rationale or apologetic for the Gospel, as if the triune God needs a defense, rather than patiently, persistently, and proficiently engaging the other for whom the Gospel is offered. In displaying the latter, Rommen's methodology describes as well as embodies an evangelistic witness. A study of evangelism does not need the endorsement of dominant cultures or to rely entirely upon an intellectual rationale for the Gospel as a proof for God through human experience. Neither can studies and practices of evangelism remain abstract as interest groups and ideologues struggle to claim strategic vantage points from which to launch their simplistic truncations or reactionary distinctions.

Fr. Rommen's analysis of the difficulties related to evangelism in the late modern era is remarkably thorough attending to the nuances and complexities of enlightenment characteristics such as: the confusion around secularism; the complexity of selfhood as being, identity, and self-awareness; the nuance of ideas such as freedom, coherence, and value; dissimulation/simulation; and the difficulty of the social discourse of self-referencing beings in the absence of the self, the other, and the transcendent. The sophisticated treatment of late modernity's implications for the self and its conversion is instructive. Fr. Rommen thoughtfully offers guidance for comprehending the circumstances and challenges we must confront as Christians commissioned by our baptisms to share the Gospel.

For Fr. Rommen, a study of evangelism depends upon an understanding of the contemporary context and the late modern self, as well as ecclesial life and practice that grows from canonical texts and Christian tradition pervaded by the Holy Spirit in Christian communities of faith to invite persons into relationship with the Gospel as person. Without sacrificing the personal nature of the Gospel, Fr. Rommen preserves and deepens a theologically robust understanding of evangelism as invitation in which conversion focuses upon participating in relationship in the midst of what can be a treacherous contemporary context. This book offers a re-calibration of the study of evangelism as central to the theological landscape, and creates an ecclesial evangelism that takes seriously the role of the self, informed by philosophical, theoretical, cultural, biblical, historical, and practical knowledge.

"You know the message he sent to the people of Israel, preaching good news of peace by Jesus Christ—he is Lord of all." Acts 10.36 RSV.

Laceye C. Warner
Duke Divinity School

Introduction

THE CHALLENGE OF THE LATE MODERN WORLD

Some years ago I proposed a model of communication[1] in which I suggested (as had so many others)[2] that communication involved a speaker encoding and transmitting some message, which was in turn received and decoded by a listener. Accordingly, the effectiveness of evangelistic communication was to be measured in terms of the listener having actually understood whatever it was the speaker had tried to communicate. As the evangelist, it was not necessarily my job to convert the listener, but rather to make sure that she or he understood the content of the Gospel. I became convinced that the effectiveness of my communication could be greatly enhanced if I could improve the process at its key points of interaction: speaker, listener, and message. This, in turn, led me to explore ways through which to improve the speaker's credibility and attractiveness. I even sought ways to enhance the speaker's control over the listener by taking advantage of what I could learn about the listener's personality and patterns of perception. I also spent a great deal of time experimenting with ways of effectively formulating or packaging the information in an attempt to minimize the ways in which cultural, linguistic, and personal factors could filter or alter the message.

---

1   Cf. Edward Rommen. *Namenschristentum* (Bad Liebenzell: Verlag der Liebenzeller Mission, 1982).

2   See, for example, Saussure's Speech Circuit *Course In General Linguistics* (Chicago: Open Court, 1997), 11-12.

In general, I think I was on the right track and did indeed make some significant improvements in the way in which I viewed and practiced missionary communication. However, when I look at the problem today I notice several things. On the one hand, my former preoccupation with the science of persuasion may have caused me to underemphasize or overlook a number of critical variables. For example: in my original model no specific attention was given to the idea of God as the source of our message; no attempt was made to factor in the enabling power of the Holy Spirit; and, although message formulation received careful attention, language as such was all but ignored. Including these topics would probably not have altered my understanding of the nature of communication. However, it would most certainly have relocated some of my emphases.

I have noticed that strategies driven by a preoccupation with the *Gospel-as-Information* have not faired well in the late modern[3] context of the last few decades. Many reasons could be given for this. It has become increasingly difficult to speak about the Christian message. The privatization of religion has all but eliminated it as a topic of public discourse, so much so that the very attempt to mediate the Christian message is often viewed as a scandalous breach of social etiquette, an unacceptable, manipulative violation of the individual's personal space. Subsequently, it has become increasingly difficult to hear or take seriously the Christian message. With the spiritualization of just about every aspect of the created order the Christian voice is all but lost amidst a cacophony of competing voices[4]—one spirituality among many. Moreover, it has become harder for our contemporaries to believe

---

3   As I will show in chapter 1, I would rather speak of late modern era, since what we are seeing is actu-
      ally the consequence of modern thought taken to its logical end—the terminal stage of modernity.
      The whole idea of a general shift to the post modern may well be the figment of the imagination of
      some very modern thinkers. See Terry Eagleton, *The Illusions of Postmodernism* (Oxford: Blackwell,
      1996). In any case, what a truly post modern framework will look like is only now being explored by
      a few elite intellectuals. Nevertheless, the vast majority of our contemporaries are still very modern.
      See Jose Lopes and Garry Potter eds., *After Postmodernism. An Introduction to Critical Realism* (New
      York: Continuum, 2005).

4   Another way of looking at this might be to speak of an "informationizing" of society—not only a
      flood of information, but the multiplication of choices creating the illusion of freedom and validity.

what they do hear. The secularization of the modern mind has deprived the Christian message of authoritative certainty,[5] relegating it to the surreality of mere human fantasy. There seem to be fewer and fewer people interested in the Christian message, there is a more pronounced separation between the shrinking pockets of Christian influence and the prevailing culture, and, as a result, Christians are having a much harder time communicating the Gospel.

There is, however, something troublesome about these explanations of our failure–something that just doesn't add up. Surely our evangelistic ineffectiveness is not merely a breakdown of discursive technique—our persuasive strategies have never been more refined, more sophisticated. Just think of the witnessing techniques used by various evangelistic organizations: tracts (Four Spiritual Laws), videos (The Jesus Film), and mass media (TV evangelists). Moreover, it does not appear to be religious information per se that is offending our contemporaries. Many religions and spiritualities are experiencing remarkable resurgence.[6] There must be something about the Christian message itself that unmasks a more fundamental discontinuity, a conflict between its very nature (not its content) and the state of the late modern individual.[7]

Certainly, the Gospel is a message—information about the death and resurrection of our Lord—and surely this information can be and has been presented in effective and understandable ways. At the same time, the proclamation of the Good News is an invitation to enter a relationship with the person referenced by our propositions. What we seek to mediate is communion with a personal being upon whose will our existence is contingent. We insist that it is only by participating in the life of that uncreated, non-contingent, personal entity that we can actually know God. It is only within the framework of such a relationship

---

5   Charles Taylor. *A Secular Age* (Cambridge, MA: The Belknap Press of Harvard University Press, 2007).

6   For example, the recent surge in interest in the spiritual dimension of human existence. Cf. Roger Walsh. *Essential Spirituality* (NY: John Wiley & Sons, Inc., 1999).

7   There is and always will be that which St. Paul refers to as the offense of the cross (1 Cor. 1:18). What I am trying to do here is re-articulate the nature of that offense in and for a late modern cultural context.

that the words of the Gospel can connote both reality and the knowledge of that reality. Our message, then, is not primarily information about some truth, but is itself a reality—communion with a personal being.

It is precisely this Gospel-as-Person that is in conflict with the late modern self. As I see it, by the mid-twentieth century the consequences of several strands of social development, all rooted in what has been called the Enlightenment Project, had created a world in which individuals appear to have largely abandoned personhood, social discourse, and, in the end, reality itself.[8] Ours is a world which seems determined to eliminate the individuality, the personhood, of each human being by reducing us to mere numbers, consumers, targets of advertising, etc. It is a world in which the truly personal dimension of social interaction is apparently rejected in favor of a kind of simulation—a game in which we all play predetermined roles, trusting in no one and nothing but ourselves. It is a world in which I believe we fabricate reality based on our own actions, ignoring or denying any and every other context of reality.

Herein lies the challenge. To the late modern mind the Gospel-as-Person is both an obstacle and the solution. How are we to speak the truth about a person to people who insist on re-creating personhood in their own image? How do we issue an invitation to communion in a context of discursive simulation? How do we establish frameworks of reality when no single object of reference (except the self) is privileged? There is, then, an essential discontinuity between the shape of the late modern mind and the Gospel-as-Person that makes it difficult to offer and difficult to receive, even though it represents the only genuine solution to the question of human ontology and the fraying fabric of the North American socioscape.

The following study is my attempt to address this challenge. It is driven by the conviction that effective communication of the Christian message depends on our ability to relate an accurate understanding of the socio-religious condition of the modern mind to the relational nature of the Gospel. In Part I I will examine the historical roots

---

8   There have, of course, been secular attempts to counteract these trends. One might point to various forms of communal living, such as eco-villages and dance communities.

of the late modern context. I begin with a general description of core enlightenment characteristics (e.g., rationalism, reductionism, consilience, freedom) showing how they have shaped both the radical inwardness and the depersonalization so characteristic of the contemporary social context. While the core characteristics of the Enlightenment were not explicitly anti-religious, they did harbor a latent skepticism that spawned a series of social and philosophical movements that became hostile and destructive to Christianity. One of the most persistent and devastating of these movements is secularism. Unfortunately, that term has been used to describe so many different phenomena that there exists today little agreement as to what it is. Therefore, in Chapter 2 I explore four generations of meaning that show how the process of secularization has progressively eroded the place of the sacred leaving only the self as a point of personal, social, and even religious reference.

Part II will continue the socio-religious analysis by tracing the trajectory of the modern self—the origins, nature and consequences of its dissimulation. When I speak of the human self, I am generally referring to an individual's awareness of who and what they are. The self is a composite whole which takes shape at the confluence of the three overlapping registers of self-hood: being, identity, and self-awareness. Thus we could say that the self is a human being whose ontic identity is actualized as being-in-the-world. In light of this, Chapter 3 will explore the notion of being and show how late modern thought challenges human existence. The extreme inwardness of modern thought and the loss of traditional coping mechanisms (kinship, community, tradition, and religion) have exacerbated what some[9] have called existential anxiety, which, in turn, has occasioned a flight from reality into the shadows of dissimulation and simulation.[10] Given the significance of

---

9   Anthony Giddens. *Modernity and Self-Identity. Self and Society in the Late Modern Age* (Stanford: Stanford University Press, 1991), 181-185.

10   According to Jean Baudrillard, "To dissimulate is to pretend not to have what one has. To simulate is to feign to have what one doesn't have." *Simulacra and Simulation* (Ann Arbor: University of Michigan Press, 1994), 3. Thus to the extent that individuals become simulacra of themselves, personhood is dissimulated and society becomes mere simulation.

being for the grounding and development of identity, I will then explore late modern notions of identity. Many today seem to assume that the individual is able to establish his or her own identity while, at the same time, declaring independence from the very webs of relationships which originally formed that identity. But can this be done? Or does the supposed autonomy of the self lead to fragmentation – a multiplicity of identities, none of which fully defines all that the self really is?

In Chapter 4 I will move on to contemporary ideas of freedom, coherence, and value. Given the radically reflexive mode of late modern being and identity, freedom, at its most fundamental level, is conceived of as a form of control over the self, a kind of self-actualization. However, no individual can exercise complete self-control. Moreover, in the multi-personed contexts of time, space, and society the individual is forced to deal with the limiting effects of competing interests. The greater the limitations and apparent risks, the more likely one is to demand the freedom (self-actualization) to retreat into the relative coherence of ones own being (self-awareness) and establish for and by itself the value of its own person (self-authentication).

Part III will relate the trajectory of the late modern self to the shape of the contemporary social bond by uncovering the ways in which the Self-in-Discourse creates the basic patterns of that socioscape. In Chapter 5 I will look at the ways in which dissimulation/simulation of individual characteristics play out in a culturally diverse context. I will suggest that anxious being seeks security in belonging, and that the resultant mode of being (seen as privilege, voluntary choice, or responsibility) reflects the way in which membership (belonging) is acquired (by ascription, achievement, or relationship). This mode of being is, of course, a determinative part of individual identity. What then is the effect of being a member of several disparate communities? Put differently, how are we to preserve coherent individual identity in the face of identity fragmentation and multiculturalism?

Chapter 6 will then examine the implications of the way in which the social discourse (if it can be called such) of self-referencing beings effectively eliminates any totalizing, grand narratives or frameworks—

such as the Creator, Revealed Truth—which might supersede the individual and thus regulate discourse. All that is left, it seems, are localized histories, a ceaselessly changing subjectivity which seeks to comprehend, i.e., assimilate, and dominate any and everything seen to be other. Here I will explore several contemporary attempts to ground ethical, moral and religious discriminations in the absence of the self, the other, and the transcendent.

Finally, Part IV will examine the specific ways in which the late modern context impedes an understanding of the Gospel and considers ways in which we might overcome those obstacles. Chapter 7 will explore the ways in which several aspects of the late modern self and discourse make it difficult (nearly impossible?) to present and receive the Gospel-as-Person. Given the personal nature of the Gospel, evangelism is best viewed as an issuing of an invitation to participate in the restoration offered by Christ. Conversion, then, involves agreeing to participate in a relationship. This message is difficult to issue, understand, and participate in because it requires: a) an affirmation of the full reality of the self, b) placing limits on freedom, c) abandoning one's self to others in trust, and d) an ability to transcend the self—the very things that the late modern mind has the most difficulty with.

What, then, is to be done? Chapter 8 will present and explore some practical ways in which we might overcome the above-mentioned impediments to evangelism. To begin with we must recognize that evangelism is itself a form of social discourse, and that in order to be effective it must under no circumstances be a simulation. That, however, can only be achieved if the individuals involved are truly personalized, and if self and society can be reintegrated within a reality that includes the sacred. Given the nature of the Gospel-as-Person and the challenges of the late modern era, I will look at how we might re-personalize the evangelistic context, rediscover real freedom, re-authenticate the witness and the Church, and reintegrate the experience of sacred reality.

If the reality-denying dissimulation/simulation matrix is as pervasive as it appears to be, the only effective path to evangelism will be a re-centering of real personhood (both divine and human) as the horizon against which to articulate human ontology, develop moral frameworks, make value discriminations, and to hear the Gospel. When I speak of the real I have no intention of entering into the centuries-old epistemological discussion of what is and is not real. Nor am I interested in revisiting the specialized usages of the term developed by psychoanalysts such as Jacques Lacan.[11] As you might imagine, I will not be able to avoid such references altogether. Nevertheless, my primary concern has to do with what it might mean to be a real human being (as opposed to a dissimulated being), and what it might look like to engage in real social discourse (as opposed to social simulation). I suppose that some sort of preliminary working definition of the real is in order (one which we will most certainly have to revise throughout our deliberations). For now I would like to think in terms of three registers of the real self.[12]

Hypostatization. The real is an actual instance of concretized, or in the case of persons, hypostasized human nature or essence. As such, said entity is either real or it does not exist—in which case the source of reality is the author of hypostatization. This is why dissimulation can only be a form of pretending (lying). We cannot actually simulate non-being. What is important here is an awareness of the nature and implications of contingent human being.

Essence or Nature. Each individual instance of hypostasized human nature is real to the extent that it conforms to its own nature or essence. This involves some level of external coercion, constitutional limitation, or intentionality. In other words, the degree to which an individual is forced to, is unable to, or chooses to affirm or circumvent the constituent aspects of human nature, that individual is more or less real, i.e., more or less human.

---

11   Jacques Lacan. *The Ethics of Psychoanalysis* (London: Routlege, 1992). Cf. Alenka Zupancic. *Ethics of the Real* (London: Verso, 2000).

12   Here I have been influenced by the thinking of Sergius Bulgakov who defines real personhood in terms of hypostasis, nature, and self-awareness. *The Lamb of God* (Grand Rapids: Eerdmans, 2008), 89.

Self-Consciousness. Each individual instance of hypostasized human nature is real to the extent that it is able to interrogate both its being and nature without pretense—without dissimulation or simulation.

As Christians we might reasonably look to the Church for the wherewithal to accomplish such a re-centering. Indeed, the doctrines of Christianity would seem to steadfastly reject the virtually real while celebrating the reality of the human person (the self) and thereby providing a stable framework for social discourse. Unfortunately, the Christian communities of North America—inheritors and developers of Western European Christian responses to the Enlightenment and modernity—seem to have compromised their own position by capitulating to prevailing social trends. As early as 1900, "mainstream Protestant denominations were beginning to bend and redefine their institutional missions in compliance with the new cultural perspectives..."[13] Throughout the 20th century most churches were moving toward a new "religious accommodation, a new ethical compromise that tried to integrate consumer pleasure and comfort and acquisition, the new 'American Standard of living,' into what was left of the traditional Christian world-view."[14]

Part of my task will be to rediscover, re-articulate, and re-center a Christian understanding of real personhood and the ways in which that understanding can help facilitate evangelism. So, beginning with Chapter 3, I will provide a preliminary review of how Christian theology and the Church help us begin the process of formulating answers to the challenges of late modern thought. For example, after the discussion of identity, I will show how Christian anthropology, with its emphasis on the iconic nature of created beings, provides a framework for discussing human being and identity. After discussing the social dimensions of identity and belonging, I will consider the possibilities afforded by the Body of Christ—ecclesial being. In exploring these Christian alternatives to late modernity, I will draw on a wide range of Christian traditions,

---

13   William Leach. *Land of Desire. Merchants, Power, and the Rise of a New American Culture* (New York: Vintage Books, 1994), 10.

14   Ibid., 194.

including those of the Eastern Church. A number of scholars have suggested that it may be time for us in the West to look to the East for new insight on perennial theological problems.[15] And as we shall see, the East provides a number of biblically based perspectives that are particularly applicable to the late modern context. I will then draw all of these theological reflections together in the final chapter where I will seek to show how the Christian message answers the challenge of late modernism, and how we can offer the invitation to Christ in an understandable way. The whole of this project is about inviting people to Christ.

---

15   Jason Byassee. "Looking East. The Impact of Orthodox Theology." *Christian Century* (December 28, 2004), 24-25

PART I.

THE CONTEXT:

THE ENLIGHTENMENT PROJECT, MODERNITY, AND LATE MODERNITY.

Chapter I

ENLIGHTENMENT ANTECEDENTS AND THE MODERN IMAGINARY

If we hope to communicate the Gospel-as-Person to our contemporaries, we will need to begin with an accurate understanding of the general socio-religious context in which they operate. It has become fairly commonplace to identify that context with either the success or the failure of the Enlightenment project.[16] Of course, to speak of a specific project is certainly to overstate the case since there is little evidence of a unified, temporally localized project.[17] Yet to declare the project a failure is to ignore the fact that recent social and intellectual upheavals are the logical outcomes of modernity, for which there still exists considerable optimism.[18] So, it would be more useful to view the challenges of our own culture as the logical consequences of the Enlightenment's effectiveness; as that toward which modernity has inexorably been moving—a kind of high or late modernism. And if we take that view it would be more accurate to speak, not of some project but of a general frame of reference; a cohesive, overarching view of the world shaped

---

16   Speaking specifically of moral theory, Alasdair MacIntyre claims that "the problems of modern moral theory emerge clearly as the product of the failure of the Enlightenment project." *After Virtue What* (Notre Dame: University of Notre Dame Press, 1981), 60.

17   James Schmidt. *What Enlightenment Project?* Paper read at the Tenth International Congress On The Enlightenment, Dublin, July 25-31, 1999.

18   In defense of continuing the Enlightenment Project Edward O. Wilson predicts "when we have unified enough certain knowledge, we will understand who we are and why we are here." *Concilience* (New York: Vintage Books, 1999), 7.

by a set of convictions that have spontaneously gained acceptance over time.[19]

Indeed the prevailing culture of Western Europe and North America has changed dramatically during the last few hundred years. This is especially true as it relates to questions of belief, which is my main concern here. At the time of the Reformation, for example, hierarchical structures of authority, basic Christian doctrines, and the existence of God seem to have been accepted by the majority of people. Today, these ideas are largely rejected and, as Taylor states, unbelief is the default position.[20] Describing how these changes came about is beyond the scope of this project.[21] However, I have a vested interest in looking into the current state of this process and asking why it has become so hard for many to believe. Yet, given the ethnic, racial, and religious diversity of the contemporary situation, that might not be as easy as it appears to be. I will need some way of speaking of the whole situation, a way to grasp, if even in a general way, a sense of the late modern culture in its entirety. This will, of necessity, require some simplification. Of course, the ongoing process of cultural homogenization[22] has already had a great leveling effect. I do not mean to underestimate the real cultural differences that exist within a population as diverse as that of the United States. Nevertheless, every one of those cultures has been exposed to the dominant themes of late modern culture and the process of hybridization has caused many of them to move in the direction of, or even adopt, those themes as their own. In other words, the overwhelming power of Enlightenment thought has not been effectively resisted by

---

19   "...the philosophers were neither a disciplined phalanx nor a rigid school of thought. If they composed anything at all, it was something rather looser than that: a family." Peter Gay. *The Enlightenment. The Rise of Modern Paganism* (New York: Norton, 1966), 4.

20   "...the change I want to define and trace is one which takes us from a society in which it was virtually impossible not to believe in God, to one in which faith, even for the staunchest believer, is one human possibility among others." " Belief in God is no longer axiomatic." Taylor. *A Secular Age,* 3.

21   This is the theme of Michael Allen Gillespie's. *The Theological Origins of Modernity* (Chicago: University of Chicago Press, 2008).

22   Speaking in the context of globalization Arjun Appadurai states that "the central problem of today's global interactions is the tension between cultural homogenization and cultural heterogenization." *Modernity at Large* (Minneapolis: University of Minnesota Press, 1996), 32.

very many. Speaking of one Enlightenment outcome, market capitalism, William Leach observes,

> no immigrant culture—and, to a considerable degree, no religious tradition—had the power to resist it, as none can in our own time. Any group that has come to this country has had to learn to accept and to adjust to this elemental feature of American capitalist culture.[23]

The same could be said for most core Enlightenment themes. So we should be able to state in a few words just what we mean by late modernism. There are several ways that I might try to conceptualize the contemporary context.

We could, for example, make use of the idea of plausibility structures.[24] These are mental frameworks that help us decide whether the things that we hear or read are believable. Such structures are shaped by individual experiences and convictions, the ideas of the groups and institutions to which the individual belongs (schools, churches, religions, political parties), as well as by the general notions of believability that dominate the culture as a whole. These structures act like filters through which we pass everyday data and spontaneously declare them believable or unbelievable. Plausibility structures do not deal directly with the actual truth or falsehood of an idea, but simply with the question of its believability. So, the plausibility structure could help us understand why today the Gospel is so difficult to accept. For example, given the contemporary predominance of a scientific (materialistic) view of life, many people would find the idea of a miracle (such as the resurrection), or the supernatural, simply implausible.

Given the nature of religious beliefs, their plausibility is often supported by religious institutions (churches), practices, and language, which create a context within which the beliefs and values promoted

---

23   Leach. *Land of Desire*, 5.

24   As does Lesslie Newbigin in his book *The Gospel in a Pluralist Society* (Grand Rapids: Eerdmans, 1989), 8-11.

appear to make sense, are plausible. But there are a host of other factors that determine the conditions of belief. The plausibility structure is limited to the believability of certain propositions and does not, for example, address social discourse, identity, freedom, conceptions of morality, and the ways in which these things affect believability. So, if we are going to grasp the contemporary context as a whole, we will need a more generalized way of conceptualizing it.

Here we might adapt Charles Taylor's idea of a Social Imaginary.[25] According to Taylor, a social imaginary has to do with "...the ways people imagine their social existence, how they fit together with others, how things go on between them and their fellows, the expectations that are normally met, and the deeper normative notions and images that underlie these expectations."[26] It is the way people imagine their social surroundings; it is carried in images, stories, and legends; and it is shared by enough people to facilitate common practices and a shared sense of legitimacy. It is a widely held sense of how things ought to go and as such it "...extends beyond the immediate background understanding that makes sense of our particular practices."[27] The social imaginary also includes moral order, notions of believability, and the practices associated with belief.

Like a plausibility structure a social imaginary has many sources and it gradually develops over time. In many cases, ideas are initially developed and promoted as theory by a small minority. That theory, then, gradually "infiltrates and transforms the social imaginary."[28] What exactly is involved when a theory penetrates and transforms the social imaginary? For the most part, people take up, improvise, or are inducted into new practices. These are made plausible by the new outlook, the one first articulated in the theory; this outlook is the context that gives sense to the practices. Hence the new understanding comes to be accessible to the participants in a way it wasn't before. It begins to define the

---

25   Charles Taylor. *Modern Social Imaginaries* (Durham: Duke University Press, 2004).

26   Ibid., 23.

27   Ibid., 25.

28   Ibid., 28.

contours of their world and can eventually come to count as the taken-for-granted shape of things.[29]

If we allow for such an overarching imaginary in the contemporary North American context, we will want to know what theories, factors, and forces have led to its current shape. As I see it our imaginary has been formed by a set of characteristics inherited from the Enlightenment that have filtered down into the general populous, albeit in generalized and transmuted forms. So then, I would like to briefly survey a series of Enlightenment characteristics which, having been developed and introduced by Protestant Reformers and philosophers, have then filtered down to the general population where they have gradually gained widespread acceptance, shaping the contemporary social imaginary and determining the believability of the Gospel and rendering its proclamation difficult.

— I —

Freedom

The most fundamental of all Enlightenment characteristics is the idea of human freedom. For some thinkers, like Immanuel Kant, this concept was primarily associated with the free and public use of reason.

> Nothing is required for his enlightenment, however, except freedom; and the freedom in question is the least harmful of all, namely the freedom to use reason publicly in all matters...The public use of one's reason must always be free, and it alone can bring about enlightenment among mankind; the private use of reason may, however, often be very narrowly restricted, without otherwise hindering the progress of enlightenment."[30]

---

29   Ibid., 29. Taylor goes on to say that this is not a purely one-sided process and it does not have to end with one transformation. "The new practice, with the implicit understanding it generates, can be the basis for modification of theory, which in turn can inflect practice, and so on." *Modern Social Imaginaries*, 30.

30   Immanuel Kant. What is *Enlightenment?* In *Perpetual Peace and Other Essays*. Trans. Ted Humphrey (Indianapolis: Hackett Publishing Company, 1983), 42.

For others the idea of freedom was considerably more inclusive. Peter Gay points out

> The men of the Enlightenment united on a vastly ambitious program,[31] a program of secularism, humanity, cosmopolitanism, and freedom, above all, freedom in its many forms—freedom from arbitrary power, freedom of speech, freedom of trade, freedom to realize one's talents, freedom of aesthetic response, freedom, in a word, of moral man to make his own way in the world.[32]

Today the notion of individual freedom is so widely accepted, enthroned in so many constitutions, and protected by such an array of institutions, that it is simply taken as a given, beyond discussion, already established. So the focus of attention has shifted away from making the case for freedom to finding or devising new ways of expressing that freedom. This has led to a gradual universalization of freedom, taking it way beyond Kant's "freedom to use reason" to a "right to choose" in any area of human life or endeavor. Life, of course, does not always provide us with a satisfying plurality of choices. But, rather than question our conception of freedom, we bolster our sense of freedom either by creating options (falsely, where there should be none) or by proliferating options beyond what is necessary, reasonable, or useful. Some of the options created by the Pro Choice movement, where the "right to choose" trumps most other considerations, illustrates the former, while a single provider's offer of over 300 cable TV channels demonstrates the latter.

As it has filtered down into the contemporary imaginary, freedom translates into the right to choose between options that are assumed to be (or made to be) omnipresent. This makes serious discussion difficult since this "right" masks or trumps the actual issues. I recently spoke to

---

31 Gay's remark should not be taken to imply some kind of unified, localized project, since the men to which he refers worked in different places and times. The Enlightenment was the work of three overlapping closely associated generations. Gay. *The Enlightenment,* 17.

32 Ibid., 3.

students at a Christian high school about the nature of worship. In the course of our conversation one of the students asked if he couldn't decide the question based on the kind of music he liked. When I suggested that his likes and dislikes were irrelevant to the question of what worship is, the whole class was seized by a wave of disbelief and consternation. The ensuing protests revealed that my statement was taken as a threat to their freedom, i.e., a violation of their "right to choose."

— 2 —

Rationalism

Another prominent characteristic of the Enlightenment is the unfettered use of human reason. As Kant put it, *"Sapere Aude!* have courage to use your own understanding." [33] According to him, this was the motto of enlightenment.

Modern thinkers held that human beings, unaided by divine revelation or signs, could, through the application of their rational abilities, come to understand the basic structure of the world. This view holds both that the world has a fundamentally rational structure to it, and that we have sufficient rational ability to uncover this structure.[34]

This faith in human reason is, of course, still with us. In fact, there is nothing to suggest that its reputation has been tarnished in any way.[35] This conviction has filtered down into the modern imaginary in several ways. First, the confidence in the human ratio translates into a wide spread, naive, unquestioned optimism. A kind of "we-can-do-this" (or

---

33 Kant. *What is Enlightenment*, 33.

34 http://www.fiu.edu/~hauptli/TheEnlightenmentProjectLectureSupplement.html

35 Although in some disciplines, such as theology, confidence may be waning. Western (Catholic and Protestant) theology, which has been extremely rationalistic, increasingly is turning to the Eastern Church for alternative ways of dealing with questions of faith. Cf. Jason Byassee. "Looking East. The Impact of Orthodox Theology" *Christian Century* (December 28, 2004), 24-25.

for that matter anything) attitude. Even though we have not, in fact, been able to solve every problem, North Americans, proud of our ingenuity, actually believe that if given enough time and resources, we can solve every problem, answer every question. Unfortunately this spills over into the religious realm in the form of an unbridled pragmatism. There is the wide spread notion that we can manage, do, program anything we put our minds to, with or without God's help. I once heard of a visitor to the United States who, after visiting a number of mega-churches, said that it was amazing what the Americans were able to do without the Holy Spirit.

Second, this faith in reason leads to the idea that human reason is omni-potent; that there is no need for any other agencies such as God and the supernatural. In fact, we have gotten so used to the exclusivity of our own thought that the possibility of divine agency is rarely even considered. To suggest that we need supernatural help is considered irrational and an affront to our own natural potency.

Third, this leads to a world without mystery. It is a world in which we claim to (or expect to be able to) understand everything. One recent expression of this might be the "medicalization" of most human problems. According to this therapeutic model[36] whatever ails us can be reduced to some disease or disorder that can be corrected with drugs or proper therapy. It is a world in which little, if anything, lies beyond the reach of reason, in which there is nothing that we cannot get our minds around. Thus, if we are going to speak of God and the supernatural it has to make sense to us.[37] The enlightened mind will brook no conundrum – no mystery.

---

36   Taylor remarks, "One of the most striking fruits of this sense of innate innocence has been the transfer of so many issues which used to be considered moral into a therapeutic register. What was formerly sin is often now seen as sickness." *A Secular Age*, 618.

37   No one had thought that Christianity might give way to rationalism until Christians tried to prove that Christianity was reasonable. Gay. *The Enlightenment*, 326.

— 3 —
Reductionism

Obviously the use of human reason was (would have to be) governed by certain methodological considerations. This has turned out to be a basically mechanistic, empiricist, and reductionistic method. Hauptli explains

> this methodology carefully examines material or natural phenom
> ena trying to break them down into (that is, to reduce them to)
> their simplest or most basic parts or units, and then it studies how
> these units combine together to produce more complex phenom-
> ena (that is, it tries to synthesize the units).[38]

But Wilson adds that

> behind the mere smashing of aggregates into smaller pieces lies a
> deeper agenda that also takes the name of reductionism: to fold the
> laws and principles of each level of organization into those at more
> general, hence more fundamental levels.[39]

This basic methodology remains the standard in almost all areas of human endeavor. For all the good that its legitimate use has done, this reductionism has been popularized into the modern imaginary with some less than helpful results.

First, we seem to have developed a kind of analysis fever, a rage to analyze[40] anything and everything. There is almost no aspect of late modern life that has not attracted a cadre of experts willing to analyze and comment. Granted, sometimes it may be reasonable to analyze, as in the case of the economy or an individual's health. But we have begun to inappropriately analyze things that don't need to be or should not

---

38   http://www.fiu.edu/~hauptli/TheEnlightenmentProjectLectureSupplement.html

39   Wilson. *Consilience*, 60.

40   Taylor speaks of Latin Christendom's concern with Reform, "a drive to make over the whole society to higher standards" and calls it a "rage for order." *A Secular Age*, 63.

be anatomized, and are doing so in ways that are insulting and which destroy the object's beauty. For example, we have pundits analyzing political speeches moments after they have been given, telling us what we have just heard, implying that it would be good for us to use our own reason, but since we (the people) are not quite up to that, it will have to be done for us. Think for yourselves, except when we think for you. Or we have detailed, play by play analyses of everything from sex to sports, a level of analysis that robs these activities of their sublime, spontaneous beauty rendering them boring, even repulsive. Of course, if everyone else can analyze, then so can we. So we analyze our diets, our free time, our relationships, our moods, and even our religion. And we do so until there is no more joy, love, and certainly no truth.

Second, we are having a hard time with some of the results of reductionism, in particular its inevitable tendency to fragment. We succeed in breaking things down into their smallest parts, but have difficulty with the synthesis, putting the pieces coherently back together.

This may be especially true of religious principles. Pavel Florensky points out what happens when a religious principle is subjected to rational analysis.

> The single and integral object of religious perception disintegrates
> in the domain of rationality into a multiplicity of aspects, into sepa-
> rate facets, into fragments of holiness, and there is no grace in these
> fragments. The precious alabaster has been smashed and the holy
> myrrh is greedily sucked in by the dry sands of the red-hot desert.[41]

This fragmentation also makes it extremely difficult to maintain our grasp on the "big picture." Late modernism is plagued by what many have called a loss of horizon and meta-narrative.[42] While there are certainly many reasons for that development, it is quite possible

---

41   Pavel Florensky. *Pillar and Ground of Truth* (Princeton: Princeton University Press, 1997), 234.

42   Jean-Francois Loytard. *The Postmodern Condition: A Report on Knowledge.* Trans. Geoff Bennington and Brian Massumi (Minneapolis: University of Minnesota Press,1984), xxiv. Of course, most late modern thinkers are celebrating, not bemoaning, the loss of meta-narrative.

that having anatomized some truth, some beauty, we are unable to reconstruct it. This is a heavy price to pay since we can no longer see the consequences of our actions; we lose our intrinsic sense of connection to a larger whole. When we then try to "'see the big picture," we try to reassemble the fragments in our minds, to list and organize all the pieces. But "as physicist David Bohm says, the task is futile—similar to trying to reassemble the fragments of a broken mirror to see a true reflection. Thus, after a while we give up trying to see the whole altogether."[43]

— 4 —
Consilience

Another characteristic of Enlightenment thought, also related to the reductionistic methodology, is the notion of consilience. In essence this is the conviction that all knowledge is unified, i.e., there is one, single pool of interrelated knowledge that can be accessed by anyone using the right methodology. Wilson speaks of the strong form of this idea, namely

> total consilience, which holds that nature is organized by simple universal laws of physics to which all other laws and principles can eventually be reduced. This transcendental world view is the light and way for many scientific materialists (I admit to being among them)[44]

In the modern imaginary the idea of consilience leads to a kind of methodological arrogance, blind belief in what are called facts, assured results of scientific study. In other words, if there is only one kind of knowledge, then there is only one legitimate way of accessing it. This, in turn, leads to a general rejection of what might be called alternative "sciences," or rather the rejection of the scientific status of anything other than the materialistic, reductionistic methodology. For example,

---

43   Peter Senge. *The Fifth Discipline* (New York: Doubleday, 1990), 3.

44   Wilson. *Consilience*, 60.

one might argue that there is such a thing as theological knowledge and that that knowledge can be discovered using a methodology and a set of tools and rules appropriate to that method.[45] One might even suggest that if this kind of research were done in a consistent and systematic manner, it could be called a science.[46] Yet, it is exactly this kind of latitude that is often eliminated in the name of consilience. If there is only one kind of knowledge, then there is only one legitimate methodology—science, the great engine of enlightened thinking.[47]

− 5 −
Criticism

Of course, Enlightenment thought promoted more than the innocent use of reason. It turned into an insistence, a demand, for the freedom to criticize. According to Peter Gay, the Enlightenment's thinkers defined philosophy as the organized habit of criticism.[48]

> The philosophers' glorification of criticism and their qualified re-
> pudiation of metaphysics make it obvious that the Enlightenment
> was not an Age of Reason but a Revolt against Rationalism. The
> claim for the omnicompetence of criticism was in no way a claim
> for the omnipotence of reason. It was a political demand for the
> right to question everything, rather than the assertion that all could
> be known or mastered by rationality.[49]

Well, it may not have started out that way, but this Enlightenment characteristic has been so widely and uncritically accepted that it is

---

45   Wolfhardt Pannenberg speaks of the scientific status of theology. *Theology and the Philosophy of Science* (Philadelphia: Westminster Press, 1976), 326-245.

46   This is, in fact, the way the word science is used, for example in German, where one can talk about theological sciences (*theologische Wissenschaften*).

47   Wilson. *Consilience*, 24.

48   Gay. *The Enlightenment*, 130.

49   Ibid., 141.

taken to be a basic human right, or to put the matter differently, it is an expression of our unshakable confidence in our own rational abilities. Recently this insistence on criticism has been incorporated into the modern social imaginary in the form of argumentativeness and an elevated sense of the importance of individual opinion.

The penchant for argument can be seen in the general loss of the art of conversation.[50] People used to get together for the express purpose of discussing different views on, let's say, politics or religion. This kind of conversation could last for hours and get rather intense. But it rarely led to confrontation, anger, or violence. Today's demand for the right to criticism is so intense that it often leads to confrontation and has made many wary of discussions in which their ideas might be criticized. It seems that we can no longer disagree without getting angry and resorting to verbal violence.[51] The more intimate the subject matter, the more likely this is to happen. Since religion has been largely privatized, any attempt to present an alternative view is going to be met with a rigorous response.

The effect of this tendency can also be seen in contemporary political debates which, of course, are not debates at all. They are strictly managed and almost completely sterilized occasions during which one can criticize an opponent without running the risk of being challenged. In most cases the participants simply ignore the question and proceed with their own agenda. The strict limitations of the format assure the speakers of sequential monolog devoid of real conversation.

As a corollary to the right to criticize others, there is the importance of one's own opinion. A somewhat humorous example are the many online news outlets that include a sidebar entitled "Have Your Say" where the viewer is provided an opportunity to give their opinion on the news events of the day. This amounts to enabling anyone to have an

---

50   Cf. Stephen Miller. *Conversation. A History of a Declining Art* (New Haven: Yale University Press, 2006).

51   Miller asks "Are Americans increasingly living in what I call anger communities? Jeanne Marie Laskas a columnist for the *Washington Post*, says: 'We the people never seem to have discussions anymore; we all just rant to our like-minded friends with our like-minded rhetoric.'" *Conversation*, 266-267.

opinion about anything (regardless of expertise). Of course, if you read the comments that are made, you quickly realize that there are very few people who are knowledgeable enough to make useful contributions. So the practice seems to be just another way to document the equi-validity of each and every opinion — of making everyone an expert. This is particularly evident in "less-than-scientific" domains, such as religion. In these cases everyone is an expert and the truth and its validation gives way to the right of expression.

— 6 —
Reflexivity

The concern for one's own opinion is also indicative of the Enlightenment's turn inward. This first-person perspective, while anticipated by Plato[52] and Aristotle,[53] is rooted in the work of Augustine. His was a turn to the self.[54] According to Taylor, "It was Augustine who introduced the inwardness of radical reflexivity and bequeathed it to the Western tradition of thought. The step was a fateful one, because we have certainly made a big thing of the first-person standpoint."[55]

But it was surely Descartes who gave this turn its most recognizable form with his maxim, "I think, therefore I am." "This new conception of inwardness, an inwardness of self-sufficiency, of autonomous powers of ordering by reason, also prepared the ground for modern unbelief."[56] This turn inward was adopted by the Enlightenment and has come into the modern imaginary in the form of a radical self-centeredness. This is more than a simple fascination with the self. There is a sense in

---

52   We are good when reason rules, and bad when we are dominated by our desires. This view of moral source leads to the need for being truly rational, i.e., self-mastery. Cf. Charles Taylor. *Sources of the Self,* 115

53   *Theoria,* or contemplation of the unchanging order, is one of highest activities of man, one which brings him close to the divine. Taylor. *Sources of the Self,* 125.

54   But our principal route to God is not through the object domain but 'in' ourselves. Taylor. *Sources of the Self,* 128.

55   Ibid., 130. But, not everyone agrees. Cf. Michael Hanby. *Augustine and Modernity* (London: Routlege, 2003).

56   Taylor. *Sources of the Self,* 158.

which the entire late modern project can be viewed as reflexive. This project is ontologically reflexive in that it seeks to ground being in a tautological reference to itself. "I exist because I exist." It is morally reflexive since it situates morality in the self by deriving moral principles from within. And it is practically reflexive in that its primary concern is the well-being of the individual. As the Enlightenment took hold, people lost interest in the supernatural, the higher order of time, the hierarchy of the Church and its mysteries. What came to dominate was a concern for a "flourishing of ordinary life,"[57] i.e., the realities of everyday living. As the Enlightenment advanced into late modernism, the risks and opportunities multiplied and "ordinary life" became increasingly difficult to define. As a result, the self, left to its own devices, is engaged in constant self-monitoring in order to secure its being, that which it perceives to be good, and its own progress.

— 7 —
Progress

The modern mindset also holds that "...as our knowledge becomes both broader and more unified, we will experience continued progress (and they have in mind not only technological progress, but also social, political, and moral progress)."[58] Consider Condorcet's [1743-1794] optimistic *Sketch for A Historical Picture of the Progress of the Human Mind* in which he declares that

> the whole foundation for belief in the natural sciences is this idea,
> that the general laws directing the phenomena of the universe,
> known or unknown, are necessary and constant. Why should this

---

57   Taylor. *A Secular Age*, 370-371.

58   http://www.fiu.edu/~hauptli/TheEnlightenmentProjectLectureSupplement.html Accessed 8/30/2008.

principle be any less true for the development of the intellectual and moral faculties of man than for the other operations of nature?[59]

The time will therefore come when the sun will shine only on free men who know no other master but their reason; when tyrants and slaves, priests and their stupid or hypocritical instruments will exist only in works of history and on the stage; and when we shall think of them only...to learn how to recognize and so to destroy, by force of reason, the first seeds of tyranny and superstition, should they ever dare to reappear amongst us.[60]

In the modern imaginary this expectation of relentless progress is reflected in a certain restlessness or dissatisfaction with the way things are. Having grown accustomed to the constant evolution of technology, the late modern individual tends to generalize and project this movement on almost every area of life. Accordingly, the economy has to grow. Relationships, friendships and allegiances have to change and evolve. Ideas (even truths) have to be developed. Speeds have to increase.[61] Superstitions have to be overcome. This often takes the form of an outright rejection of the past. The beliefs, values and aspirations of those who have gone on before us are thrown off simply because they are of the past. Like everything else these things have been modernized and improved upon. Those no longer on the progressive side of life's curve are shunned and hidden away. The immanent obsolescence of just about everything leads to an idolization of the new and improved.

Subsequently, any argument based on past practice or its antiquity is, as a matter of principle, going to be suspect. Ideas rooted in historical continuity, such as Christian Tradition will have no authority. The prospect

---

59   Marquis de Condorcet. *Sketch for A Historical Picture of the Progress of the Human Mind.* trans. J. Barraclough (London: Weidenfeld and Nicholson, 1955), 173. Cited by Bruce W. Hauptli at http:// www.fiu.edu/~hauptli/ TheEnlightenmentProjectLectureSupplement.html

60   Condorcet. *Sketch,* 199. Cited by Hauptli at http://www.fiu.edu/~hauptli/TheEnlightenmentProject Lecture Supplement. html

61   This is an interesting side-effect of the idea of progress. Cf. James Gleick. *Faster. The Acceleration of Just about Everything* (New York : Pantheon Books, 1999).

of a constant, stable relationship with a Savior who lived centuries ago will be unacceptable for several reasons. In short, the Gospel-as-Person is going to be difficult to accept and difficult to present.

This, then, is the general shape of the modern imaginary and its implications for the communication of the Gospel. We are the inheritors of Enlightenment thought. Thought which has undergone a degree of generalization, popularization, and even transmutation. The contemporary social imaginary is the context in which we operate. It is the air we breathe; it is in the water we drink. As a result, we are hard pressed to escape its influence. Any presentation of the Gospel-as-Person is going to confront a context dominated by the continuing effects of these basic Enlightenment (modern) characteristics. For that reason, I am reluctant to speak of a post modern environment. It seems to me that the vast majority of our contemporaries are wrestling with very modern ideas and that the post modern is limited to the small cadre of elite thinkers, who are even now laying the foundation for a future imaginary. But, as things stand, we are still very, very modern.

Chapter 2

SECULARISM AND BELIEF

As already indicated, the core characteristics of the Enlightenment were not explicitly anti-religious,[62] but they did harbor a latent tension, which, over the course of time, did undermine belief. One of the most persistent and devastating of these movements is secularization. There has been a great deal of discussion as to the exact nature and outcomes of secularization, and, given the wide range of definitions ascribed to this phenomenon, there appears to be little agreement as to what it is.[63] Yet everyone agrees that something has taken place. The conditions for belief today are not what they were at the beginning of the Enlightenment period. A number of definitions have been offered, but each one seems to have its limitations.

First, secularism has often been associated with the general decline of religion; that is, it has been identified as a process by which religious thinking, practice, and institutionalization have lost prestige and influence. But the changes in existing institutions and traditional practices are not necessarily synonymous with the demise of religion itself. Here one need only point to the recent interest in all manner of spiritualities in spite of the highly secularized nature of contemporary society. Another difficulty arises when one seeks to identify the

---

62 Of course, some of the Enlightenment's advocates were definitely anti-religious and in particular anti-Christian. Cf. Voltaire's "Candide" *The Portable Voltaire*, Ben Ray Redman, ed. (New York: Penguin Books, 1977), 229-328.

63 Cf. Taylor. *A Secular Age*, 1-22 and Rodney Stark and Roger Finke. *Acts of Faith. Explaining the Human Side of Religion* (Berkeley: University of California Press, 2000), 57-79.

religious "peak" from which society has declined. Was there a golden age of religion?

Second, secularization has been linked to the disengagement of religious institutions from society. As society separates itself from religious legitimization and constitutes itself as an autonomous reality, it gradually assumes many primary functions formerly performed by the Church, i.e., economic, welfare and health services, family assistance and education. Religious institutions are, thereby, stripped of societal relevance and are pushed to the periphery. Once religious institutions have lost their public role, religion becomes increasingly a matter of private choice. In its completely secularized form religion would have "a purely inward character, influencing neither institutions nor corporate action outside its own immediate sphere of influence."[64] Disengagement, however, is not necessarily a sign of religious collapse, but rather a shift in function. There are obviously certain areas that are today better left to governmental agencies. And why not? Christianity itself differentiates between the community of faith and society at large. In keeping with the increasing differentiation of society, religion has simply had to adjust its practice and its self-conception.

Third, secularism has been equated with moral erosion, that is, with a dissolution of religious control over and/or motivation of values, beliefs and behavior. As diversity increases, the normative code needed for integration is of necessity generalized, i.e., the common denominator is lowered. What begins as a comprehensive set of specific, religiously motivated norms held by each subgroup, gives way to an ever-expanding area of flexibility—generic religious commitment, a kind of benevolent coexistence. Believe in God and, for the rest, do as you please. This notion has two significant limitations: (1) it is difficult to determine the content of such a generic religion. To what extent are its values actually held by the members of society? Are religious values generalized, implying some residual religious content, or simply abandoned? (2) the values of such a generic religion may be inherent in the culture. It is, for

---

64   L. Shiner. "The Concept of Secularization in Empirical Research." *Journal for the Scientific Study of Religion* 6 (Fall 1967): 212.

example, difficult to distinguish between generalized religious values and nationalism. Of course, the religious could be abandoned in favor of a code of behavior based exclusively on secular principles—a code of duty founded on considerations purely human.[65]

Moral erosion might also have something to do with a transmutation of beliefs, which are retained in some form but are no longer grounded in the sacred—as in the case of the transformation in the Calvinistic system of a disciplined attitude toward life, the by-product of which was the accumulation of wealth and the development of capitalism. In other words, capitalism developed its own momentum and the original religious underpinning became superfluous.

Finally, secularization is sometimes thought of in terms of the liberation of human ratio with its emphasis on the autonomy of human reason the subsequent transformation of attitudes toward truth. Accordingly, independent and self-sufficient reason takes the place of revelation and of a divinely wrought, life-unifying system, liberating academic disciplines from theological domination and leading to the absolute autonomy of technology, which is then viewed as a "closed organism," [66] an end in itself with no particular responsibility for politics, morality or spiritual values. In the end, the human beings are themselves set up as the measure of all things—a self-contained law acknowledging no limitation, value, or law imposed from without. Morality is pegged to the "normal," i.e., whatever the majority of individuals accept as good. Responsible to no one, each person is the master of her own destiny.

While each of these definitions contributes something to our understanding of secularism, each one is limited to one facet of the process, or fails to take actual developments into account. For that reason, it might be more useful to trace the development of the concept through what I believe must be at least four generations of meaning— expedience, emancipation, progress, surrender—none of which were

---

65   For example John Dewey's *A Common Faith* (New Haven: Yale University Press, 1934).

66   Jacques Ellul. *The Technological Society* (New York: Vintage Books, 1964), 133.

completely abandoned as its scope was refined, as the movement closed in on belief.

— I —

Ecclesio-Political Expedience

The term "secularize" was first used during the negotiations which led to the Peace of Westphalia. In April 1646 the French representative introduced it as a possible solution to the extremely delicate situation. The only way to satisfy the Swedish demand for reparations was to consider the transfer of certain properties owned by the Roman Church. Catholic sensitivities had already been inflamed by the loss of some areas to the Lutherans. Any further expropriation by a civil authority would have been interpreted as a kind of sacrilege and, therefore, intolerable. The German word *Verweltlichung* could have been used to describe the exchange. But the French translation would have implied a "disposing of" (*Verausserlichen*) and, therefore, profaning of the sacred and had to be abandoned. Secularization, though similar in meaning, had no anti-sacral overtones. It could be used to describe the transfer of property without necessarily implying the abrogation of its original religious purpose. As in the case of secular-priests, who were no less committed to religious pursuits than their monastic counterparts, the secular was not necessarily anti-church. This neutrality satisfied the claims of each participant, although nothing was decided, i.e., each delegation clung to its interpretation and the religious wars were brought to an end.[67]

This original religious neutrality was, however, doomed from the start. Secularization had already been used for the legitimate regress from a monastic order. Without nullifying his religious character, an indult could "effect the complete severance of the bond between the religious and his institute."[68] But it did smack of spiritual degeneration. Secularization disqualified the religious who was, therefore,

---

67   Martin Stallman. *Was ist Säkularisierung?* (Tübingen: J.C.B Mohr, 1960), 5-7.

68   *New Catholic Encyclopedia*, 1967 ed., s.v. "Secularization of Clerics," by E. L. Schneider.

debarred from; (1) every office, every benefice in major or minor basilicas and cathedrals; (2) every position as teacher and every office in greater or lesser clerical seminaries; in other houses for the instruction of clerics, in universities or institutions conferring degrees by apostolic privilege; (3) every office in Episcopal curia..."[69]

This reluctant tolerance of the secular flared into open hostility on February 25, 1803. The Kaiser of the Confederation of the Rhine instituted sweeping land reforms, which included the secularization of monasteries and bishoprics. In addition to staggering material losses, the Church was made subservient to civil authority. The events of 1803 fixed in the Catholic mind an understanding of secularization limited to the usurpation of sacred law and the illegitimate expropriation of Church properties. The victims saw it as a cheap triumph of thoughtless selfishness, an ugly breach of law.[70] Yet to others it signaled a long awaited breakthrough. To them ecclesiastical participation in government was an anachronism—an obstacle to progress. Secularization simply buried something that was already dead.

— 2 —

Separation of Church from Culture

What began as the neutral language of political expedience soon became the slogan of those seeking society's emancipation from the restrictive tutelage of Christianity. Ironically, "Christian conscience was the force which began to make Europe secular."[71] Hegel, for example, argued that it was Christianity that brought the Germanic nations of Europe to the realization that man as man is free.[72]

---

69   *The Catholic Encyclopedia*, 1912 ed., s.v. "Secularization," by A. Boudinhon.

70   Herman Lübbe. *Säkularisierung* (München: Karl Alber, 1975), 27-30.

71   Owen Chadwick. *The Secularization of the European mind in the 19ᵗʰ Century* (Cambridge: Cambridge University Press, 1975), 23.

72   Individual freedom in religious matters had, of course, been expounded earlier. "None, therefore, neither individuals, nor churches, nor even commonwealths have any just title to invade civil rights

With the Christian religion the doctrine arose that all men are free before God, that Christ has freed men, has made them equal before God, and freed them for Christian freedom. These notions made freedom independent of birth, class, education, etc., and this means immense progress.[73]

Self-determination, of course, included the freedom of thought, i.e., the right to dissent. It was with one such dissenting free thinker[74] that secularism as a program for societal improvement was associated. In 1846 George Holyoake organized the secular society in order to propagate the principles of secularism, which, it was hoped, would aid in the coming of the kingdom of man.[75]

These principles being few, practical, and demonstrable to any capable of observation and reflection, they constituted an independent code of conduct which, owing nothing to ancient revelations, adherents of such views were under no obligation to waste time in reconciling the truth of today with the error of the past.

My mind being given to open thought, I came to consider whether a simple theory of ethical duty was possible, which regarded the theology then in vogue, uncertain, irrelevant, or untrue.[76]

---

and rob each other of worldly goods on the plea of religion." John Locke. *A Letter on Toleration*, trans. J. W. Gough (Oxford: The Clarendon Press, 1968), 85.

73   Carl J. Friedrich. The Philosophy of Hegel (N.Y.: The Modern Library, 1953), 171. See also Richard L. Schacht, "Hegel on Freedom," in Hegel, ed. Alasdoir MacIntyre (Notre Dame: Univ. of Notre Dame Press, 1972), 289-328.

74   "Not seeing in my youth what better I could do in a world, here no one seemed infallible, than to think for myself led to my acquiring opinions different from other people. For a time it distressed me very much to find that I differed from the world, until it occurred to me that the world differed from me: Then I had no more anxiety." G. J. Holyoake. *Sixty Years of an Agitator's Life*, 2 vols. (London: T. F. Unwin, 1892), 2:290.

75   "Professor Clifford exclaimed: 'The kingdom of God has come; when comes the kingdom of man?' A secularist is one who hastens the coming of this kingdom; which must be agreeable to heaven if the people of this world are to occupy mansions there." G. J. Holyoake. *The Origin and Nature of Secularism* (London: Watts, 1896), 62.

76   Holyoake. *Sixty Years of an Agitator's Life*, 7:292-293.

According to Holyoake secularism was not necessarily anti-Christian. It was not committed to any hostile attitude towards theology, nor did it imply atheism.[77] Secularism, like mathematics, is independent of theistic doctrines. Religion was simply irrelevant.

> We know the laws of sanitation, economy, and equity, upon which health, wealth, and security depend. All these things are quite independent of any knowledge of the origin of the universe or the owner of it.[78]

As the implications of Christianity's irrelevance gained acceptance, the clamor for emancipation grew and took on a decidedly anti-Christian character. For Marx, religion was not only irrelevant; it was the source of alienation, a cruel illusion, which gave divine justification to social evil. As such, it had to be abolished. Even religion as a man's private concern, as proposed in the Gotha Program,[79] was intolerable.

> But the workers' party ought at any rate in this connection to have expressed its awareness of the fact that bourgeois 'freedom of conscience' is nothing but the toleration of all possible kinds of religious freedom of conscience, and that for its part it endeavors rather to liberate the conscience from the witchery of religion.[80]

Although no use was made of the term secularization, it can be said that Marxist theory is the most influential of all symbols for the progress of secularization in the nineteenth century.[81]

---

77 G. J. Holyoake and C. Bradlaugh. *Secularism, Scepticism, and Atheism* (London: Austin and Co., 1870), 1-36.

78 Holyoake. *Sixty Years of an Agitator's Life*, 7:294.

79 Chadwick. 81.

80 Karl Marx. "Critique of the Gotha Program," in *The Marx Engels Reader*, ed. Robert Tucker. (N.J.: W. W. Norton and Co., 1978), 540.

81 Chadwick. 69.

In 1889 Friedrich Jodl called for the secularization of philosophy,[82] i.e., freedom from its scholastic servility to theology. This was applied particularly to ethics, which should be grounded in individual autonomy rather than the imposed will of some transcendent being. Based on a similar ethic, Emil Laas envisioned a peaceful federation of nations which he referred 'to as a secularized analogy of the medieval papacy.' Jodl and Laas were among the leading intellectuals who organized the German society for ethical culture (*Deutsche Gesellschaft für Ethische Kultur*) in 1892. Its political goal was the realization of a technocratic vision in which society, in complete independence of religious premises, would solve its own problems through technology.[83]

By the end of the century secularization had swept into philosophy, ethics, politics and education.[84] It had become a platform for social reform and in some cases an ideological assault on Christianity.

− 3 −
The Reprogramming of Culture

A lecture given by Richard Fester in 1908 signaled an important change in the use of the term secularization.[85] Speaking to the International Historians Congress, Fester called for, or more accurately, celebrated the secularization of history. In concert with the free thinker's call for emancipation, he declared the final and ultimate unshackling of history from the chains of the biblical-theological world view. The significant difference was his use of the word as a scientific term, which described secularization as the process of societal emancipation.

---

82   Friedrich Jodl. *Geschchichte der Ethik in der neueren Philosophie*, 2 vols. (Stuttgart: Cotta, 1882-1889), 2:364.

83   Lübbe. *Säkularisierung*, 41-48.

84   One of the stated aims of the "Leader" newspaper, of which Holyoake was commissar, was "the complete freeing of secular education from all restraints of sect or dogmatical religion." Holyoake. *Sixty Years of an Agitator's Life*, 2:236.

85   Richard Fester. "Die Säkularisation der Historie," *Historische Vierteljahresschrift Schriftreihe* 2 (1908): 441-459.

This was in keeping with the then revolutionary concept of sociological facts. Emile Durkheim, applying the approach of the natural sciences, developed a set of rules for the study of society. In order to isolate sociological facts one had to ask whether the phenomena under consideration were: (1) general throughout the extent of a given society, and (2) whether there was any manner of exercising an exterior restraint over the individual.[86] In this way society could be examined phenomenologically. Thus, the term secularization could be (re) neutralized and applied, without evaluation, to an observable process. Pioneers of this procedure were Max Weber and Ferdinand Tonnies.

In examining the relationship between confession and social status, Weber noticed that Protestants held more influential positions than did Catholics. ". . . Business leaders and owners of capital as well as the higher grades of skilled labor, and even more the higher technically and commercially trained personnel of modern enterprises, are overwhelmingly protestant."[87]

This, he concluded, was directly related to the Protestant mentality, which openly encouraged the accumulation of material wealth. "We must admonish all Christians to gain as much as they can and save as much as they can the result of which is to become rich."[88]

But this precipitates a struggle with the problem of the secularizing effect of possessions.[89] The original religious motivation is gradually replaced by the dictates of economic reality. Under the pressure of secularization the "religious root dies and makes room for a utilitarian this-worldliness."[90]

Ferdinand Tonnies described the resultant society (*Gesellschaft*) as a secularized (*verweltlicht*) form of community (*Gemeinschaft*).[91]

---

86   Emile Durkheim. *On Morality and Society* (Chicago: The University of Chicago Press, 1973), 772-777.

87   Max Weber. *The Protestant Ethic and the Spirit of Capitalism* (N.Y.: Charles Scribner, 1958), 35.

88   Max Weber. *Soziologie-Weltgeschichte-Analysen* (Stuttgart: A. Kroner, 1968), 374.

89   Ibid., 373.

90   Ibid., 375.

91   Lubbe. *Säkularisierung*, 62.

Community was the result of what he called "essential will," i.e., the objectification of man's basic nature. Society, on the other hand, was based on rational will as in the individualistic society of modern capitalism. He observed the transition from a predominantly communal to a predominantly societal order, as a "consequence of increased commercialization together with the rise of the modern state and the progress of science."[92] This included the transposition of the validity of organized religion.

Secularization, then, was a supposedly neutral sociological fact. By neutralizing[93] it, i.e., freeing it from the polemic of the nineteenth century, these sociologists opened the way for its use by Protestant theologians.

— 4 —
The Christian Re-Incorporation of Culture

The secularization of the nineteenth century European mind spawned the critical questioning of the biblical texts, the historicity of Christ, and the traditions of the Church. In rapid succession a series of cardinal truths were jettisoned. With Strauss, Bauer, Feuerbach and Nietzsche[94] "German religious thought was well on its way past orthodoxy and enlightenment, past absolute spirit and myth- to the edge of the grave of God."[95] Against this backdrop three distinct theological approaches developed. Protestantism could be viewed as the source of secularism, as the last bastion of defense against it, or as the realistic interpreter of inevitable social change.

---

92   *International Encyclopedia of the Social Sciences.* 1968 ed., s.v. "Tonnies, Ferdinand," by Rudolf Heberle.

93   That is by initiating the process of neutralization. Sociologists are still in pursuit of this elusive goal. "I am afraid, however, that the careless and partisan use of 'secularization' is so general that its polemical connotations will continue to cling to it despite the social scientists' efforts to neutralize it." L. Shiner. "The Concept of Secularization in Empirical Research." *Journal for the Scientific Study of Religion* 6 (Fall 1967): 220.

94   It should be noted that it is primarily Protestant theology which is associated with the secularization of theology whereas Catholic theology tended to be anti-modernistic.

95   Martin Marty. *Three Paths to the Secular* (N.Y.: Harper and Row, 1969), 47.

According to Ernst Troeltsch one of the most important theological developments has been

> ...the separation of church and state, the toleration of a variety of co-existing religious communities, the principle of volunteerism in the development of church groups and the freedom of opinion and conviction in all matters of world view and religion.[96]

The secularized or totally this-world state of affairs is not to be interpreted as a sign of degeneration, or even the sinful disorientation of the world, but rather as the secularization of a religious idea, i.e., the autonomy of the individual.[97]

Since Protestantism has actively promoted religious individualism, it is one of the principle architects of the modern world.[98] It broke up the Catholic monopoly[99] and fathered the free Churches, which Troeltsch calls the stepchildren of the Reformation.[100] The idea of individual freedom was intensified by the free Churches and eventually secularized, i.e., overpowered by nationalism, skepticism, and utilitarian tolerance. Although

> a large part of the modern world's foundations in the state, in society, economics, science and art did develop in complete independence of Protestantism... its significance for the development of the modern world can obviously not be contended.[101]

In one sense, contemporary society is the logical, inevitable outcome of Protestant thought. Not everyone agreed. For some secularism was

---

96 Ernst Troeltsch. *Die Bedeutung des Protestantismus für die Entstehung der Modernen Welt* (München: 1928: reprinted ed., Aalen: O. Zeller, 1963), 63.

97 Stallman. *Was ist Säkularisierung?* 15.

98 Troeltsch. *Die Bedeutung,* 23.

99 Ibid., 46.

100 Ibid., 62.

101 Ibid., 23.

an unmitigated evil. Assailed from within and without, the Church was called to join in the "decisive battle between genuine Christianity and a religion of secularism."[102] In 1931 Cannon S. M. Warner declared that "never since pre-renaissance times have the ideas of the Christian community been impelled to face the haunting menace of wide-spreading secularism as it confronts us today."[103] The threat was considered particularly insidious since the line between the Church and the world, although fundamentally contrary to one another, had faded.

> Now it may be said that this confusion between civilization and Christianity, between Satan's world and God's rule, has been un-mistakably advanced by the assumption on the part of professing Christians that such evolutionary progress, popular as it is amongst our religious leaders, philanthropists and modern thinkers is fundamental to the Christian project... nothing could be more alien to God's revealed plan of redemption than such teaching.[104]

With new battle fronts between Christ and the world being drawn up everywhere, Protestants were compelled to resist or be swallowed up by this perversion of Christian assumption.

That mankind was approaching a completely religionless era could hardly be denied, but it need not be interpreted as a cause for desperate polemic. Dietrich Bonhoeffer viewed it as the sign of a world come of age. Since this cannot be altered (nor should one want to prevent it), the fundamental question is: How can Christ be communicated in a worldly way? Traditional apologetics are clearly meaningless and unchristian. That approach would be like trying to push an adult back into adolescence, i.e., to make him dependent on things from which he had already attained freedom. It has become superfluous and insulting to present God as a working hypothesis to fill the gaps of our dilemma. Our real task is to

---

102   Ibid., 23

103   C. W. H. Amos. *The Church or the World. The Crisis of Christendom* (London: Marshall, Morgan and Scott, 1931), 7.

104   Ibid., 58.

reinterpret the message, i.e., to develop a non-religious interpretation of biblical terms. This emphasis on a this-worldly Gospel, it was hoped, would uncover godlessness and bring men to a recognition of their true standing before God. Thus, in his godlessness, modern man may well be closer to God than those who have not yet come of age.[105]

Since Bonhoeffer, Protestant theologians have no longer been able to interpret secularization as a culpable turning away from God. For him it was a Christian event in which modern man's religious destiny was fulfilled.

Another decisive step towards theological legitimation was made by Friedrich Gogarten's distinction between secularization and secularism. According to Gogarten secularization is the process whereby ideas and knowledge are loosed from their original source, and become accessible to human reason. Man begins to recognize his own potential, his own ability to understand and administer the world, i.e., is in possession of himself and responsible for the world. This process, says Gogarten, is the "necessary and legitimate consequence of the Christian faith. It was faith in a created order that first freed men from their metaphysical fears of the material world. Once freed, they were able to experiment and the resulting experience confirmed their independence. Christian faith enabled the freedom that led to the advancement of humanity.

This could lead to an attempt at atheistic profanation, or secularism. Impressed by his own abilities man begins to search for the answers to all questions and ultimate meaning within himself. Secularism appears to be a degeneration of secularization, which seeks to advance beyond the limitations imposed by human reason. The task of faith, therefore, is to help it remain in its secularity by remaining true to its nature by continually distinguishing between the divine reality of salvation and the earthly-worldly meaning of human action. "Therefore, faith and secularization relate to each other in the sense that there can be no

---

105   Dietrich Bonhoeffer. *Widerstand und Ergebung* (Gutersloh: Verlagshaus G. Mohn, 1978), 132.

faith without secularization of the relationship between the faithful and the world."[106]

Post-Christian society has been deeply affected by Christianity, and bears the latter's mark . We have not ceased to be products of the Christian era, but we have managed to reject what is specifically Christian and retain only its psychic aspect. Thus, many of secularism's ideals are not necessarily derived from human nature but may represent residual Christian influence.

– Conclusion –
Secularism's Effect on Individual Commitment

In the end it is the individual, that most elementary of societal components, who determines the complexion of society, including its religious visage.

Both organizationally and theologically the heart of religion is commitment. Historically, the primary concern of all religious institutions has been to lead men to faith, and the continued existence of any religion would seem to depend on accomplishing this task. The degree of secularization, then, is a reflection of the extent to which the Christian mind has been able to maintain its commitment and resist the secular.

> It is common place that the mind of modern man has been secularized. For instance, it has been deprived of any orientation towards the supernatural. Tragic as this fact is, it would not be so desperately tragic had the Christian mind held out against the secular drift. But unfortunately the Christian mind has succumbed to the secular drift with a degree of weakness and nervelessness unmatched in Christian history.[107]

---

106   Friedrich Gogarten. *Verhängnis und Hoffnung der Neuzeit* (München: Siebenstern Taschenbuch, 1966), 143.

107   Harry Blamires. *The Christian Mind* (London: S.C.K., 1966), 3.

Religious commitment (belief) always has an object, usually greater than the individual, and is either partial or total depending on the nature of the object. As the changes wrought by secularism are applied, this object of faith has shifted from a personal God to a system of thought (truth), to religious institutions, and finally to the self.[108]

If a personal God is the object of religious commitment, the individual relinquishes all claim to self-rule and seeks to order all of life according to the dictates of his Lord. This is a total life orientation that denies neither the sacred nor the secular and seeks to keep them in perspective. Its characteristics would be a carefully delineated belief system, a high degree of public and private religious practice, personal experience of supernatural agency, and a causal link between belief and values, behavior, and ethical norms. God is the only object which can command total commitment, since He pervades every aspect of daily life.

Another object of belief might be some system of thought. Since the sacred-secular separation calls the supernatural into question, the individual may be tempted to abandon the commitment to a personal God in favor of a more concrete or even material object. Thus, she may focus her attention on a cognitive object, such as a system of truth. If the scope of separation is limited, this could be Christian dogma. Commitment would then be measured in terms of varying degrees of orthodoxy. If separation became total, the object of commitment could be ethics, a philosophy, or perhaps some cause, such as the struggle for justice. Obviously, these objects can never exact absolute commitment. Public opinion and doctrinal plurality would always mitigate the intensity of individual commitment.

As the effects of generalization begin to erode the authority of doctrine, the individual will feel compelled to anchor her commitment in something more solid. Institutionalized forms of religion become the focus of attention. Participation in corporate church activities, church sponsored projects, ritual and membership are the standards

---

108   Rommen. *Namenschristentum*, 56-59.

of commitment. This will often be related to doctrine as formulated by the particular institution. But, as we shall see, there is no necessary connection between ritualistic practice and understanding of, or acceptance of specific beliefs. Once this kind of segmentation is allowed, total commitment becomes impossible. The secular counterpart takes the form of obligation to a company, government agency, social club, or sports club. These functional substitutes for religion become more predominant as secularization advances and commitment is increasingly limited to that sphere of life dominated by each particular institution.

Although the need for commitment is generally fulfilled by an object other than one's self, the increased individualization of society can give the impression that the only constant factor is the individual herself. Self-fulfillment is taken to be the object of commitment. It is evidenced in all the narcissism of a consumer-oriented society. But "existence, which revolves totally around one's own personal needs is finally experienced as empty and meaningless."[109] It is a narrow commitment that inevitably leads to bitterness and isolation.

---

109   Donald E. Miller. "Some Reflections on Secularization," *Religion in Life* 48 (Winter 1979), 495.

Part II.

The Trajectory of
the Late Modern Self.

In this section I intend to explore the trajectory[110] of the late modern self. The term trajectory implies movement along a specific route or path, movement under the influence of certain forces, as well as a current position from which continued movement might be projected. This approach to the development of the self should facilitate an accurate assessment/evaluation of its current condition and, depending on our findings, suggest corrective alteration of the trajectory. With this in mind I will seek to identify and elaborate on several prominent features (phenomena) of the late modern self that mark its position/condition on the plane/horizon of (human) being. I will then propose alternate trajectories privileged by a Christian perspective.

In doing so, I am not interested in developing a traditional phenomenology of human being, since pure description tends to disallow critical evaluation and will not advance the present trajectory-altering project—the re-centering of the real. Yet, given the Matrix-like[111] environment of denial, some phenomenological investigation will be necessary in order to part the veil of similitude that blankets us in unreality.

Indeed, we will have to explore the questions that define the individual and social context of the late modern condition:[112] what we do, how we act, who we are – questions which, according to Giddens, are central "…for everyone living in circumstances of late modernity—and ones which, on some level or another, all of us {have to} answer, either discursively or through day-to-day social behavior."[113]

But it is precisely on the plane of day-to-day discourse that the late modern self abandons reality—it dissimulates with shamefaced and

---

110 Giddens used this idea in his book *Modernity and Self-Identity* (Stanford: Stanford University Press, 1991). I realize that the term is somewhat overused and therefore limited. However, my intent is to signal (in good post modern fashion) the possibility of multiple extensions of the trajectory—dependent on which forces we choose to apply to the self.

111 As in the film "The Matrix."

112 "We will also ask, if these concerns are historically distinctive? Can we really say that they are specific to our era? That they are the consequences of our past, the enlightenment project or its failure? Indeed, it has been suggested that this search for self-identity is, in fact, a late modern problem, perhaps having its origins in Western individualism." Giddens. *Modernity and Self-Identity*, 70.

113 Giddens. *Modernity and Self-Identity*, 70.

submissive denial of its own personhood—rendering social discourse mere simulation and leaving all phenomenological description thereof askew. The only escape from the vortex of the unreal is an honest investigation, driven by an aggressive apologetic agenda—namely an anti-dissimulational defense, a reassertion of the very essence of our human nature. I do not want to simply describe the self, I want to make a case for its reinstatement. It is to this apologetically informed description that we now turn.

Chapter 3

Being and Identity

The biggest danger, that of losing oneself, can pass off in the world as quietly as if it were nothing; every other loss, an arm, a leg, five dollars, a wife, etc., is bound to be noticed.[114]

— I —

Being: The Passage from Ontological Security to Existential Anxiety and Back

When we speak of the human self, we are generally referring to an individual's awareness of who and what they are. The self is a composite made up of three elements: being, identity, and self-awareness. The first, being-as-such, includes both the corporeal and incorporeal elements of human existence. It is, on the one hand, the self as defined by the fact of material existence; the body and its various abilities and needs. On the other hand, it is human existence as evidenced by the thoughts, desires, and hopes—the spirit, the ontic essence—of an individual. The second element, identity or being-in-the-world, involves the individual's relationship to external frameworks of reality, in particular other human beings. This is the self as viewed through the ongoing history of one's interface with the physical as well as social and cultural dimensions of the world. It is the self established as and identified by participation in goals, values, and languages shared with others. The third element, self-

---

114   S. Kierkegaard. *The Sickness unto Death* (London: Penguin Books 1989 (1849)).

awareness, is an active reflection on the other two. This is an ordered and stable self, realized by a process of self-interrogation,[115] constant self-monitoring whereby it answers questions, manages threats and generates a confidence in the persistence of its being and the continuity of its identity.

Taken together, then, the three registers yield a kind of ontological security. That is, they would if the individual would consciously participate in the whole process. But if, for example, the self is unable or unwilling to interrogate its own being, and if the external threats to its existence and identity cannot be managed effectively, security quickly morphs into an existential anxiety. In other words, the individual loses the ability to say anything certain about his or her own existence and anything coherent about identity—it loses the self. This, unfortunately, is the condition facing most late modern human beings.

In fairness it should be pointed out that the problem of one's own being is the least natural of all problems—the one that common sense never poses.[116] This may be true because we simply take for granted that which is so "luminously evident."[117] Or is it because we harbor an innate, primal fear of the question itself—somehow recognizing the enormity of what is at stake, the paucity of our language[118] and the inability of our minds to reach beyond this self-evident horizon of human existence? Indeed, I submit that the question is so deeply troubling that most human beings eagerly bracket the question.

---

115   "Derives from the human capacity to make both the world and our own existence objects of our active regard, to turn a kind of mirror not only on phenomena in the world, including our own bodies and our social relations, but our consciousness too, putting ourselves at a distance from our own being so as to examine, judge, and sometimes regulate or revise it… we are what our attention to ourselves makes us be." Seigel. *The Idea of the Self* (Cambridge: Cambridge University Press, 2005), 6.

116   Aubenque as quoted by Umberto Eco. *Kant and the Platypus* (San Diego: Harcourt, 1999), 15. And quoting Heidegger, goes on to conclude, "being as such is so far from constituting a problem that apparently it is as if such a datum 'didn't exist'" (Heidegger 1973: 1969).

117   Eco. *Kant and the Platypus*, 9.

118   Umberto Eco, quoting Paschal, points out the essence of our dilemma. "One cannot begin to define being without falling victim to this absurdity: one cannot define a word without beginning with the term *is*, be it expressly stated or merely understood. To define being, therefore, you have to say *is*, thus using the term to be defined in the definition." *Kant and the Platypus*, 9.

Nevertheless, knowing that we have not answered, or cannot answer, the most fundamental question of human existence leaves us in an irremediable state of ontological insecurity. Why, then, do we accept this condition of anxiety? Three aspects of late modern context suggest themselves as possible causes: radical reflexivity, depersonalizing of social institutions, and what might be called the dilemma of bad faith.

A. RADICAL REFLEXIVITY

One reason for the presence of such widespread anxiety is the radically reflexive[119] and self-referencing nature of the late modern ontological project—the extreme inwardness fostered by the Enlightenment (modernity). This turn inward is sometimes expressed as an extreme confidence in human ability to define itself. That idea is rooted, in part, in the assumption that *existence precedes essence.* In other words, the human subject just

> ...exists, turns up, appears on the scene, and, only afterwards, defines himself... Thus, there is no human nature, since there is no God to conceive it. Not only is man what he conceives himself to be, but he is also only what he wills himself to be after this thrust toward existence.[120]

There are two problems with this. One is that if man is nothing else but what he makes of himself, then the human being bears the full responsibility[121] for the outcome, every choice, every discrimination of good and evil, every framework of meaningful life, with no external standards, no tutors, and no one to share blame for eventual mishaps. But, given the universality of less than perfect outcomes, the isolating reflexivity

---

119 At this point it is difficult to know whether to use the word reflexive or reflective.

120 Sartre, Jean-Paul. *Essays in Existentialism* (New York: Citadel Press, 1988), 35-36. Yet, there are limits. "...if it is impossible to find in every man some universal essence which would be human nature, yet there does exist a universal human condition, the *a priori* limits which outline man's fundamental situation in the universe." (52)

121 Ibid., 36.

of absolutized inwardness must eventually issue onto an equally inward and overwhelming anguish/forlornness—existential anxiety.

The other problem with this approach is that we can never really be sure who we are, since every new action changes the human subject. In other words, there is no stable core of identity that operates outside the vicissitudes of one's personal history. Whoever I am at any given moment is not who I am in the next moment—another source of existential anxiety.

B. DEPERSONALIZING OF SOCIAL INSTITUTIONS

Another reason for the prevalence of late modern existential anxiety is the depersonalization of the social institutions needed to establish identity and manage the risks associated with the opportunities afforded by modernity. Obviously, the Enlightenment has brought significant advances in our knowledge of the natural world, medicine, transportation, communication, commerce, etc. Yet those very advances have also amplified the types and consequences of the threats: nuclear fallout, biological contamination, terrorism, identity theft, and so on. The anxiety caused by these threats is inescapable and "…filters into most aspects of day-to-day life, at least as a background phenomenon."[122] In this context ontological security is a matter of trust in the perceived reliability and predictability of those individuals and institutions needed to balance risk and opportunity.

Traditionally, trust has been expressed within the context of actual relationships with other people. But the combination of social complexity and inwardness has caused us to replace those relationships with what might be called Expeditious Associations,[123] such as those between a merchant and a customer, or a doctor and a patient. These are transitory commitments in which what is important is some semblance of utility within a given arena of action. In effect, we minimize the role of

---

122 Giddens. *Modernity and Self-Identity*, 181.

123 Giddens refers to this as *facework* commitments in which what is important is indication of the integrity of the other, but only within the given arenas of action. *The Consequences of Modernity* (Stanford: Stanford University Press, 1990), 88.

others—trusting ourselves—choosing and managing select associations only as need requires.

Just how far this is sometimes taken can be seen from an XConomy report on a new voicemail service called Slydial.

> Here's the paradox that Boston-based MobileSphere is exploiting: We all want to own a cell phone. But a lot of the time, we don't actually want to talk with our friends, family, co-workers, and all of those other people who are just trying to suck the life out of us. So when we absolutely have to reply to a message they've left, or tell them we're too busy to meet them for lunch, or offer some other minimal gesture of recognition, calling them is far too risky: they might actually pick up, forcing us to interact. It would be far better if we could simply leave a voicemail message, without ever causing their phone to ring. That way, there'd be no muss, no fuss; no dealing with an actual human and all their demands and sensitivities.

> They're openly pitching it as a way to avoid unpleasant conversations, annoying people, or any situation where you might have to take responsibility for something. "Checking-in with a boss, friend, significant other or parent has never been easier as Slydial provides *the illusion of communication* without the hassle of engaging in a time-consuming conversation." I added the italics, but I am not making this up; it's right in Slydial's press release.[124]

We have also tended to replace traditional institutions (kinship, family, religion) with what might be called Abstract Systems of knowledge or expertise. These are mechanisms, such as commercial distribution networks and the Internet, that provide access to threat management, while minimizing the need for placing trust in another person—the direct presence of the other is essentially removed from the encounter—we neither have nor are other. What makes trusting some system of

---

124   http://www.xconomy.com/boston/2008/07/22/slydial-voicemail-service-offers-the-illusion-of-communication/ Accessed July 25, 2008.

expertise necessary is the sheer complexity of modern life that precludes an individualized working knowledge of all the systems/mechanisms needed to survive. It is the acknowledgement of our own lack of expertise that forces us to "trust" abstract systems. The average motorist, for example, cannot verify the chemical integrity of gasoline purchased any more than the patient can actually authenticate a physician's diagnosis. Thus, the unavoidable encounters of the multi-being-ed world are reduced to the pragmatics of "faceless commitments,"[125] a kind of civil indifference—merely using (not really trusting) others to balance a possible threat against potential benefits.[126]

And herein lies the greatest threat of all, personal meaninglessness—the loss of self. If exaggerated inwardness prevents me from actually trusting (depending upon) a person(s) other than myself, and if I have no control over or understanding of the abstracted systems of expertise required for day-to-day living, then of what significance is my own person? Is it not lost in the futility of vacuous activity?

C. The Dilemma of Bad Faith

A third reason for this late modern anxiety is the practice of dissimulation.[127] While I am convinced that this existential anxiety is pandemic, there are many people who do not appear to be anxious. However, I suggest that they are actually hiding their anxiety, that many are fleeing from[128] their anguish and doing so in "bad faith"[129]—

---

125 Giddens. *Consequences*, 88.

126 Of course, the opposite is also true, i.e., if I conclude that my own expertise is sufficient—that there is no need for expert assistance—I simply ignore institutions associated with those domains.

127 A form of dishonesty or hypocrisy, to state something one knows to be false, cf. Rom. 12:9, Gal 2:13.

128 Sartre. *Essays in Existentialism*, 38.

129 Sartre, 68. For the existentialist this anguish can actually lead to freedom. "One who realizes in anguish his condition at being thrown into a responsibility which extends to his very abandonment has no longer either remorse or regret or excuse; he is no longer anything but a freedom which perfectly reveals itself and whose being resides in this very revelation."

lying about it, masking it under a cloak of the dissimulating denial of responsibility and the hyper-real "white noise"[130] of frenetic activity.

The basic structure of this bad-faith-lying involves: a) a basic affirmation, negation or action, which b) conflicts with reality, and c) a second level affirmation, negation, or action designed to mask the dishonesty. For example: a) I affirm the need for sexual purity, b) but that conflicts with my own life, c) so I aggressively affirm my opposition to homosexuality. Or a) I claim to care about other people's well being, b) but actually, I couldn't care less about others, c) so I support a hungry child in Asia.

With respect to the self, we lie by insisting that we have no anxiety, as if the confidence in continued existence were not shaken by the encircling threats. We lie by pretending that the stability of persistent personhood does not really matter, that the carousel of fugacious associations is an adequate foundation for being-in-the-world. But, if the presence of existential anxiety is an ever-present aspect of self-awareness, then it is indeed bad faith, for to lie in this way is to hide the truth known by the self from self[131]—it knows that it is lying to itself, and that in doing so the once unified notion of the human self is shattered.

The only way to prevail in the face of such obvious deception is to radically repress it—to lie about the lying—in order to expunge it from consciousness. One way of doing that is to emphasize the importance of the self (personalized home page, personal computer, personal evangelism, etc)—narcissism as a cover for the loss of self, relentless activity as a cover for the loss of contemplation. But, alas, to be dishonestly dishonest is to abandon the self to the vortex of unreality, rendering it a being that in being denies being.

I realize that some of this is difficult to follow in the abstract, so let me illustrate with a brief case study (something which really happened).

---

130   Cf. Don DeLillo. *White Noise* (New York: Penguin, 1986).

131   There is a scene in the film *The Matrix*, in which the traitor is being offered a meal by the group's enemy. He takes a slice of steak and says, "I know this is not real, but I am going to enjoy it anyway."

A thunderstorm menacing, the biker deftly rolls his fuel-starved Harley to a neat stop at a remote filling station. Repeated attempts to activate the pump fail. Then, suddenly, as if out of the ether itself, a disembodied voice admonishes…

"Sir, you have to pay in advance. There are dishonest people who drive off without paying, so I'm afraid we can't trust you."

"But," protests the biker, nervously eyeing the storm "I'm not dishonest. Why are you punishing me for the crimes of others?"

"That's not it at all," sniggers the voice, temper shortening "It really has nothing to do with you as a person."

"Well, that's a relief." "But, wait" protests the anxious biker, "you don't even know me, a family man, a tax payer, a churchgoer . . ."

"Please," chides the ether "don't make this harder than it has to be. Everyone knows that family, community, and especially religion are irrelevant."

"Ok, Ok" capitulates the dejected biker, as it begins to rain. "So, how does this work?

"It's quite simple. Come in, leave $20 at the register, go pump gas, come back in for the change."

"But… How do I know you encased in your bulletproof cage will give me change? How do I know that what is being pumped is actually gasoline?"

"Really, Sir, you just have to trust me!"

This encounter illustrates the three aspects of late modernity of which I have spoken—the loss of self, the depersonalization of social discourse, and bad faith.

First of all, you will notice that there is no place for the self in this exchange. "It has nothing to do with you as a person." In other words, the biker's person, identity, human existence is eliminated from a transaction that should (actually does) require mutual respect, recognition, and trust. He is simply the non-personal, abstracted consumer (functionally no more significant than the fuel itself) in an utterly one-sided exchange. The biker is powerless. If he wants fuel, he has no choice but to acquiesce, to abandon his own personal identity and play the game.

Second, you will notice that social discourse has become a mere simulation. The event at the gas station—buying and selling—would ordinarily require the presence of more than one person and a relationship based on mutual trust. But as you can see, the two persons involved have been removed from the transaction, i.e., separated by technologies such as the intercom and reduced to abstracted symbols of themselves. One is a customer, the other a vendor, and beyond that who and what they are is completely unimportant. Obviously, this cannot be seen as the interaction of two individual persons. And it is certainly not based on mutual trust. The technologically enabled gas station attendant creates an utterly one-sided situation in which she alone is safe, and powerful. Actually, the biker has no choice but to "trust" the experts who produce and distribute fuel, determine fair (?) market value, and guarantee the "integrity" of the product. But, the imposition of blind, one-sided trust in some depersonalized system of experts actually removes personhood from the transaction, redefining the very nature of trust—both participants, having been abstracted, their presence obviated, engage in a mere illusion of social discourse.

Third, you will notice that the biker has little choice but to dissimulate, i.e., to pretend that his own identity does not matter, to "just deal with it" as if he were not a person even though he is.[132]

---

132   The Lie of Bad Faith: a) my person is not important, b) yet I know that my person is important, c) so I emphasize the convenience and security of the depersonalized transaction.

As deeply troubling as this incident is, I have found very few people who are disturbed by it. Having randomly presented the case to numerous individuals in a variety of settings, I have been repeatedly told that this is simply the way things are and that we just have to deal with it.

— 2 —
Identity: Self-Narrative, Reflexivity, and Expression

The question of identity is closely related to the issue of being and involves answers to the question "Who am I?" as opposed to "What or How I am?" Obviously, identity is a complex, puzzling structure which involves personal (private, psychological) and public aspects and has both historical and momentary (and perhaps proleptic) elements.

The roots of our contemporary understanding of individual identity lie in the philosophy of Frederich Hegel and John Stewart Mill. According to Hegel, an individual's consciousness is a movement of the intellect by which it apprehends an object(s) in terms of difference. It can thus distinguish itself from the world of things around it. Self-consciousness, on the other hand, is an awareness of the self as an object in which case there is no difference between the subject and the object.[133] This, he says, amounts to a motionless tautology, I am I, with no difference, merely being or desire. Self-consciousness achieves satisfaction of that desire only in another self-consciousness.[134] But self-consciousness, inevitably faced by another consciousness, must go out of itself and apprehend the other and then supersede the other in order to be sure of itself. In so doing, "they recognize themselves as mutually recognizing one

---

133 Friedrich Hegel. *Phenomenology of Spirit* (Oxford, 1977), 113 "Self-consciousness is, to begin with, simple being-for-self, self-equal through the exclusion from itself of everything else. For it, its essence and absolute object, is 'I', and in this immediacy, or in this [mere] being, of its being-for-self, it is an individual."

134 Ibid., 110.

another."[135] In this way, over against another self, the self can begin to answer the question of who it is. Identity is then created in response to others in a matrix of mutual recognition.

> This is the sense in which one cannot be a self on one's own. I am a self only in relation to certain interlocutors: in one way in relation to those conversation partners who were essential to my achieving self-definition; in another in relation to those who are now crucial to my continued grasp of languages of self-understanding and, of course, these classes may overlap. A self exists only within what I call 'webs of interlocution.'[136]

But to what extent does the individual have control over the development of her own identity. John Steward Mill suggests that the individual (identity) can be shaped in two ways. One can proceed in terms of what he calls authenticity, that is discovering and being true to oneself. In this case one posits the self (identity) as something given *qua* existence, something that can be uncovered, perhaps even developed and expressed. While the late modern individual is certainly interested in being true to herself, the idea of accepting certain aspects of identity as given seems unacceptably limiting. The more popular path to identity formation is an Existentialist one. Here, as Mill argues, one accepts existence (not identity) as a given and then goes on to describe or define what one is to exist as, i.e., to make up the self (identity). This freedom to develop one's own identity is seen as essential to well-being.[137]

Freedom is sometimes expressed in the form of a life-plan, a mode of living. Princeton philosopher Kwame Appiah reemphasizes Mills assertion.

---

135   Ibid., 112.

136   Taylor. *Sources of the Self*, 36.

137   J.S. Mill. *On Liberty* Chapter III, 1 "If it were felt that the free development of individuality is one of the leading essentials of well-being; that it is not only a coordinate element with all that is designated by the terms civilization, instruction, education, culture, but is itself a necessary part and condition of all those things; there would be no danger that liberty should be undervalued, and the adjustment of the boundaries between it and social control would present no extraordinary difficulty."

Individuality is not so much a state to be achieved as a mode of life to be pursued. Mill says that it is important that one choose one's own plan of life, and liberty consists, at least in part, in providing the conditions under which a choice among acceptable options is possible. But one must choose one's own plan of life not because one will necessarily make the wisest choices; indeed, one might make poor choices. What matters most about a plan of life…is simply that it is chosen by the person whose life it is…"[138]

Individuality, then, is not a matter of diversity, but rather the value of creating or constructing individual identity. It is developed as a matter of chaining a series of overlapping private and public[139] factors around the central fact of individual existence (being).

Perhaps we should speak in terms of a dynamic interplay between being and identity, a core identity around which chained identities (roles?) are arrayed. The human subject is, on the one hand, initially determined by the nature of human being (an *ontic identity*) and, on the other hand, the manifold roles required of life. However, because modern culture has had to dissimulate, denying being's role in establishing identity, we will have to re-explore identity as a rather messy composite of overlapping factors.

To begin with, consider a few examples of the private factors that help determine or impose identity.

Biological/Racial History. We are who/what we are physically. Physical identity is defined by what I am like—tall, short, fat, skinny, etc. We are very sensitive about our appearance or the way we think we appear to others. This is obviously one of the primary means of identification and recognition, as in the use of picture IDs, passport photos, and the like. Other physical components of identity include race, gender, and age. Age, for example, is an advantage or a disadvantage,

---

138 Kwame Anthony Appiah. *The Ethics of Individuality.* (Princeton: Princeton University Press, 2005), 5

139 When I speak of private factor, I am referring to those things which primarily affect our own understanding of who we are. Public factors tend to shape our identity in the context of social discourse.

depending on the cultural context. One might be honored and respected as an elder, possessing wisdom or one might be disregarded, rejected, and abandoned as someone no longer up-to-date, vibrant, beautiful, etc. And obviously, the way these factors play out affects the way in which the elderly view themselves.

Kinship Relationships. Blood relationships have a powerful effect on the ways in which we experience our own identity. This is often the first thing we mention when asked who we are, especially if our kin are well known. As my children were growing up, I was known to their friends as my son's or my daughter's father. I had no independent identity. Who I was, was tied to them. The importance of this kinship factor has been fading as the traditional institutions are undermined.

Cultural/Ethnic Tradition. The context in which we have grown up, have been reared, leaves a lasting imprint on identity. It has to do with a commitment to a body of shared knowledge which governs the ways in which we interpret and respond to the world around us, a certain mentality. We are also dealing with recognizable traits or characteristics such as behavior/speech patterns. Something like one's accent, for example (in Germany as an American, in the South as a Northerner, etc.) can profoundly affect the way that one is viewed and the degree to which one is made to feel part of the larger group. A mildly British accent might be associated with erudition and dignity, while an accent from Eastern Europe might be considered indicative of lower economic and educational standing, which in turn might lead to certain, often false, conclusions about the person's social, political, and even religious identity.

Religious/Moral Orientation. Spiritual commitments and notions of what is right and good also affect identity.[140] While this may be less important in our secular age, it nevertheless does play into one's identity. This is particularly evident in the sense of belonging mediated by one's religious identity. Note the camaraderie experienced by, for example, Pentecostals and Episcopalians among themselves. This can easily spill over into other areas. During the height of the Cold War, for example,

---

140   Taylor. "The full definition of someone's identity usually involves not only his stand on moral and spiritual matters, but also some reference to a defining community." *Sources of the Self*, 36.

American Orthodox Christians became very reserved, unwilling to identify themselves as Orthodox, because they were often associated with Russia and, therefore, with communism.

Now consider a few examples of the more public kinds of things that shape identity.

Language. This is probably the most fundamental element of one's public identity. It is the ability to share cultural knowledge and engage in social discourse. It can identify your cultural heritage, your social standing, even your profession (psychobabble, lawyer-speak, etc.) While it is used in the public arena, language is closely associated with one's view of the self. Any criticism or ridicule of one's language ability is taken personally, as a challenge to one's legitimacy or intelligence.

Relationships. Associations with other, especially well known, individuals or groups often shape identity by association. Like the old adage "it is not what you know but who you know." This dynamic can be seen in the endorsements politicians give one another during election campaigns. Just recently Ted Kennedy threw his backing behind presidential candidate Barack Obama and, without explicating the relationship, the endorsement associates the candidate with a particular brand of democratic liberalism. In other words, it contributes to the shape of Obama's public identity.

Education/Profession. What one does for a living and one's level of education are common elements of individual identity. When asked who we are, we frequently answer by stating our profession, our level of education, or both. And this is often done in order to gain some advantage—of status, position, or just to support the ego. Consider our fascination with academic titles. I recently heard a speaker introduced as Rev. Prof. Dr. Dr. So-and-So. It has become a common practice for students to sign their emails with information on the degree program they are enrolled in. Notice how often speakers refer to their education or perhaps more importantly the place of their education, e.g. "When I was ... at Harvard"). All of this, of course, to help establish who one really is.

Economic. This is closely related to the previous factor and is essentially the status that society assigns to wealth. While wealth can be and often is flaunted, economic status is not always immediately observable. At times, the identities afforded by riches are the creation of mass media and advertising, and become the object of emulation even when the resources are not present. In any case, the public use of certain brands of clothing, automobiles, etc, may reflect an actual state of wealth, or it may point to an attempt to define identity.

Moral Stance/Orientation: We can summarize this discussion by pointing to the fact that when we are speaking of human personhood—the self—we are focusing on identity in terms of the "place" from which I answer the question "Who am I?"

To know who I am is a species of knowing "Where I stand." My identity is defined by the commitments and identifications which provide the frame or horizon within which I can try to determine from case to case what is good, or valuable, or what ought to be done, or what I endorse or oppose. In other words, it is the horizon within which I am capable of taking a stand.[141]

This has both private and public aspects. "We are all framed by what we see as universally valid commitments... and also by what we understand as particular identifications,"[142] which serve as the background, framework, for our own understanding of ourselves. At the same time, we interact with others from a particular standpoint. Thus our orientation defines where we answer from, hence our identity.

× × × × ×

Much of late modern discussion adamantly denies the presence of anything like a stable or persistent human subject. Having rejected the notion of a totalizing human essence/nature, the whole decentering project would have us believe that the self and, thereby, identity are not rooted in a stable ontic core, but altered by every act of discourse,

---

141   Taylor. *Sources of the Self,* 27.

142   Ibid., 29

by every movement of self-monitoring. What we are left with is an unstable context populated by isolated fragments of identity. Identity, then, is essentially the evolving *history* of an individual—a combination of constantly changing[143] biological factors outside the will of that individual or group, rendered meaningful when expressed socially, i.e. in relation to other individuals or other groups.[144] But notice how the characteristics of late modern society exacerbate the fragmentation: dissimulation, depersonalization, violence, and simulation.

A. DISSIMULATION:
SELF-REFERENCING IDENTITY

As already indicated, by bracketing the question of being and by acquiescing to the depersonalization of society, the late modern individual has essentially lost the self, the ontic core of being. Ironically, one of the most common coping mechanisms is a radical reflexivity that seeks to self-define. This, in turn, has lead to a kind of individualism which pictures the person as, at least potentially, "finding his or her own bearings within, declaring independence from the webs of interlocution, which have originally formed him/her, or at least neutralizing them."[145] People are (put themselves) under a great deal of pressure to abandon formative associations and identifications (family, church, ethnicity, moral orientation) all in the name of independence, maturity, and the freedom to create, on their own, a life plan.

While under that pressure they experience significant internal conflict since they are abandoning things which have actually contributed to their identity. Moreover, they do so in an attempt to reshape that identity based primarily on aspects of self-perception, who they think they are or who they want to be. Thus, we notice the shift away from having one's image defined by traditional identifications and by public perception

---

143   Amilcar Cabbal. "Identity and Dignity in the Context of the National Liberation Struggle." In *I Am Because We Are* (Amherst: University of Massachusetts Press, 1995), 79.

144   Ibid., 79. Here you see the dialectical character of identity, which lies in the fact that an individual (or a group) is only similar to certain individuals (or groups) if it is also different from other individuals (or groups).

145   Charles Taylor. *Sources of the Self*, 36.

within networks of mutual recognition to defining and projecting an image chosen by the self in order to maximize the impact of one's own person.

It takes a great deal of effort and energy to reinvent and maintain a coherent identity in the absence of an ontic core. What you wind up with is a host of loosely related identity fragments. Without a totalizing core and the influence of community, kinship, etc., we develop multiple identities—none of which define all that we are.

B. DEPERSONALIZATION: RECOGNITION VS. IDENTITY

Late modern life has forced us to accept the necessity of what is best called recognition. In pre-modern society identity was established within the context of community, kinship, religion, and tradition. You didn't need any ID because you were known by the other members of the community. It is only the recent advent of mass mobility, depersonalized abstract/expert systems, and distansizing technologies that has rendered identification a problem and transmuted our whole notion of identity. Today we use passport photos, picture IDs, and computer log in sequences in order to assure correspondence between an individual and the identity she claims—to prove that she is who she says she is. Yet, the official at the border checkpoint does not actually identify her, he simply confirms that the picture on the passport corresponds to her person. This is not identifying, but merely recognizing. Another example: when you try to use the university's computer network, it very politely and asks you to "Identify yourself to the network." But what does identity mean in this case? Isn't it simply a mechanism for matching a specific activity with a certain individual precisely *without* having to know them? We can also think of the dreaded identity theft. Is it not simply the theft of that matching mechanism and not a personal identity? In these and many other ways we have cheapened (depersonalized) the whole concept of identity.

C. VIOLENCE: IMPOSITION OF IDENTITY

The disembedding technologies of our age exert tremendous power over identity in that they are capable of imposing identity fragments onto the individual against or without their will. Consider Taylor's reference to the plight of women who have been "induced to adopt a depreciatory image of themselves... internalizing a picture of their own inferiority..."[146] Another example is Kellner's argument about the ways in which television and advertising create identities and seduce the consumers into emulating those images.[147] It would seem that mass media actually has the power to impose identity fragments.

I recently saw an article in a motorcycle magazine in which riders were categorized (stereotyped) according to the type and make of bike they rode. BMW riders were shown to be sophisticated, with every article of clothing matching, and prepared for all emergencies. The so-called Rice Burners were characterized by a random mix of dress, running shoes, being primarily interested in high performance, and willing to take risks. Harley Davidson riders appeared in big boots, black leathers, and were gruff and nonconformist. Given the wide range of professions, personality types, and income levels actually present in each group, one wonders where these images come from. I believe that they are created by the manufacturers of the bikes, who specifically target a certain type of rider, thereby imposing an identity fragment. Of course, the riders appear to "willingly" buy into the stereotypes.

What about in the church? Do we also have the power to impose identity fragments on those we seek to minister to? We seem to have labels for just about everybody: seekers, singles, students, survivors, seniors, etc. In many cases we segregate the thus labeled populations

---

146   Charles Taylor. "Politics of Recognition." In *Multiculturalism.* Amy Gutmann, ed. (Princeton: University of Princeton Press 1994), 25.

147   Douglas Kellner. "Popular culture and the construction of postmodern identities." In Scott Lasch and Jonathan Friedman. *Modernity and Identity* (London: Blackwell Publishers, 1993). "...popular culture provides images and figures which its audiences can identify with and emulate." (150) Speaking of *Miami Vice,* Kellner observes that the "chief characters... All have multiple identities and multiple pasts which intersect in unstable ways with the present." (151) "Postmodern identity, then, is constituted theatrically through role playing and image construction... Identity revolves around leisure, centered on looks, images, and consumption." (153)

into special groups, each with its own specific activity, status, and, yes, identity within the larger ecclesial community.

D. SIMULATION: IDENTITY FRAGMENTS AS TOOLS OF SOCIAL DISCOURSE

As we have seen, social discourse in the late modern context tends to take place in the context of identity fragments (expeditious associations, expert systems) rather than on the basis of some coherent, unified sense of who one is. In this regard, our dealing with other people is similar to that of our interaction with the computer network—identification (recognition) without a knowledge of the person. As a result, we exist in extremely superficial networks of relationships.[148]

Now, if identity is made meaningful within such networks and those networks are shallow, then the resulting sense of identity will be equally fragile. My discourse with the medical specialist, the gas station attendant, the government official, even my pastor contributes little to my own understanding of who I am. If this kind of relational simulation characterizes a large part of my being-in-the-world, it will have a profoundly disorienting effect, leading to confused, vague answers to the question and, therefore, what we might call identity anxiety.

These, then, are some of the identity related discontinuities of late modern life. What do we as Christians have to offer?

— 3 —
Theological Perspectives on Being and Identity

A. BEING AS COMMUNION:[149] ON THE POSSIBILITY OF ONTOLOGICAL SECURITY

The late modern bracketing of and rejection of ontological contingency leaves us with little choice but to reference the self. Who I am is what I

---

148 Of course, this is not always the case and is not true of everyone. That a good friend is hard to find has never been more true and goes without saying, but friendship is also valued because it's rare and priceless for our own identities.

149 John D. Zizioulas. *Being as Communion* (Crestwood: St. Vladimir's Seminary Press, 1997).

perceive myself to be in any given context, which amounts to a kind of dissimulation leading to the loss of self behind a veil of the non-real. One way forward would be to replace this self-referencing with the stability of human being viewed as contingent communion. Here I think it is possible to speak about the ontology of divine being in relationship to the ontology of creation, and the human being in particular.

According to Christian teaching the three Persons of the Trinity are of one essence, they share unmediated participation in every aspect of divine being—all knowledge, every thought, and all truth. The fact that the Son and the Spirit are of the same essence or substance as the Father implies that divine substance "possesses almost by definition a relational character."[150] It is only in the Father-Son-Spirit relationship that God fully and eternally exists as uncreated divinity.[151] For God to *be* means that He must be in relationship.[152] In other words, the very substance—the ontological essence—of God can be conceived of as communion.[153]

Given the ontological significance[154] of God's being for all existence, created beings can only exist in communion with God, i.e., they possess

---

150 Ibid., 84. Zizioulas points out that by connecting the being of the Son with the substance of God, Athanasius develops the relational aspect of divine being as an ontological category, i.e., "that communion belongs not to the level of will and action but to that of substance." *Being as Communion*, 85-86.

151 Cf. Athanasius. *Contra Arianos* I:20 "If the Son was not there before He was born, there would be no truth in God, which implies that it is the Father-Son relationship that makes God be the truth eternally in Himself." Cited in Zizioulas. *Being as Communion*, 85.

152 Speaking of the Cappadocians' identification of *hypostasis* with *prosopon*, Zizioulas states that "this latter term is *relational*, and was so when adopted in Trinitarian theology. This meant that from now on a relational term entered into ontology and, conversely, that an ontological category such as *hypostasis* entered the relational categories of existence. *To be* and *to be in relation* becomes identical." Zizioulas. *Being as Communion*, 88.

153 Zizioulas asserts that "if God's being is by nature relational, and if it can be signified by the word 'substance' can we not then conclude almost inevitably that, given the ultimate character of God's being for all ontology, substance, inasmuch as it signifies the ultimate character of being, can be conceived only as communion?" *Being as Communion*, 84. What Zizioulas means is that "communion is not added to the being of God, as something transitory, but is the being of God and as such is an eternal 'being' or reality." Aristotle Papanikolaou. "Divine Energies or Divine Personhood: Vladimir Lossky and John Zizioulas on Conceiving the Transcendent and Immanent God." in *Modern Theology*, 19 (2003), 366.

154 The basic idea here is the noncontingency of God's uncreated existence over against the contingent character of everything created.

being itself only as it is granted by the creative will of God and, because of that contingency, their existence is of necessity a being in relation.[155] If a created being were nothing more than a cognitive potentiality—divine images or thoughts of the world—it would possess no substantial reality and it would make little sense to speak of its being at all. But because divine thought has been concretized, the resultant created being must be viewed as being in relationship,[156] i.e., dependent upon that in which it participates.[157] In other words, the ontological potential of created being can only be realized if it participates in the life of communion with God.

Having been created in the image of God the relational aspect of created being includes the possibility of communion with beings of like substance. Indeed, since there is a plurality of created, personal beings, being in relation might reasonably be expected to entail some form of substance sharing—an inner-creational communion analogous to inner-Trinitarian communion. In general terms this takes place by means of the God given faculty of speech[158]—an ability that makes possible the concrete expression of thought by means of language not simply for the inter-personal transfer of information, but the very instrument needed to establish relationships, i.e., communion. This can also take place through participation in the Eucharist, which itself mediates being, life, and knowledge to the individual and creates a form of communion (1 Cor. 10:16-17).

Understanding human being as contingent makes it possible to avoid the primary causes of contemporary existential anxiety, to experience ontological security. Reflexivity is replaced by contingency: existence does not precede essence. This means that human being is seen as a

---

155   Zizioulas. *Being*, 88.

156   Athanasius. *Contra A.* I:9 46-48, III:40 Note the distinction between communion (koinonia) and participation (metoxh\), which is never used of God in His relationship to creation.

157   Creaturely truth is dependent upon something else in which it participates; this is truth as communion by participation (as compared with God, who is truth as communion without participation). Ibid., 94.

158   Cf. Edward Rommen. "God Spoke: On Divine Thought in Human Language. *Pro Ecclesia* 15 No. 4 (Fall 2006), 387-402.

concretization of human essence, (hypostatization), the individual is not defined on the basis of self-awareness and behavior, but references to the real nature of human existence. Some of what it means to be human is given. This means that we are not alone, solely responsible for every aspect of our being. Thus, we avoid the despair of reflexivity. We are not constantly changing, but have an ontic core rooted in the stability of divine will.

Dissimulation is replaced by the real (Truth): It is no longer necessary to bracket the question of being. The lies of bad faith become unnecessary. There is a basis for insisting on the importance of personhood in spite of contemporary challenges.

Discursive simulation is replaced by relationship in community: Based on the relational nature of creation, we can re-personalize institutions that help manage the risks of modern life, and in particular the Eucharistic community where we relate to one another in the context of our relationship to the divine.

I have no illusions about altering the course of modern society, but viewing my being as contingent on the will of God has enabled me to establish a small zone of ontological security that frees me from existential despair and anxiety and allows me to maintain a vibrant sense of personhood in the midst of the depersonalizing pressures of our society—a counter-dissimulational reality mediated by the Gospel of Christ.

B. IDENTITY AS ICON: ON THE POSSIBILITY OF STABLE IDENTITY

The late modern rejection of ontological contingency leaves us with little choice but that of self-referencing. That, in turn, destroys the totalizing ontic core of identity, forcing an atomization of being-in-the-world governed by a process of reflexive self-monitoring: who I am is what I perceive myself to be in any given context. This gives way to dissimulation and simulation leading to the loss of self behind a veil of the non-real.

The only way forward is to replace self-reference with the stability of human being viewed as contingent communion, and to replace the self-monitoring horizon with an identity centered on a stable ontic core. If ontological security is provided by a recognition of human being's contingent communion with the creator and created order, what of identity? Here Christian doctrine provides a framework for identity by speaking of human beings as having been created in the image and the likeness of God.[159] Scripture teaches that God created man in His own image and after His own likeness (Gen. 1:26, 27). Many modern exegetes do not accept the distinction between the two, suggesting that in Hebrew the two terms are synonymous.[160] However, the Eastern Church has long considered the two terms "image" and "likeness" to be distinct, and that distinction provides the framework within which a concept of identity can be developed. The *iconic* (image) aspect provides a basis for the ontic core of identity while the notion of *theosis*[161] (the process of becoming like God) orders the chaining of the phenomenological aspects needed for coherent human identity.

---

159 Were we to speak in soteriological terms, it could be pointed out that in order for language to be restored to its intended use as an instrument of communion, several things would have to happen: a) human nature would have to be healed of corruption, freed from death and brought back into communion with the divine uncreated being of God; b) the tainted human will need to be cleansed and forgiven of its manifold sins renewing the possibility of communion; c) the linguistic consequences of the fall and the divine confounding of human language would have to be reversed. The first two things were accomplished in the incarnation, death and resurrection of Christ, the third through the coming of the Holy Spirit at Pentecost. Cf. Rommen. "God Spoke." 398.

160 Keil and Delitzsch, for example, state, "modern commentators have correctly suggested, that there is no foundation for the distinction drawn by the Greek and after them by many Latin Fathers, between *imago* and *similitudo*, the former of which they supposed to represent the physical aspect of the likeness to God , the latter the ethical; but that, on the contrary the older Lutheran theologians were correct in stating that the two words are synonymous, and are merely combined to add intensity to the thought..." Biblical Commentary. The Pentateuch. Vol. I (Grand Rapids: Eerdmans, 1968), 63. They go on to compare the difference to certain German word pairs, such as *Bild* and *Abbild* or *Umriss* and *Abriss*. Two comments are in order. First, the physical/ethical distinction they read into the Fathers is inaccurate. Second, although the terms are similar there are subtle differences even in the German pairs, which translate into the English as "likeness" and "copy," and "outline" and "sketch."

161 While the doctrine of deification is often associated with the Eastern Church, it has been rediscovered and is being actively discussed in the West. Cf. Daniel A. Keating. Deification and Grace. (Naples, FL: Sapientia Press of Ave Maria University, 2007).

The image of God is that which reflects God's nature in human beings; that which we all have in common; that which constitutes our very being. As such, the image is the ontic core, presupposing the divine prototype, thereby defining the nature of that being. Each hypostatized instance of human nature is stamped with an original identity. There have been many suggestions as to the exact nature of the image, such as human intellect, the capacity for reproduction, and free will.[162] It is the common property of all human beings, and that without which they could not be considered human. It is a static term and "signifies a realized state, which in the present context constitutes the starting point for the attainment of the 'likeness.'"[163] It is one pole of the identity axis.

Likeness is a dynamic term and points to a potential—something we must acquire ourselves, having received the possibility of doing this from God. To become "in the likeness" depends upon our will; it is acquired in accordance with our own activity. (Phil. 2:12b) "Likeness to God, while it constitutes the goal of human existence, is not imposed, but is left to the individual's own free will. By submitting himself freely to God's will and being constantly guided by His grace, man can cultivate and develop the gift of the 'image' making it a possession, individual, secure and dynamic, and so coming to resemble God."[164] (Eph. 4:13)

This resemblance of God, then, is the other pole of the identity axis. Usually referred to as deification, it is defined as a union or communion with God, which is so complete that it can be said of man that he is like God. Adam was not created perfect in an absolute sense. But he was created without sin, in communion with God and, therefore, with the potential to achieve that for which he was created—deification. Man, being created, could, of course, never acquire what the uncreated Trinity was by nature. But, by God's grace, it was possible for mankind to advance towards God-likeness. Because God alone possesses holiness as an attribute of His very nature, the only way contingent beings can

---

162 Georgios I. Mantzaridis. *The Deification of Man* (Crestwood: St. Vladimir's Seminary Press, 1984), 22.

163 Ibid., 21.

164 Ibid., 21-22.

become holy is by participation in the holiness of God—to become "partakers of the divine nature." (2 Peter 1: 4)

The possibility of such participation is restored in the incarnation. For by taking on human nature without abandoning divinity, Christ brought about the regeneration of the "image" and its elevation toward the archetype. Consider the words of St. Gregory Palamas.

> God's Son became man to show to what heights He would raise us; to keep us from self-exaltation through thinking that we ourselves have secured the revocation of our fall; to join together, as a true mediator, and as Himself being both divine and human, the sundered aspects of our nature…; to make men sons of God and participators in divine immortality…; to show how human nature was created in the image of God above all other created things, for it is so kindred to God that it can form a single hypostasis with Him…; to unite what is separated by nature, mankind and God, since He became a mediator both human and divine by nature.[165]

This communion can become a concrete reality only by the mediation of the Holy Spirit.[166] The Spirit of God residing in the spirit of human beings makes them participants of God's grace. Listen again to St. Palamas:

> As the beam of the eye, uniting with the sun's rays, becomes actual light and thus sees sensible things, so the intellect, become one spirit with the Lord clearly perceives spiritual realities.[167]

As I have said before, I have no illusions about changing the course of late modern society. However, I am quite optimistic about the possibility of overcoming identity fragmentation and anxiety. The process of *theosis* gives us the opportunity to enhance the meaningfulness of every identity

---

165 St. Palamas's Holy Saturday sermon, as quoted by Mantzaridis. *Deification*, 26-27.

166 Ibid., 34.

167 St. Palamas as quoted by Mantzaridis. *Deification*, 34.

fragment. If the idea of *theosis* means we are to become more God-like (by participating in divinity) then the behaviors and relationships associated with each fragment would be transformed by the power of the Holy Spirit into something that respects and honors God and his creation. We could overcome the superficiality of expeditious associations, resist the negative images imposed by the powerful, and accept the biological/personal aspects of identity. We could also relate those fragments to a stable core of identity (the image) rooted in God. The various fragments would build a whole and all would be unified by a common root and goal.

Chapter 4

Self Awareness: Freedom, Coherence, and Value

In this chapter I will continue to trace the trajectory of the late modern self by looking at the ideas of freedom, coherence, and value. Because of the reflexive mode of late modern being and identity, freedom is basically conceived of as the unimpeded liberty to choose and, above all, express anything the self wills or desires. This is a process whereby the will imposes itself on various aspects of its environment (time, space, social) in an effort to actualize its own desires. Unfortunately, this self-actualization is often limited by the conflict of interests generated in a multi-individual world. There are times when one simply cannot self-actualize in the larger social context. As a result, the late modern self will often view its own body as an initial field of self-actualization. Assuming the close coherence between the self and the body, the will finds a compliant partner. This tightly controlled body is then "used" to negotiate the larger context and achieve a degree of self-actualization. In all of this the self will have had to make choices relative to the importance, goodness, and value of the things it seeks to actualize. The late modern base line for these decisions is, of course, the self. Before any valuation of others and actions can take place, the self has to establish its own value, has to legitimize itself. Once that is done, the late modern notion of freedom is complete and operable.

— I —
Freedom and Self-Actualization

As I stated above, freedom is one of the most fundamental characteristics of Enlightenment and, therefore, late modern thought. Yet freedom seems to have become more of an illusion than a reality. The more we insist on the primacy of an individual expression of freedom, the more we wind up denying the reality of true personhood, thus dissimulating and rendering the expression of that supposed freedom a mere simulation.

Given the radically reflexive mode of late modern being and identity, freedom, at its most fundamental level, amounts to a form of control over the self, a kind of self-actualization. The self, however, is not only controlled internally (within its own private environment) but externally, i.e., in a public context of time, space, and society. But this multi-personed context also forces us into the freedom-limiting matrix of risk and opportunity, i.e., of competing interests. The more limitations we are subjected to and the greater the dangers to our continued existence appear to become, the more we feel the need to demand the freedom to self-actualize, to self-express.

A   On the Nature of Freedom

I could spend considerable time tracing the idea of freedom through endless iterations of philosophical discourse. However, for my present purposes, I would like to limit the discussion of the contemporary struggle for freedom to only two of its aspects, i.e., will, the capacity of the human will for spontaneous activity, and expression, in particular the conditions (empirical, psychological, spiritual) under which that spontaneity is articulated. Taken together these two aspects of freedom lead to a preliminary working definition: Freedom is a state in which the will can choose to activate and apply any inherently human faculty or combination thereof at a specific time and in a particular place without condition or necessity.

At the very heart of our notion of freedom lies the concept of choice, i.e., the ability to pursue the fulfillment of the desires of the will without coercion or restraint. In most cases this will involve something required for continued existence, such as food, shelter, etc. Of course, the will is wont to desire beyond the limits of necessities and can easily envision (and thus desire) power, wealth, or the various commodities our respective cultures consider desirable. In order to realize such desire, the process of choice engages one or more human faculties, such as speech, mobility, love, etc. This inevitably involves time in some way: In terms of time allotted to, required by, elapsed in the course of, allowed, available, momentary, or continual. This includes questions of whether to wait, postpone an action, and what a decision's effect will be over time. Choice also involves place: In terms of space requirements, availability, appropriateness, distance, and mobility. Place localizes choices and their consequences. So we have a sliding scale of freedom depending on where it is or can be expressed. Where decisions are made may, in some cases, be as important as when they are made and by whom.

The other key aspect of freedom is the opportunity to express that freedom, be it freedom of speech, of vocation, or of movement. To put it negatively, freedom, or at least the perception of freedom, largely depends on the limitations placed on its expression. There is little value in speaking of a freedom, which, for whatever reason, cannot be actualized in time and space. Thus, the degree of freedom, actual or perceived, is derived from the reasonableness and the effectiveness of opposition to the expression of choice. Note the difference in the way in which freedom is perceived in the case of a speed limit and of speaking one's mind. Most people do not consider the posted speed limit to be a serious violation of personal freedom. There seem to be good reasons for moderating speed. Yet, speed limits are so irregularly enforced that many drivers feel free to exceed the posted limit and do so without much thought or emotion. In other words, on both sides of the equation a speed limit does not generate a strong sense of freedom or limitation, even though that is exactly what it is. However, honestly speaking one's mind, stating one's opinion, is a different matter altogether. In this case we are hard pressed to see the reasonableness of any limitation of our right to express. Yet, it is often severely limited by social settings, notions of political correctness, the possibility of negative consequences, and so on. Given the strong commitment to self-expression, these limitations are resented and taken as a violation of one's personal freedom.

B. FREEDOM IN THE LATE MODERN CONTEXT

The radical reflexivity of late modernity leads to an increased desire for self-actualization (self-determination). This grows out of the reciprocal play between constant self-monitoring and a proliferation of choices. Part of the difficulty this creates is that while late modernity confronts the individual with a complex diversity of choices, because the mode of presentation is non-foundational, it offers little help in making those choices.[168]

Of course, I am speaking of more than a series of isolated decisions. It might be better to use Giddens' concept of a lifestyle. A lifestyle can be defined as a more or less integrated set of practices which an individual embraces, not only because such practices fulfill utilitarian needs, but because they give material form to a particular narrative of self-identity. The notion of lifestyle may sound somewhat trivial because it is so often thought of solely in terms of a superficial consumerism: lifestyles as suggested by glossy magazines and advertising images. But there is something much more fundamental going on than that common definition suggests. Under the conditions of late modernity, all of us not only follow lifestyles, but in a more important sense are forced to do so—we have no choice but to choose choosing.[169] In addition, Giddens suggests that all such choices (including the more consequential ones) are decisions not only about how to act, but who to be. The more post-traditional the settings in which an individual moves, the

---

168   Giddens. *Modernity and Self-Identity*, 80.

169   Ibid., 81.

more this lifestyle impacts the very core of self-identity, its making and remaking.[170]

(1) Will (Choice)

In the late modern context this will to choose is not simply the impulse to freely fulfill desires, but it is almost a demand for unlimited choices in every area of life. It is as if the reality of our own freedom to choose depended on the proliferation of options. The plurality of choices, which confronts individuals in situations of late modernity, derives from several influences.

First, there is the fact of living in a post-traditional order. In the absence of traditional coping institutions (family, church, etc), the individual is left to make most decisions on their own. Even within the late modern marriage, decisions are often taken individually, e.g. where to go to church, whether to baptize children, etc. Second, there is what Berger[171] calls the 'pluralization of life-worlds,' the segmentation of life into public and private domains. These are what we could call lifestyle sectors or time-space slices, each of which generates a different set of desires and requires a different set of choices. A third factor conditioning plurality of choice is the existential impact of the contextual nature of conditions of belief in the modern context. What is believable or not is often a function of expert opinion, an outgrowth of specialization. Since we choose what is, for us, believable, and since experts can be cited for almost every conceivable position, we seem to have an almost unlimited supply of believable choices. Fourth, the prevalence of mediated experience undoubtedly also influences pluralism of choice. The impact of mass media as a source of alternative lifestyle options supports the idea of choosing an overall style of choosing (mega-choice), life-planning (calendars). Fifth, in the name of profit the free market environment of North America tends to expand customer choices to the extent that the market will bear them. In many cases these are not even real choices, but simply two manufacturers selling essentially the

---

170   Ibid.

171   Peter Berger. *The Homeless Mind* (New York: Vintage Books, 1974), 63-82.

same product. But, this practice does support the late modern desire for more choice.

There is, of course, something illusory about the freedom promised by this proliferation of choice. It only seems to support an increased freedom and may actually limit it. Consider, for example, the variety of breakfast cereals available at a typical late modern grocery store. There are literally hundreds of possibilities, some touted as new, such as flax seed flakes, other variations on older themes such as chocolate, strawberry, and honey coated corn flakes. Now the consumer may well take this variety as an indication of expanded freedom of choice. However, that, it seems to me, is just an illusion, since in the end there is no way of choosing all of the options. Presumably the customer will choose just one (or perhaps no) cereal, in which case freedom to choose would retain its full effect even if there were only one cereal to choose. Freedom is not simply a function of the number of choices. I would also suggest that the unlimited proliferation of choice actually limits freedom by making it more difficult to choose the best option. The cereals are presented in such a way as to suggest that they are all equally valid choices, even though some of them are definitely not in one's best interest. Since the presentation of choice offers no help, the consumer is left with the daunting task of sifting through the options, something they may not wish to do, in which case they forfeit something of their freedom. I realize that this is not the most consequential of examples. However, it does illustrate the point that even in the realm of something as mundane as breakfast cereal, the trend toward proliferation of choice is observable. What, then, of more significant areas of life, such as relationships, sex, charity, etc. Are we to say that more partners, more variety, greater frequency translate into more freedom? Or is it an illusion, which has no qualitative affect on freedom, but may well destroy it?

Next, note that late modern technologies have greatly extended the range and effects of human faculties. This can be seen in increased mobility, communication, access to knowledge, web-commerce, etc. These are technologies that, in many cases, are said to make possible and preserve more choice, i.e., hold at bay the undecidables, the uncertainties of life and give us the feeling of freedom. For example, it is now possible to know the gender of a baby before birth. While this technology is obviously useful in preventing and treating potential disorders, its freedom enhancing effect seems to lie in its ability to remove uncertainty. Given the vast array of such technologies, much of individual freedom is experienced in the context of the performative use of these technologies—knowing how to use the internet, computers, automobiles, motorcycles.

Our notions of freedom also have much to do with the late modern ability to control time: based, in part, on recent normalization, standardization of time. As a result, we are able to divide our lives into time-segments over which we have greater or lesser control: work, leisure, etc. Our notion of freedom is derived from our perceived ability to control the overall use of time (the uncontrollable portions embedded into a context of managed time). We tend to rank the time slices in terms of relative control and often engage in time related behavior in order to enhance our sense of control. For example, it has been suggested that to overcome the panic of a lost sense of control, a "door close button" was added to elevators.[172] Similarly, we engage in various activities such as listening to an audio book during a traffic jam in order not to "waste" the time. Of course, the modern concept of the perpetual present makes the notion of waiting (for anything, including traffic) rather intolerable.

Self-actualization, then, implies the control of time—essentially, the establishing of zones of personal time, which have only remote connections with external temporal orders (the routinized world of time-space governed by the clock and by universalized standards of measurement).[173] It has even become vogue to manage the whole of one's life in this way, by viewing it as a series of passages leading to the idea of life cycles, life calendars, etc. Of course, this was done in

---

172   James Gleick. *Faster. The Acceleration of Just about Everything* (New York: Pantheon Books, 1999), 23-30.

173   Giddens. *Modernity and Self-Identity,* 77.

pre-modern times as well. But there the idea was that of historical continuity and tradition, where they thought primarily of the context into which the individual was incorporated as opposed to self-actualized life cycles—designer lives.

The reason we think we can actually control time is linked to two modern developments:

First, time has been divorced from Divinity, i.e., from anything outside of or beyond ordinary human experience. Time is simply a given, a phenomenon rooted in human experience itself. Of course, this makes it very difficult to talk about things like eternity or the biblical idea that time will, at some point, actually end (Rev. 10:6).

Second, time has been homogenized,[174] i.e., there is only one sort of time: Every day, every season, every moment relentlessly ticking away in their monotonous uniformity, no one moment different or more valuable than another. What has been eliminated by this approach is the idea of a hierarchy of times. For example, the concept of sacred time, of a feast day, or of the Sabbath, is rendered incomprehensible. How could one day be any different than another? That is why it has become so difficult to distinguish between a workday and a Sunday, as evidenced by the growing number of businesses and trades that maintain full operations on Sundays. Indeed, if all time is the same, there is no reason to reserve one day, that is, no reason not to use Sunday for the same activities engaged in on the other days.[175]

One of the problems with this approach is that it becomes difficult to see time as meaningful. We have all experienced the painfully slow passage of time, the monotonous grinding away of day after day, no one more or less important than the other. It is almost as if time itself were an enemy, we are afraid of it, have no way to save it, don't want to waste it. We can't stop it, we simply have to endure it, fill it, all the while threatened with a profound sense of the meaninglessness of it all.

---

174   Taylor. *A Secular Age*, 271.

175   Ibid., 208-209.

As for place, the late modern technologies of distancization mitigate the effect of distance as a limiter of freedom by multiplying the choices and stretching the horizon of appropriateness. Consider the cell phone and wireless networks—because they are available almost everywhere, they are used almost everywhere; cell phones disrupting the quiet of the library, students checking their email and the weather during the lecture. Notions of etiquette and respect for others might, at one time, have limited the use of such technologies in these places. In that case, the freedom generated by the choices would be, at least practically, illusory, something that could not or should not be used. But, what is happening in the late modern context is that availability itself overrides traditional restraints, driven by the supposed right to express.

(2) Expression

Thus, the fact that we now place such importance on expressive power means that our contemporary notions of what it is to re-spect people's integrity includes that of protecting their expressive freedom to express and develop their own opinions, to define their own life conceptions, to draw up their life-plans.[176]

As this quote from Taylor indicates, freedom is also tied to the idea of an absence of limitations on the overt expression of the will. Here we need to distinguish between the ways in which our perception of freedom is affected by choices made in private and those made in public.[177]

Private expression of choice is, for the most part, taken for granted and therefore not immediately associated with the feeling of freedom.

---

176   Taylor. *Sources of the Self*, 25.

177   Note how Kant used the terms private and public in his piece on the Enlightenment. For him the "private use of reason may... be very narrowly restricted, without hindering the progress of enlighten-ment. The public use of one's reason must always be free...By the public use of one's own reason I understand the use that anyone as a scholar makes of reason before the entire literate world. I call the private use of reason that which a person may make in a civic post or office that has been entrusted to him. *What is Enlightenment*, 42.

Here it seems that the only restraint is that of imagination. No one can limit my absolute freedom to think, feel, or criticize at will.

However, the boundary between the private and public has become increasingly porous. External or public frameworks can impinge upon internal (personal) freedom, as, for example, in the case of guilt experienced at thoughts, which violate some existing relationship or accepted norm. We also see this in the concern for "image" that invades the private, and in the way in which private opinion is imposed on the public sphere.

This imposition of the private upon the public takes place with such frequency because *public* expression of will is taken to be the individual's right—is equated with freedom. This is often observed in Church related Bible Study groups where everyone has the right to give an opinion on the meaning of a text, whether they have the requisite knowledge, training, or not. "To me this text means" becomes the mantra of such discussions, as if one's opinion were rendered accurate or truthful by virtue of having been expressed. Nevertheless, even this supposed freedom is governed by a complex set of limiting factors (elements of the modern social imaginary). Once again, the degree of perceived freedom, in this case the freedom to express, is related to: *the possibilities,* which are enhanced by technologies such as mnemonic devices, communication networks, presentation software; *the appropriateness,* perceived level of acceptance; and *the effect,* that is, the degree to which the desired self-actualization succeeds.

— 2 —

Coherence and Self-Awareness

According to Terry Eagelton, "the postmodern subject, unlike its Cartesian ancestor, is one whose body is integral to its identity."[178] The body's recent rise in popularity should not really surprise us. As we have seen, the pressures of modern life and thought have exacerbated

---

178   Eagelton. *The Illusions of Postmodernism,* 69.

existential anxiety and undermined the self and self-identity. Since the self is always *embodied*,[179] the body remains one of the few constants of our experience. It is, therefore, quite understandable that we should look to the body for coherence. "…[T]he contours and properties of the body are the most immediately observable, the most original and intimate components of human self-image. It is the agent by means of which we experience (control) the fact of our own existence in the day-to-day praxis of the world."[180]

So it is that pictures identify us with our physical makeup. It is this aspect of our individuality that is said to be recognizable. The body is ever present and a primary source of pleasure. It is the most readily available, unresisting field in which to express the desire to exercise freedom. However, "…it is not just a physical entity which we 'possess', it is an action-system, a mode of praxis, and its practical immersion in the interactions of day-to-day life is an essential part of sustaining a coherent sense of self-identity."[181] Moreover, the constant self-monitoring generated by the reflexivity of the late modern project quite naturally elevates the importance of the body. The body, then, is not simply an object, it is experienced as a (the) primary means of monitoring both other and self.

Given the simplicity of the body's proximity to the self, one might think that its function is more easily understood than either being or identity, and given its subservience, that it remains a compliant, willing servant of self-authentication. But, quite to the contrary, the current preoccupation with the body has actually imbued the body with a power that distorts its relationship to the self. It is either vested with the interactional autonomy of the self (as if it were the self) or reduced to a mere instrument of the human subject. And this should give us pause. For no relationship, be it ontological, psychological, or physical, can retain its simplicity if it is unhinged by dissimulation. By

---

179 Giddens. *Modernity and Self-Identity*, 58.

180 Ibid., 58.

181 Ibid., 99.

not participating in the source of its being, by divorcing the body from the self, all semblance of balance, proportionality, and coherence is lost. So rather than enhancing human coherence, the late modern fascination with the body actually disrupts coherence and ends in disembodiment, a rupture between the self and the body, which is particularly unfortunate since there are several aspects of the body that have special relevance to the self and self-identity.[182]

A. APPEARANCE

Bodily appearance concerns all those features of the surface of the body including modes of dress and adornment which are visible to others and serve to document one's identity and to provide the clues needed to interpret actions.[183] In pre-modern settings, appearance tended to be standardized in terms of social identity signaling gender, class, and occupation. This can still be seen in the late modern context in the dress of police, medical personnel, and military personnel. In my case, I wear a clerical collar as a sign of my office. It does two things:

First, it is a statement of who and what I know myself to be (aid to self-determination). I wear it almost all the time, no matter what else I might have on (leather jacket, HD vest, or a black suit jacket. The collar is an underlying theme that provides a certain amount of coherence to my understanding of my own identity and the way in which I present that identity to others.

Second, it is a signal to others that they are to treat me in a certain way and that I, in turn, can be expected to display certain behavior. That this actually works is evidenced by the people who apologize for, or refrain from using profanity in my presence, or by those complete strangers who occasionally ask me to pray for them.

While dress may still serve that function, standardization – the idea of uniform – is more likely to be rejected in the late modern context where appearance is used to express or connect the various fragments

---

182   Ibid., 99.

183   Ibid., 99.

of an individual's identity or desired identity. Appearance may indicate a desire for success that is actualized by association. Take, for example, those people who wear upscale business attire when the situation does not require it. Similarly, many use sports apparel, especially foot ware, t-shirts and sweat shirts displaying the names of particular brands or institutions, in order to express a desired identity. Appearance may also express the desire to belong. There is a kind of safety in numbers that bikers express in their use of assorted Harley Davidson, Honda, BMW paraphernalia. Of course, conversely, a desire not to belong may characterize one's appearance as in the case of various sub-cultures,[184] the use of tattoos, body piercing, and the like.

So, appearance can be an expression of actual or desired identity. But these uses of the body often undermine coherence because of the inherent dissimulation: I couldn't get into Harvard so I wear their sweat shirt; I'm not an NBA athlete, but I wear the same shoes as the star; I don't know how to ride a motorcycle, but I wear an HD patch; I am only different by virtue of the excessive use of the ordinary; this, as opposed to the use of a uniform, which indicates who I really am (not just a desire), and who I am all the time.

B. DEMEANOR

Demeanor determines how appearance is used by the individual within generic settings of day-to-day activities.[185] It is how the body is mobilized in relation to constitutive conventions of daily life. It is possible to distinguish between two modes of demeanor: passive and active.

In its *passive* mode the use of appearance is determined by the expectations or limitations of the specific setting as in the appropriateness of attire at a ball game as opposed to a board room meeting. The individual is expected to adjust to each given situation. Since demeanor is dictated by the situation, this use of the body could easily undermine the coherence of identity. The identity projected through appearance

---

184   Dick Hebdige. *Subculture. The Meaning of Style* (London: Routledge, 1979).

185   Giddens. *Modernity and Self-Identity,* 99.

would change from place to place, in which case it would not be an expression of one's core identity. [186] However, maintaining certain elements of demeanor across various situations[187] would be one way of maintaining a stable identity. But, that would assume some core identity with which one was sufficiently comfortable.

In its *active* or aggressive mode the body is merely a tool (an object) of the will, used to express desire, leading to a rupture between the self and the body. It is as if the body were the other, creating an ontological stress by introducing difference into the self. This also raises the possibility of using the body to do violence, as is the case with the seductive clothing worn by some women, or the intimidating appearance favored by some bikers.

C. REGIMES

In order to use the body to these ends it is necessary to subject it to certain disciplines, in particular eating habits and health care. In general terms, it can be reduced to the idea that body-care delivers body-power. Taking care of the body can help a person retain, and even improve on, her or his appearance, based on an understanding of how the body functions and on closely monitoring those functions. Cosmetics, cosmetic surgery, dieting, dietary supplements, exercise, and tanning are all part of a growing industry designed to help the individual reshape the body.[188]

The body, then, has become part of the general reflexivity of modernity, i.e., "body regimes and the organization of sensuality in high modernity are opened up to continuous reflexive attention, against the backdrop of plurality of choice."[189] Indeed, we have almost unlimited opportunity to (re)design the body. At least that is what the advertisers would have us believe, even though, given the physical limitations of the body, there is only so much that one can do. Yet, as the focus of intense

---

186   Ibid., 100.

187   As in the case of the clerical collar mentioned above.

188   Ibid., 102. I'm not suggesting that there are no legitimate uses of these things, but that they often become the means by which we subject the body to the desires of the will.

189   Ibid., 102.

monitoring the body takes on a prominent role in identity formation. "Who I am" becomes "what I look like," which easily morphs into "I am my body." The extremes of this extraordinarily reflexive activity are Body Building through which one can sculpt a specific look by exercising specific muscle groups, and weight loss programs that become self-destructive (anorexia).[190]

All of this puts enormous stress on the individual, since our society seems to have accepted the idea that we are our bodies, as can be seen with the enormous popularity of pornography, common notions of beauty, and the fascination with sports. But this backfires on most individuals. How many of us are 6'10," highly coordinated basketball players? Yet, we have been convinced that with the proper regimes, almost anything is possible.

D. SENSUALITY

A final aspect of the body, sensuality, refers to the dispositional handling of pleasure and pain. [191]This is rooted in the idea of self-love. If one actually does love the self, then no limits can be placed on the pursuit of pleasure. This, combined with the proliferation of choice and the supposed right (freedom) to express every and all desires has led to the boundless hedonism of our age. If it feels good, it is right. Again we are faced with dissembling, as in "I am my feelings, my pleasure," and a disembodying occurs which views the body as a mere object owned by the Self.

I don't need to comment further on this phenomenon. However, I would like to point out that all this freedom has been limited (further distorted) by two intensely depersonalizing mechanisms:

First, there is avoidance which confronts us in two forms. On the one hand, there is the attempt to remove from our immediate purview anything "painful, e.g. death. Note, for example, the media

---

190   Ibid., 103-108.

191   Ibid., 99.

coverage of 9/11 which showed none of the victims.[192] On the other hand, there is what amounts to accountability avoidance made possible by the depersonalizing, distancizing technologies. For example, the use of pornography on the Internet has become so accessible and so anonymous as to render accountability meaningless. Anyone can engage this information from the shaded sanctuary of their own computer.

Second, there is what we might call an unnatural amplification of sensuality. Again, we are confronted with several forms. One is the grotesque exaggeration and imbalance of things like extreme sports, sex, and body-building. The combination of unrestricted freedom and limitless choices is a recipe for boredom, which drives the search for ever more exciting variations. The other form of this amplification is the craving for what is touted to be real. In some cases this involves reducing things to such bizarre levels of detail that they become repulsive.[193] In other cases it is the addiction to the supposedly real, as in reality TV. But this "'passion for the Real': culminates in its apparent opposite in a theatrical spectacle."[194] This kind of extreme behavior[195] inevitably leads to a kind of disembodiment—a rupture between the body and the self. Unfortunately, the modern fascination with the body has not brought the desired coherence, but leads, rather, to disembodiment and dissembling of the self.

---

192 This points to what Slavoj Žižek calls a derealization of horror "...which went on after the WTC collapse: while the number of victims—3000—is repeated all the time, it is surprising how little of the actual carnage we see—no dismembered bodies, no blood, no desperate faces of dying people... in clear contrast to the reporting on Third World catastrophes, where the whole point is to produce a scoop of some gruesome detail." *Welcome to the Desert of the Real* (London: Verso, 2002), 13.

193 Žižek. *Welcome,* 6. A level of detail at which point "...a shift occurs: when we get too close to the desired object, erotic fascination turns into disgust at the Real of the bare flesh."

194 Ibid., 9.

195 As can be seen in the phenomenon of "cutters" who deliberately slash themselves with razors in order to regain some hold on reality. Cf. Marlie Strong. *The Bright Red Scream* (London: Virago, 2000).

— 3 —
Value and Self-Authenticity

If we are correct in assuming that life is a voluntary and reflexive enterprise over which the individual has, if not complete, then extensive control, then the self is faced with choices, not as an expression of freedom, but which arise with respect to the value of the self, of the other, the nature of the good life. Much of what we have come to value is viewed in the context of the flourishing of ordinary human life. Yet, these discriminations have become difficult in light of the loss of a (self) transcendent horizon. What makes the self (human being) valuable? Here we are hampered by the dilemma of reflexivity. Are we, for example, to suggest that the self simply declares itself valuable by a process of self-authentication, the self-evidence of its existence? Is this any more effective or satisfying than bracketing the question of being? Or is it not the same move? How are we to decide what is a good and meaningful life, what is to be valued? Again we face the dilemma of the late modern self's reflexive stance—the pragmatic application of narcissistic principles which determine meaning in terms of how much pleasure or respect the individual derives.

These and related questions fall under the general rubric of what Charles Taylor calls moral thinking. According to him there are three distinct axes of moral thinking: 1) dignity, our sense of ourselves being worthy of respect; 2) respect for and obligations to others; and 3) understanding of a meaningful life.[196] A brief look at these three axes reveals the fundamental difficulties of late modernity.

A. VALUE OF THE SELF

Late Modern context requires something akin to self-respect (self-authentication). In the absence of traditional support mechanisms and the depersonalizing effects of technology and expert systems, it would be very difficult to survive without some confidence in the worth

---

196 Taylor. *Sources of the Self*, 15.

and dignity of the self. In fact, we ascribe a whole host of pathologies (depression, anxiety, inferiority) to the absence of such confidence. And our mass media, especially advertising, constantly proclaims our individual value, the fact that we "deserve," are worthy of, whatever it is they think we should be buying.

The whole idea of the value of a given objective is, aside from its monetary value, determined by a number of factors, particularly, admirable qualities. Value can be thought of in terms of what is real, genuine, or authentic, such as a Rolex watch. Value is also associated with the uniqueness of a one-of-a-kind object. It may have to do with the usefulness of an item. Beauty, in its most general sense, as in elegance, miniaturization, efficiency, is yet another measure of value. We can also interrogate by asking how value is determined. Is the object intrinsically (self-evidently) valuable, instrumentally valuable (for specific use), or relatively valuable (to certain individuals)?

But if we try to apply these ideas of value to the late modern self, we are immediately faced with a whole range of discontinuities caused by the dilemma of reflexivity. Is the self intrinsically (absolutely) valuable? That is hard to answer, since the question of being has been bracketed and the unity (coherence) of the human composite fragmented. We could seek validation through other human beings, in which case the self might be instrumentally or relatively valuable. Or one could self-authenticate, declare one's own value to be self-evident.

What, then, of the individual qualities ordinarily associated with value? As it turns out, they are just as difficult to apply. Is the self *real*? If, as we have seen, the late modern self is merely a sign of itself, then in what sense can we speak of its being real?[197] Is the self unique? Again, with the question of being bracketed, without the idea of hypostasis, a concrete instance of human nature, how can we speak of uniqueness?

---

197 Remember that our working definition of a real Person involved three registers: Hypostasization: The Real is an actual instance of concretized or, in the case of persons, hypostasized human nature or essence (no longer mere potential). Essence: Each individual instance of hypostasized human nature is real to the extent that it conforms to its own nature or essence. Self-Acknowledgment: Each individual instance of hypostasized human nature is real to the extent that it is able to interrogate both its being and nature without pretense—without dissimulation or simulation. Again we might speak of a range of, or degrees of reality.

Does the self have other admirable qualities? Perhaps, but by what standards are they to be determined? Does the self have a purpose? With the elimination of teleology, without an idea like *theosis,* how can we speak of purpose? Does the self have beauty/dignity? Without the ideal of the divine prototype, all beauty and dignity is relativized. The individual is left with only one path to value—self-authentication, but this, according to a Christian perspective, is self-defeating.

B. VALUE OF THE OTHER

The second axis of moral thinking is respect for the other. Speaking of value as a dimension of the self implies the other, perhaps more than the other dimensions. The problem is that in order to authenticate the self we have to extend our understandings of worth to others. If I expect to be treated with respect and dignity (worthy of respect) then, at the very least, I will have to assume the other capable of recognizing my value and acting accordingly.

This amounts to a kind of mutual recognition. The self is the other of the other, but this tends to blur the distinctions since I am basically loving myself through the other. I have to value the other in order to authenticate myself. There can't be any self-authentication in solitude. In other words, it is still a reflexive move and subject to the disintegration just mentioned. As I will illustrate in Part IV, the only non-reflexive possibilities would be to a) extend the reality of the image and likeness to the other, b) accept the idea of being as communion, in which case the other becomes part of the definition of the self and, c) offer the other charity, neighborly love.

Not long ago I went out to lunch with a colleague. We had about an hour to discuss several issues that deeply affected both of us. During the lunch, his cell phone rang four times and each time he took the call. None of the calls were of an emergency nature, yet he spent the majority of our time together talking on his phone. What can explain this kind of behavior? Perhaps my friend was driven by an elevated sense of his own importance. Perhaps he simply could not bear the idea of not being instantly accessible. In any case, the experience does point to a reversal of social priorities. There was a time when the person, whose face you saw, took priority over those who were absent. Now, however, the distancizing technology reverses that and gives priority to everyone but those present. The clear message is "I'll talk to you, as long as my phone doesn't ring." I, the other in this case, was obviously not very valuable.

C. VALUE OF ACTION (LIFE)[198]

The third axis of moral thinking is an understanding of a meaningful life. Is this self-evident? Can we rely on our intuition? During the modern era much of our attention has been focused on what Taylor calls the affirmation of ordinary life. "With the Reformation, we find a modern, Christian-inspired sense that ordinary life was... the very centre of the good life. The crucial issue was how it was led..."[199]

During the modern era several points of departure have been suggested. Hegel speaks of duty,[200] Levinas starts with the Face of the Other,[201] and more recently, Badiou wants us to consider the truth of each situation.[202] But all of this is made difficult by the dilemma of reflexivity, that is the combination of radical reflexivity, leading to self-love, and a disintegration of the self through the passions and the misuse of human faculties. From a Christian perspective, a meaningful life is one characterized by the virtues. Thus, the good life would be characterized by a positive use of the faculties integrated by the double character of love. Love/Charity becomes the integrating feature of a meaningful life.[203]

---

198 We will take a closer look at this in chapter 6.

199 Taylor. *Sources of the Self*, 13.

200 Immanuel Kant. *Groundwork of the Metaphysic of Morals* (New York: Harper Torchbooks, 1964).

201 Emmanuel Levinas. *Totality and Infinity* (Pittsburg: Duquesne Univ. Press, 1969).

202 Alain Badiou. *Ethics. An Essay on the Understanding of Evil* (New York: Verso, 2001).

203 Lars Thunberg. *Microcosm and Mediator: The Theological Anthropology of St. Maximus the Confessor* (Chicago: Open Court, 1995). 298.

— 4 —
Theological Perspectives on Freedom, Coherence, and Value

In this chapter I have argued that the reflexive nature of late modern being has reduced the idea of freedom to the unimpeded liberty to choose and express anything the self wills or desires. I have also argued that the perceived right to self-actualization has quite naturally led to a demand for more options and that this proliferation of choices creates only the illusion of freedom. Next, I observed that the late modern tendency to use the body as a tool of self-actualization leads to a disembodiment, a rupture between the self and the body. Finally, I suggested that these notions of freedom involve making choices based on the value given the self, others, and actions, and that the self-referencing mode of late modern existence makes that valuation difficult. What, then, does Christian teaching have to contribute to this discussion? In what ways does it address the questions of freedom, coherence, and value?

A. FREEDOM

Freedom of human will is a major theme in Christian theology. It is, however, a freedom anchored in the context of the real; not an absolute freedom, but one conditioned by the contingency of our being and the communality of our essence.

According to St. Maximus the Confessor the will, or self-determination, is a constitutive faculty of human nature and represents the very core of the image of God. As a result, human beings have the ability to self-actualize, that is, to make choices, and are in that regard free. In seeking to understand this freedom of the will, Maximus makes a sharp distinction between natural will and what he calls the gnomic will.

"Natural will" is the *rational* faculty of self-determination inherent in man, "gnomic will" is the free and *ambiguous* (εφ εκατερα)

desire and motion active in concrete man, and called forth by
man's sense of pleasure (spiritual or bodily). "Natural will" is based
on God-given human nature and thus closely related to the *logos*
of human nature; "gnomic will" is based on the γνωμη, i.e., the
habitus of desire man has acquired through his use of his capacity
for self-determination.[204]

While these faculties are God-given and therefore inherently good,
the whole faculty of self-determination has been perverted by the
fall into sin. Positing their own being with reference to themselves
rather than the uncreated being of God, human beings abandon the
contingency of participation, which would have brought fully realized
being and freedom. However, this refusal to participate in the life upon
which created existence depends has fragmented the unity of human
being, disrupted inter-personal discourse,[205] and turned freedom into
a form of self-love or self-satisfaction.

The Fathers sometimes refer to these sin-damaged faculties as the
passions[206]—all those loudly raging emotions and actions, such as anger,
greed, despondency, gluttony, and slothfulness. True freedom is achieved
only when the self achieves a state called *dispassion* (apathia), in which
the passions have been replaced by their corresponding virtues.[207] This
can be seen when fasting overcomes gluttony, service to others overcomes
greed and self-love, and physical discipline defeats despondency and
slothfulness. Dispassion, then, represents true freedom of the will.

Dispassion, however, is not to be measured in terms of isolated acts
of restraint, such as skipping a meal, or holding one's tongue in spite
of being provoked. As good as that might be, what Christian thought
envisions is an all encompassing life of discipline rooted in repentance

---

204 Maximus cited by Thunberg. *Microcosm*, 211.

205 Ibid., 226-227.

206 In particular the Desert Fathers. See, for example, Evgrius. "Texts on Discrimination in respect of
Passions and Thoughts." In St. Nikoimos and St. Makarios. *The Philokalia* Vol. 1 Transl. G.E.H Palmer,
Philip Sherrard, and Kallistos Ware. (London Faber and Faber, 1979), 38-52.

207 Cf. John Cassian. "On the Eight Vices." In *Philokalia* Vol 1, 73-93. Virtues are the undamaged human
faculties.

and a desire for the Kingdom of God; a spiritual state where the passions no longer exist. As John Climacus put it:

> By dispassion I mean a heaven of the mind within the heart... A man is truly dispassionate—and is known to be such—when he has cleansed his flesh of all corruption; when he has lifted his mind above everything created, and has made it master of all the senses; when he keeps his soul continually in the presence of the Lord and reaches out beyond the borderline of strength to Him. And there are some who would claim that dispassion is resurrection of the soul prior to that of the body, while others would insist that it is a perfect knowledge of God, a knowledge second only to that of the angels.[208]

As mentioned above, the notion of freedom also has a temporal component. A Christian approach to time is based on the conviction that true freedom comes not from our ability to control time, but rather from a participation in and sanctification of time. This is done in several ways.

First, it is done by viewing time as a divine gift, which can be used and abused. There was a time when there was no time—before creation. The world was not created at some particular point in time, but was created with time.[209] In other words, until God created there was no time.[210] Time is a God-given aspect of the created order, a gift, which facilitates self-awareness as well as self-actualization. As such, we should not be seeking to control time, but rather participate in it—moving with it in ways that conform to its purposes.

---

208   St. John Climacus. *Ladder of Divine Ascent,* cited by John Mack. *Ascending the Heights* (Ben Lomond: Conciliar Press, 1999), 165-166.

209   As St. Basil affirmed, "The beginning of the road is not yet the road, and the beginning of the house is not yet the house; so the beginning of time is not yet time and not even the least particle of it." St. Basil. Hexaemeron. I, 6, *Nicene and Post-Nicene Fathers* Vol 8. Philip Schaff and Henry Wace, eds. (Peabody: Hendrickson Publishers, 1994), 55.

210   The absence of time does, of course, not imply the non-existence of the divine. Modern researchers have confirmed this understanding of time. Cf. Ilya. Prigogine and Isaaabelle Stengers. "Rediscovering Time" In *Order Out of Chaos* (New York: Bantom, 1984), 213-232.

Second, if time is not subject to our control, that is, if we cannot force our meaning or purpose on time, then we must accept its inherent multiplicity of purposes. Not all time is the same, some times are special. For example, during a Liturgy ordinary time is said to be suspended and we enter into a sacred space, in the presence of one who is above time. Here there is no interminable ticking away of moments. The Sabbath is different time, a day set aside and sanctified for the purpose of worship and rest. The great feasts of the Christian calendar are special time, each for its own reason. We mark this time by fasting, by holding services, and in some cases, with special events. If we cannot control time, then freedom is gained only by submitting to, participating in, and sanctifying the time that is so graciously given to us.

As with time, Christian thought views place as a resource given *qua* creation. As such, freedom is found in participation or acceptance of the divinely ordained order of place. This includes the idea of a hierarchy of space, i.e., not all space is the same and must thus be accepted as a gift and used according to its purpose. Place is sanctified by proper use. This can be seen in the layout of the Church, where some space is considered sacred.

How does this affect our right or ability to express the freedoms we do have? As indicated above, the idea of freedom is closely associated with the perceived (or actual) absence of limitations or constraints. We think we are free when we are able to act without condition and necessity. However, since the very being of the human subject is contingent upon the will of the Creator, its freedom can only be realized within the constraints of that contingency. Any attempt at self-determination that is divorced from a relationship to the Creator becomes an exercise in self-love and ends in bondage. In the Christian frame the freedom to express the will is governed by:

Self-Transcendence: Freedom of will is human existence invested with the possibility of self-determination within the bounds of being-in-communion. Self-determination is only possible when the other is the point of reference.

The Ecclesial Community: Given the recapitulation[211] made possible by the work of Christ, human beings need a renewed context within which to live out that new life. The Church provides the essential helps such as the Eucharist, the Scriptures, and the communion of the faithful.

Sanctification/Deification: The overall purpose of self-determination is the sanctification of the individual and the surrounding world. As such, a primary element of a Christian's self-determination will have to be service.

Freedom, then, is the dispassionate use of the faculties, which participate in the cycle of sanctified time as service to and through the Eucharistic community.

B. Coherence

The Christian perspective on the coherence of human being is based on assumptions about a) the unity of body and soul, b) the effects of the fall, and c) what might be called an asceticism of hope.

Unity of Body and Soul. Human beings have, from the first moment of creation, consisted of a material body and of a soul, which, while it (the soul) cannot be reduced to matter, both permeates and transcends the material body creating a union of the two, a third reality the purpose of which is to bring about a dialogue (communion) between the supreme personal reality and these created persons. Body and soul are produced by the Eternal Conscious Spirit—conceiving the rational principles of matter and molding them into material form (body), also bringing into existence in this body His own image—a conscious soul.[212]

St. Maximus the Confessor held that no part of man-the-hypostasis comes into existence at some point after creation, since the union transforms both elements whenever they are united, and the human

---

211 A term used by some of the Fathers to sum up all that Christ has accomplished for us. See, for example, Irenaeus "Against Heresies", Book 5, Chapter 21, *Ante-Nicene Fathers* Vol 1. Alexander Roberts and James Donaldson, eds. (Peabody: Hendrickson Publishers, 1995), 548-551.

212 Dumitru Staniloae. *The Experience of God. Orthodox Dogmatic Theology. Vol. 2 The World: Creation and Deification* (Brookline: Holy Cross Orthodox Press, 2000), 67.

being would not be human before the union of body and soul.[213] St. Maximus also pointed out that the soul and the body cannot be united under the pressure of an exterior force (even sin) or of any natural affinity, since in either instance their union would be derived from impersonal forces devoid of freedom, and in which case, the human would not be a free being. "At the beginning through creation, and afterwards through birth[214] and by the will of God, the soul and the body come into existence simultaneously as a unity, not as a unity of substance, but as a unity formed from both elements."[215]

The body, then, is not identical with the soul (self), nor is it merely a part of the soul, but rather the agent by means of which the soul can gather together and exert influence on the created order—a link between the eternality of the Creator and creation itself. However, this should not be taken to mean that the body is simply an instrument "owned" by the self. With the breath of life God implants

> more than just biological life within the human frame (for animals also have this and they do not receive the divine inbreathing, it did not happen at the creation of subsequent human beings, Eve, being fashioned from the already animated material of Adam); it bestows the life of understanding and also of communion with God, that is to say, spiritual life.[216]

St. Symeon the New Theologian states that "as a result of this inbreathing the created being burns with the Spirit and becomes in his soul wholly a flame. He also shares this radiance with the body, in the way that visible fire shares its own nature with molten iron. St. Symeon continues by quoting St. Gregory Nazianzus who said, "the soul becomes to the body what God has become for the soul. For as the soul

---

213   Ibid., 71.

214   Significantly, for which two human beings are required. "New human beings are then born from a pair of other human persons through the power of God who enters into dialogue with them." Ibid., 71.

215   Ibid., 71.

216   Ibid., 84.

is unable to live without being illumined by the Creator, neither does the body live without being empowered by the soul."[217]

As the soul extends throughout the whole body and no part of the latter lacks its share, so is it necessary that the flesh, in turn, being inseparable from the soul—indeed, unable even to live without it—be wholly directed by the soul's will; and, as it is not possible for a body to live without a soul, neither can the body, in that case, have a will which is foreign to the soul.[218]

Any dissembling use of the body, then, will ultimately undermine coherence and the integrity of self-identity. To use appearance and demeanor to project a lie is to dissolve the probity of the self. To use the body to do violence to others is to fragment the unity of human being. And any activity that ruptures the bond between body and soul has to be rejected, since every form of disembodiment will damage the union and therefore both the body and the soul (self). For example, the idea that we have the freedom to use the body as a platform for unrestricted sensual pleasure without lasting effect on the self is simply absurd.

The Effects of the Fall. As Nellas points out, the conditions of creation described above are altered by humankind's fall into sin. As he puts it, a third state is occasioned by the introduction of sin, a state which awaits complete restoration at the resurrection. In patristic teaching this third state is often described with reference to the "Garments of Skin." (Gen. 3:21). The skins are not the body and they do not refer to gender—all of this existed in their pre-lapsarian state. The garments of skin represent the mortality which man put on after sinning. It is not primarily about death, but rather "life in death." Life transmuted into survival.[219] Therefore, the post-lapsarian state represents God's gracious condescension in anticipation of final restoration. This mercy has a two-fold character.

---

217   As quoted by St. Symeon the New Theologian. *On the Mystical Life. Ethical Discourses.* Vol. 2 Translated by Alexander Golitzin. (Crestwood: St. Vladimir's Seminary Press, 1996), 68.

218   Ibid., 69.

219   Nellas, Panayiotis. *Deification in Christ. The Nature of the Human Person.* (Crestwood: St. Vladimir's Seminary Press, 1997), 47.

On the one hand, then, the garments of skin are the physiological
result of sin, constituting an obscuring of the image, a fall from what
is according to nature and introducing hubris, penalty, and trauma;
on the other hand they constitute a remedy and blessing, introducing
a new potentiality which God gives to man enabling him, since he has
forfeited life, to survive in death and even to survive in the right way
so as to reach the point of finding again the fullness of life and the
beauty of form that belongs to his nature in Christ.[220]

Anthropological dimensions of the Garments of Skin speak to the
late modern addiction to bodily pleasure.

The new reality created by sin, that is, the sinful union of pleasure with pain, was compassionately used by God after the fall to
grant the human race survival—just as with the law he granted it
morality.[221]

Garments of skin do not refer exclusively to the body. However, when
human beings were clothed in the garments of skin, they lost something
of the "light and aerial beauty," the divinely woven image of dispassion
and incorruptibility. It became coarse, gross, passionate, and heavy. In
essence, this points to the general association of human beings with
the perpetually fluctuating material world, which is why Gregory of
Nyssa says they are inescapably transient and why the satisfactions of
the flesh are fading—yet redeemable.

An Asceticism of Hope. If human being is a unity of body and soul,
and if that unity is a faculty (or set of faculties) given for the purpose of
communion with God, then the way in which its components interact
will define its life—its spiritual life. Implied in this conviction is the
hope that these various elements of being can overcome sin and function
as they were intended to function. How can this happen? Taking his
queue from 1 Thess. 5:23, St. Theophan explores three aspects of human

220 Ibid., 63.

221 Ibid., 72.

spirituality: body, soul, and spirit.[222] Each has its proper function and all three aspects are necessary to our nature.

The life of the body has three major parts: the digestive system, and the musculoskeletal system, and the nervous system. These serve for nourishment, movement, and the senses.[223] The life of the soul has three major parts: the intellectual, the desirous (will), and the heart. The intellectual is understood as imagination and memory, ability to reason, and knowledge.[224] The desirous part is the will,[225] which is governed by the "pleasant, beneficial, and necessary." The heart[226] is the center and root of life; all that man encounters passes through the heart and there is found his treasures. "For out of the heart a man speaks." The heart is the source of zeal. The aspect of spirit serves as the meeting place for communion with God.[227] It is seen mostly as the fear of God, the conscience, and longing of God. This longing for God teaches man to be satisfied in God alone and also creates in man a general dissatisfaction with everything created. The spirit of man is the breath of God which He breathed into him when He created him in His "likeness."

St. Theophan goes on to explore the implications of this structure by assuming that the spiritual state of an individual depends on which one of these aspects dominates the person. By divine intent the spirit should dominate, with the soul and the body carrying out the will of the spirit and maintaining communion with the Trinity through the Holy Spirit. However, sin disturbed this proper order, resulting in confusion and disharmony. Once communion with God had been broken, the spirit lost its authority and the soul and body cried out for satisfaction as a result. Along with this the force of passions entered

---

222 St. Theophan. *The Spiritual Life and How to be Attuned to It* (Forestville: St. Herman of Alaska Brotherhood, 2000), 61. This is just one of many possible interpretations of the elements of human being, but it illustrates the way in which we can envision the elements working together as a whole.

223 Ibid., 45-48.

224 Ibid., 49-51.

225 Ibid., 53.

226 Ibid., 56-60.

227 Ibid., 60-64.

into man, which were foreign to him, but were of the devil, the serpent who tempted them.

Since the fall, human beings have lived in confusion with themselves, and as a result, have lived four kinds of fallen life: the carnal; the intellectual; the carnal-intellectual; and the intellectual-spiritual. There is also a fifth life, the spiritual life of true Christians. The carnal life is a life where the body dominates the soul and the spirit. This life produces every sort of uncleanness and defilement of the flesh. Although the soul and spirit are still present in man, they are suppressed, almost being completely unnoticed. Then man lives worse than an animal, being destroyed by the passions (Jude 10). The intellectual life is a life in which the soul drives the body and the spirit. All that a person takes into himself in this state is governed by his reason, concepts, presuppositions and opinions. The carnal-intellectual life seems to be life dominated by the body and the soul, seeking to please their longing and needs above all else. The intellectual-spiritual life is a religious life that is dominated mostly by the mind. These persons profess God or a god but do not know God. Although the spirit makes its appearance, ultimately these people answer to themselves.

The spiritual life. All of the above lives are unnatural to man and sinful. These people rule themselves. They are separated from God and would perish if God had not provided a means to reconciliation, to commune again, to live as God created us. The means God has provided are the incarnation, the life, crucifixion, resurrection, and glorious ascension of our Lord and Savior Jesus Christ and the coming and abiding presence of the Holy Spirit in the Church.[228] When a person believes the gospel of God his spirit is revived and is united to God. This is the new birth. As the Scripture says, "Awake, sleeper, and arise from the dead, and Christ will shine on you" (Eph. 5:14). This is the awaking of the spirit. Through child-like faith and dependence on God, a person's spirit, then, is united and strengthened with the Holy Spirit.

---

228   St. Theophan. *The Spiritual Life*, 108-120.

Then the soul and body are naturally harmonized and there exists the possibility of true coherence.

C. VALUE

The dilemma of self-authentication can be seen in the fact that it inevitably leads to self-love. Being a combination of a passionate attachment to the body (sensuality) and pride (the demands of the ego), late modern self-love answers the question of value by simply assuming its own value. The difficulty with this is that there is no basis, no intrinsic standard, and the self-assigned value is easily undermined by the plurality of completing values. In this case, the self faces the never ending necessity of shoring up its own value, trying to convince others that it is valuable. Yet one may or may not be valued, considered beautiful by others, and whatever worth is ascribed may fade depending on circumstances.

The Church's teaching on the creation of human beings in the image and likeness of God represents the only solid basis upon which the value of human being can be established. As the image of the infinitely good, divine prototype, human beings reflect that goodness. They are declared good by the Creator (Gen 1:31). And this can be expressed in terms of the admirable qualities (faculties) of the human being independent of specific situations. Moreover, as we have seen, contingent being implies love, creation without necessity, rendering the object of divine love, the human being, infinitely valuable. This fact is underscored by the willingness of God to sacrifice His only begotten Son on behalf of humankind. Human value is also rooted in the idea of deification, that is, it is grounded, teleologically, in the ultimate purpose of human existence. The self is valuable both intrinsically and instrumentally.

This understanding of the value of the self is extended to others. Thus, the good life would be characterized by a positive use of the faculties integrated by the double character of love. Love/Charity becomes the integrating feature of a meaningful life.[229]

---

229 Tunberg. *Microcosm*, 298.

As we have already seen, replacing the passions with the virtues leads to a life of dispassion (apathia), or a state of detachment. In most cases this is not simply a passive state, but rather one of active/deliberate "participation of the soul in divine life and the imitation of the divine nature."[230] The concept of detachment is stated in terms of its positive content: It is the life of Christ himself with his charity;[231] not passive, but an active balance held together by love. Detachment is, then, a state of equilibrium, excluding both positive and negative excess. But, overall, charity as the offspring of detachment emphasizes the positive function of the three aspects of the soul:[232] rational; love of God, knowledge of God, concupiscible; love of God, holiness, irascible; love of neighbor, patience and kindness.[233]

The dual character of love reintegrates the self by restoring the participation in the divine life (real not a sign) and reintegrates the other by reestablishing social discourse (real not a simulation). As such, the good life can be tied back into the ultimate purpose of human existence, namely deification. The whole process of dispassion/charity is a step along that path. It is in this context that St. Maximus brings in the other two theological virtues, *faith* and *hope*—as agents of deification.

Finally, if deification is, in fact, a participation in divine life, then we can assume a kind of reciprocity in the sense that divine characteristics (virtues) are being manifested (incarnated) in human life. It is this, perhaps more than anything else, that gives us reason to think that, in spite of all their shortcomings, human beings can lead meaningful lives and rediscover the real self and true social discourse.

---

230   Ibid., 301.

231   Ibid., 301.

232   Ibid., 308.

233   Ibid., 315-316.

Thesis: *Late modern reflexivity creates a context in which individuals become simulacra of themselves and in which social discourse is reduced to mere simulation. A Christian Theological framework offers a means of recentering the Real, i.e., recovering the self and restoring discourse.*

Trajectory of the Self

	Late Modern	Result	Christian	Result
Being	Self-Referencing	Loss of the Self	Being as Communion	Recovery of the self—human personhood
		Loss of the Other	Human being as contingent communion	
Identity	Self-Defining	Loss of Ontic Core	Image of God	Provides a stable Ontic Core
		Identity Fragmentation	Likeness of God	Deification as a chaining mechanism
Freedom	Self-Actualizing	Self-justified Contexts of Unlimited Choices	Passion/Dispassion Time/Tradition	
		Chaos of Unrestrained Expression	Expression as Service	Freedom anchored in the real
Coherence	Self-Monitoring	Disembodiment	Unity of Body and Soul	Kinship with God
		Body Power	Asceticism of Hope	Control & Communion
Value	Self-Authenticating	Dilemma of Reflexivity	Image and Likeness	Value of Self
		Loss of Value	Virtues (e.g., Charity) Deification	Value of Other Value of Action

PART III.

SOCIAL DISCOURSE IN THE LATE MODERN CONTEXT.

In this section I will relate the trajectory of the late modern self to the shape of the contemporary social bond by seeking to uncover the ways in which the Self-in-Discourse creates the basic patterns of that socioscape. I do not mean to imply a one-to-one relationship between the points on the trajectory of the self and particular elements of the social bond. But they are related in a recursively dynamic way. The discursive self creates the basic features of the socioscape, and is, in turn, constantly reshaped by the socioscape. To uncover these patterns, I propose an archeology of the contemporary social bond. I will look at a number of domains of social discourse, beginning with the ideas of belonging and diversity in a pluralistic, multicultural society and followed by questions of order, ethics, and religion.

While there is some justification for seeing Enlightenment thought as the dominant narrative of Western European and North American culture, this section will introduce an array of other narratives that have and are informing the contemporary social imaginary. The cognitive patterns inherited from the Enlightenment are still strongly held and still dominate certain domains of North American culture. But, the forces of globalization have brought a wealth of other cultural, ethnic, linguistic, economic, and religious narratives that contribute to social discourse and are transforming the other narratives represented in the social bond. For example, the religious part of our imaginary once held that one faith (Christianity) had an absolute corner on the truth. As it now stands, that conviction is being replaced by "a broad trend toward tolerance and an ability among many Americans to hold beliefs that might contradict the doctrines of their professed faiths."[234] A Pew Foundation report, *U.S. Religious Landscape Survey,* shows that 70 percent of Americans affiliated with a religion or denomination said they agreed that "many religions can lead to eternal life," including majorities among Protestants and Catholics. Among evangelical Christians, 57 percent agreed with the

---

234 http://www.nytimes.com/2008/06/24/us/24religion.html?em&ex=1214452800&en=c75daf04e6c17 7a6&ei=5087%0A Accessed 06/24/2008.

statement, and among Catholics, 79 percent did.[235] This development is, no doubt, the result of the increasing multiplicity of our society, as well as the logical implications of modernity. It leads to a complex environment full of discontinuities. These we will seek to uncover.

---

235   http://www.nytimes.com/2008/06/24/us/24religion.html?em&ex=1214452800&en=c75daf04e6c17 7a6&ei=5087%0A Accessed 06/24/2008.

Chapter 5

Belonging and Diversity

Next, I would like to explore the ways in which the late modern ideas
of being and identity play out in the context of social discourse. I will
begin by arguing that the anxious being seeks security in belonging and
that the resultant mode of being, seen as privilege, voluntary choice,
or responsibility, reflects the way in which membership was acquired.
Then I will suggest that the fragmentation of identity is exacerbated by
the pressures to diversification inherent in a multicultural environment.
In each case (being and identity) there is a recursive dynamic between
the self and the social bond similar to what Foucault calls *doubling*.

> The mobility of the system of formation appears in two ways.
> First, at the level of the elements being related to one another:
> these in fact may undergo a number of intrinsic mutations that
> are integrated into discursive practice without the general form of
> its regularity being altered... But inversely the discursive practices
> modify the domains that they relate to one another.[236]

When I speak of discourse I am not referring simply to the isolated
events and actions of language or social interaction, but rather to the
whole context in which the interests and power (faculties) of human-
being(s) are channeled or linked to specific domains, such as being and
belonging, religion, and ethics. My understanding of the social bond

---

236   Foucault. *Archeology of Knowledge*, 73-75.

is rooted in the conviction that human being, in particular being-in-the-world, is unavoidably relational. With the possible exception of a few reclusive ascetics, every human being will, of necessity—in order to apprehend being, to form identity, to order life, and to value self and others—relate to other human beings.

In speaking of an archeology of the social bond I am not inferring some pre-existing structure or order below the surface of the socioscape, but I am seeking insight that is tied to uncovering the history of the changes wrought by discourse within the context of the social bond (what has happened, what is happening, what will happen). Now, this process of 'digging' is going to be a messy business. Messy because, a) it does not lend itself to neat, clearly distinguished categories, causes and effects, b) I will not be able to neatly compartmentalize the religious aspects of culture, since I intend to describe religious components of the larger domains, such as being and belonging, and c) while repeating some basic doctrine, I will not be able to isolate Christian alternatives as easily, since what I will be describing is, in part, Christianity's own struggle with the same context that all other faiths are struggling with. Thus, part of what can be learned from the Christian experience will come from its own performance within the North American context.

Yet, I believe that this "digging" is necessary because we are, as Nietzsche says, not naturally beings of knowledge, at least not with respect to ourselves.

We are unknown to ourselves, we men of knowledge-and with good reason. We have never sought ourselves—how could it happen that we should ever find ourselves? It has rightly been said: "Where your treasure is, there will your heart be also." Our treasure is where the beehives of our knowledge are. We are constantly making for them, being by nature winged creatures and honey gatherers of the spirit; there is one thing alone we really care about from the heart—"bringing something home." Whatever else there is in life, so-called "experiences"—which of us has sufficient earnestness for them? Or sufficient time? Present experience has, I am afraid, always found us "absent-minded:" we cannot give our hearts to it—not even our ears! Rather, as one divinely preoccupied and immersed in himself into whose ear the bell has just boomed with all its strength the twelve beats of noon suddenly starts up and asks himself: "what really was that which just struck?" so we sometimes rub our ears afterward and ask, utterly surprised and disconcerted, "what really was that which we have just experienced?" and moreover: "who are we really?" and, afterward as aforesaid, count the twelve trembling bell-strokes of our experience, our life, our being—and alas! miscount them.—So we are necessarily strangers to ourselves, we do not comprehend ourselves, we have to misunderstand ourselves, for us the law "Each is furthest from himself" applies to all eternity—we are not "men of knowledge" with respect to ourselves.[237]

— I —

Belonging: Being in a Pluralistic Society

The first domain of social discourse in which I would like to "dig" is that of belonging. Obviously, this is tied to the relational aspects of human being and identity. If I exist relationally, then my relative position among other human beings will be of vital interest, since that defines, not only the context of my being—belonging—but also the mode of being-in-the-world. Note the reciprocal, recursive dynamic.

The benefits of belonging have been established by psychological studies which indicate that belonging is one of our basic human needs, second only to physiological and safety needs. This is generally satisfied by sharing thoughts and feelings; acceptance, confirmation, understanding, and influence with others we deem to be significant. When this need is unsatisfied, a person will feel its absence in the form of loneliness, ostracism, rejection, friendlessness, and rootlessness. It has

---

237   Freidrich Nitzsche. *On the Geneology of Morals* (New York:Vintage Books, 1967), 15.

been said that this need to belong is universal and that belonging to a community organization, school, profession, social circle, athletic team, church, or any group that unconditionally welcomes and accepts you for who you are now, not who you've been or who you might become, is a key factor in human well-being.[238] Of course, belonging may also provide access to resources and services otherwise unavailable.

But, I wonder how this need manifests itself today and how it is satisfied in the late modern era with its depersonalizing institutions, its collapse of community,[239] and its distancizing technologies. What does it mean to belong in light of the fact that loyalty in the work place[240] is a thing of the past? What can it mean to belong when membership is electronic[241] and the members never even see each other, never get to know one another? What of financial or consumer cooperatives[242] that call us members, and give us certain privileges, but do not introduce us to other people? What does it mean to be a part of a religious group now that they too are characterized by a high degree of mobility?[243]

As I see it, belonging in the late modern context is a function of the way in which one becomes a member and the resultant state or mode of being. This mode of being can be described in terms of the strength of affiliation, the view of membership, and the sense of belongingness.

A. ON THE NATURE AND PROCESS OF BELONGING

Generally speaking, individuals acquire membership in three basic ways, each producing its own mode of being.

---

238 Abraham Maslow's hierarchy of needs in *Motivation and Personality*. (New York: Harper and Row, 1970).

239 Robert D. Putnam. *Bowling Alone. The Collapse and Revival of American Community* (New York: Simon and Schuster, 2000).

240 Jill Andresky Fraser. *White Collar Sweatshop. The Deterioration of Work and Its Rewards in Corporate America* (New York: W. W. Norton, 2001).

241 According to Putnam modern technologies such as mailing lists and online membership has created an "entirely new species of 'tertiary' association whose members never actually meet. At the same time active involvement in face-to-face organizations has plummeted." *Bowling Alone*, 63.

242 Such as American Express and Sam's Club.

243 Pew Survey 2008, 44% of adults have shifted allegiance. http://religions.pewforum.org/reports# Accessed 8/18/2008.

Ascription. In some cases membership is ascribed or attributed without any particular action on the part of the individual as is the case, for example, with citizenship. Having been born in this country, I don't have to do anything in order to belong to the citizenry of this country, in contrast to the requirements (language, knowledge of history and politics, taking an oath) imposed on immigrants seeking to become citizens. In any case, I was born here and membership has simply been ascribed—it is a kind of belonging by default. Of course, this lack of requirements has an effect on the resultant right to be an American. It leads to a mode of being in which affiliation is taken for granted, membership is thought of primarily in terms of entitlements, rights, and privileges, and the sense of belonging is impersonal and weak (unless challenged). In my case, I don't think I understood my status as a citizen until I lived overseas where I did not belong, was an outsider.

Achievement. In other cases membership can be acquired or earned through some form of effort, a purchase, the fulfillment of requirements, or through relationships of convenience. You see this, for example, in athletic clubs, hobby groups, and business associations. In each case the member belongs by virtue of having demonstrated some skill, expressed some particular interest, or purchased membership as in the case of an automobile club. In these cases affiliation is strong, something like a badge of merit. Membership itself is thought of in terms of voluntary choice, freedom to choose, since the individual provides the occasion or rationale for membership. But the sense of belonging is depersonalized, based on the shared interest, and remains relatively weak.

Relationship. Another possible path to membership is a relationship of some sort. This could be kinship or having been invited by current members. This is very often the case with golf/country clubs, business clubs, and even churches. Since the individual is responding to a personal invitation, affiliation tends to be stronger (a privilege, an honor). Membership is thought of in terms of ownership, responsibility, and participation, and the sense of belonging is stronger or weaker depending on the level of participation.

I realize that these distinctions are a bit messy, since there is quite a bit of overlap, both in the role of the individual, the role of current members, and the resultant right to be. Observe the range of involvement: a) the individual does nothing, does everything, or simply accepts, b) current members do nothing, set conditions, or invite, and c) the mode of being ranges from a set of rights to an array of responsibilities. If what we have said about the reflexive nature of the late modern self holds true, then we would expect the bulk of late modern belonging to fall into the second category, membership by achievement.

When it comes to belonging in the religious realm, there are at least three culturalisms which bear directly on the paths taken to membership and belonging. This is most easily demonstrated with respect to various religioscapes[244] and allows us to refine the description of belonging.

Monopoly. Is a situation of absolute religious hegemony as one used to find in places like Greece, Spain, and Norway. Consider the 19th Century Norwegian Lutheran hegemony that molded the way its members and their descendants came to view becoming and being Lutheran. Religious identity became a part of cultural identity—to be Norwegian was, by default, to be Lutheran. No one chose to become Lutheran, they simply were Lutheran by virtue of the dominant culture. This kind of situation often leads to belonging by default, in which case Being is seen as an entitlement, much like the idea of citizenship. Note the close relationship between nationality and religious identity.

Duopoly (Pseudo/Shared Monopoly). In this case, two hegemons share power, such as in 19th and early 20th century Germany. Here Catholic and Protestant allegiances were divided up according to geography, with every village, every province, every State being either primarily Catholic or Lutheran. Belonging still comes by default, but here with the added component of a contrast. It is not that there are no choices, but rather only one of two is legitimate. There is no real

---

244   Arjun Appadurai proposes an elementary framework for exploring cultural flow that includes ethnoscapes, mediascapes, technoscapes, financescapes, and ideoscapes. Interestingly he does not include the religioscape. *Modernity at Large. Cultural Dimensions of Globalization* (Minneapolis: University of Minnesota Press, 1996), 33-37. Cf. David Martin, *A General Theory of Secularization* (New York: Harper and Row, 1978), 1-10.

possibility of free choice, since you are either a member by default or by conversion (which would be considered highly suspect). Being, then, remains a form of entitlement, but it is intensified by apposition—a sense of belonging achieved at the expense of the broadest aspects of discourse.

Pluralism. All of this changes in the case of a pluralistic context. All hegemony, all monopoly is abandoned in favor of a completely leveled playing field, which transforms the domains into a market place in which an increasing number of vendors are vying for a share (allegiance).[245] This form of socioscape has, of course, reached its zenith in the North American context (cf. our discussion on freedom and choice). This context taken together with the radicalized reflexivity of the late modern self leads to what I would call belonging by subscription. The individual freely (voluntarily) chooses membership, in which case being is viewed in terms of autonomous choice, i.e., in the end it is the individual, not the group of which she is a member, that determines the mode of being—the level of, terms of, timing of participation. Thus, allegiance is primarily a matter of choice or basically utilitarian. Membership is experienced on one's own terms and is measured by varying levels of participation. The sense of belonging is, for the most part, self-generated, based on common interest and on one's ability to control participation.

Finally, belonging is also about trust. Membership is almost inconceivable without the element of trust. Membership by ascription involves a high level of trust in the larger community and those who make membership decisions. Membership by achievement implies, at the very least, the belief that I will get what I have paid or worked for. Obviously, membership by relationship would indicate trust in other individuals. But all of this has been put under tremendous pressure in the late modern context. The post-traditional context has effectively robbed us of faith in the institutions we once trusted; family, community, church. Much of our social discourse is with abstract, expert systems. So who, in that case, do we trust? Not a person, but a system. To become

---

245   C. Peter Berger. *The Sacred Canopy* (New York: Anchor Books, 1969).

a member of an on-line organization is to have faith in a system which will keep my information secure, and which will deliver what I have signed up for. But, this is not the kind of trust that leads to a strong sense of belonging. It is depersonalized and distancized. As for membership by relationship, most of our interpersonal connections are based on convenience, need, or some shared interest. Again, this seems like a very narrow form of trust, unlikely to lead to a stable sense of belonging strong enough to counter the existential anxieties so prevalent. The reflexive nature of the late modern self leads to a kind of self-trust, really a mistrust that makes the desire for belonging hard to satisfy.

B. WELCOME TO AMERICA: A CASE STUDY IN MOBILITY AND CULTURAL TRANSPLANTATION

One of the more interesting aspects of the increased diversity[246] of immigrants to the United States is that even after immigration, the ethnic and religious aspects of it remain largely in tact.[247] So much so that many immigrants, while living in adopted geographic spaces, remain, e.g., solidly Indian, Russian, etc. This may be in part due to the continuing, if not intensifying, role of religion as a provider of the social context needed for expressing ethnicity,[248] as well as the social mechanism needed to preserve ethnic identity and govern cultural assimilation.[249]

Belonging to a religious community in a newly adopted geographic space directly affects the degree to which an individual's ethnic identity is perceived, maintained, or modified. Some research has explored the ways in which religious community enables the individual to process

---

246 Ebaugh, Helen Rose, And Janez Saltzman Chafetz. *Religion And The New Immigrants: Continuities And Adaptations In Immigrant Congregations* (Walnut Creek, CA: Altamira, 2000). Warner, R. Stephen, Judith G. Wittner, Eds. *Gatherings In Diaspora: Religious Communities And The New Immigration* (Philadelphia, PA: Temple University Press, 1998).

247 Arjund Appadurai. *Modernity at Large. Cultural Dimensions of Globalization* (Minneapolis: Univeristy of Minnesota Press, 1996).

248 Gary A, Kunkelman. *The Religion Of Ethnicity. Belief And Belonging In A Greek-American Community* (New York: Garland Publishing, 1990). This study indicates that the Church experienced a reversal of roles and became the guardian of Greek culture, not Christianity.

249 Martin Marty. *Pilgrims in their own Land* (New York: Penguin Books, 1984).

ethnicity. It has been suggested that the retention/assimilation strategies and their outcomes depend on the relative strength of the religion in the home and host geographies, i.e., the shift in majority/minority status caused by geographic transplantation.[250] What follows is the experience of one of the many immigrant groups[251] that have wrestled with questions of religious belonging.

> *Some parishioners are sitting near the entrance to the Church when a complete stranger bursts in and asks, "What kind of Church is this?" "We are Orthodox" comes the reply. "Ah! Greek or Russian, right?" Following an uncomfortably long moment of silence, someone manages to say, "No! American! We are Americans." "Well then," calls the stranger as he turns to leave, "welcome to America."*

Welcome to America, indeed! This exchange encapsulates many of the paradoxical patterns that have come increasingly to define Orthodoxy in the United States. Most of the people involved in the exchange described above were born, raised, and educated in the United States. They hold positions in the business, academic, or scientific communities and, given their knowledge of and participation in American cultural paradigms, there can be little doubt that they are American. Even within the context of their own religious practice these descendants of not-so-recent immigrants have achieved a high degree of conformity to American culturalisms. These individuals are—as any *recent* Greek or Russian immigrant would attest—definitely *American* Orthodox.

Yet, in spite of their assimilation into American modes of cultural life, society tends to interpret American Orthodox religious identity in terms *other* than American. One reason for this is that the Orthodox

---

250 Yang, Fenggang, Helen Rose Ebaugh. "Transformations In New Immigrant Religions And Their Global Implications." *American Sociological Review* 66(2) (2001): 269-88. "Religion And Ethnicity Among New Immigrants: The Impact Of Majority/Minority Status In Home And Host Countries." *Journal For The Scientific Study Of Religion.* 40(3) (2001), 367-378.

251 The basic patterns described here are being repeated by more recent immigrants such as Korean, Chinese, and Eastern Europeans. I myself grew up in the Scandinavian subculture of New York City and can attest to similar experiences.

retain—and I would argue deliberately maintain—a separate identity, which is shaped by their membership in the ethno-religiously bounded community associated with the Church. That community's distinguishing markers are, moreover, located primarily in the very fabric of the boundaries themselves and only secondarily in the culturalisms contained within those boundaries.[252] This intentionally diasporic identity ultimately determines societal perceptions of Orthodox believers, as well as Orthodox assessments of their own identity. Thus, no matter how American they might actually be, their understanding of themselves, as well as their discourse with other members of society—at least at the level of religion—is dominated by the boundaries of the religious community to which they have come to belong.

Complicating this state of affairs is the fact that as Orthodoxy underwent translation into the diverse, North American ethno-religious context, several distinct paths to belonging developed, each with radically different outcomes and implications for Orthodox individuals, as well as the Church. Initially, belonging was a matter of *default*, typical of contexts in which one religion is associated with the dominant culture and so closely connects faith to ethnicity that religious and cultural identity are practically synonymous and religious being is considered a birthright approached with an attitude of entitlement. This conflicted sharply with the pluralistic context of the new world in which religious belonging was a matter of *subscription*, that is, a conscious choice of faith more-or-less independent of ethnic considerations. In this case, religious identity was tied to the content and practices of the religion, and religious being was viewed as a privilege expressed through deliberate participation. Subsequent generations of diasporic communities began to conflate these two paths in such a way as to render belonging a matter of *ascription*. Loyalty to one's cultural heritage privileged a kind of "belonging by default" while the prevailing religious plurality encouraged being by free choice and voluntary participation.

---

252 Fredrich Barth. *Ethnic Group and Boundaries. The Social Organization of Culture Difference* (Prospect Heights: Waveland Press, 1969).

Today Orthodox Churches in America are comprised of members who have come to Orthodoxy through each of these patterns of belonging and are thus faced with a complex environment. Internally, the presence of all three modes of being creates tensions, misunderstandings, and programmatic difficulties. Externally, the nature of the boundaries forces these communities to wrestle with the question of what it can mean to be Orthodox in America today. In order to address these challenges, I would like to explore the ways through which individuals come to belong to Orthodox Churches in America in order to determine how the manner of *becoming* Orthodox affects the nature of *being* Orthodox.

(1) Belonging by Default

The first path to membership is that of "*belonging-by-default*"—a situation in which religious hegemony, real or simulated, admits no other alternative. In this case, Orthodoxy and ethnic content are so closely related that they combine to create a religious being or identity based on the notion of entitlement.

The roots of this phenomenon lie, I believe, in the 19th century Russian and Greek[253] Orthodox hegemony that molded the way its members and their descendants came to view becoming and being Orthodox. Because being Orthodox was included in the hegemon's catalog of concerns, religious identity became a constitutive part of cultural identity—to be Russian or Greek was, by default, to be Orthodox. Few deliberately chose to become Orthodox, they simply were Orthodox by virtue of the dominant culture's power to make that decision for them.

Theoretically, this approach to belonging could have and, to a certain extent, did work to the advantage of the Church. The dominance of the Orthodox faith made the decision to baptize children routine and nearly universal,[254] securing a demographically stable membership. Thus initiated into an Orthodox identity, these children were supposed to have

---

253 This is, of course, not limited to these two regions. The same thing could be said of most geographies in which Orthodoxy dominates, Serbia, Romania, etc.

254 Obviously, this practice is also rooted in and facilitated by a theological context, which allows for—expects—the children of Orthodox parents to be baptized.

had their religious being shaped by the various educational mechanisms of the Church—godparents, pastoral instruction, church schools, and the like. Ideally, this indoctrination/enculturation should have culminated in the individual's active appropriation of membership—and in some cases it did. However, since belonging was conferred as a matter of course, being was taken for granted and the motivation for intentionally investing in its development was undermined. Moreover, since neither the content of the faith nor the dominant culture were being challenged, religious education could be focused on facilitating conformity to the religious consensus, i.e., correct religious behavior. There was little perceived need for apologetic, biblical, or theological instruction. But people did need to know what to do and how to do it during the services—when to make the sign of the cross, when to genuflect, how to approach the chalice, etc. In this context, one simply was Orthodox and nothing more needed to be done to establish or ensure the vitality of that being short of formal (correct, occasional) participation in ecclesial events such as confession and the Divine Liturgy.

Transplanting Orthodoxy from Russia/Greece to the United States deprived it of its privileged place within a hegemonic elite. The Orthodox emigrating to the East Coast of the United States at the turn of the 20th century soon discovered that the prevailing culture had relegated their religion, and with it their culture, to a position of societal insignificance—one-among-many. It also became apparent that an insistence on "belonging by default" was not likely to be tolerated by the prevailing culture of diversity, in which "belonging by choice" was the norm.

One approach to this dilemma might have been to simply abandon Orthodoxy and buy into the religion of the prevailing culture, as, for example, the Russian Orthodox lady who told me that she became a Baptist so that she and her children would "fit into their new home."[255] However, rather than simply surrendering their own understandings or translating them into the idioms of the host culture, the Orthodox

---

255   Interview at Holy Transfiguration Orthodox Church, May 2004.

immigrants adopted a dualistic retention/assimilation strategy,[256] which depended on simulating the strength of the religion in the home geographies, as well as assimilation into the culture of the diasporic space. Resisting the changes that diversity demanded of the Orthodox notion of becoming, while, at the same time, taking advantage of diversity's tolerant attitude toward being, they established clearly demarcated enclaves[257] within which their own religion was granted hegemony. Individuals became and were Orthodox as if the Church were still the sole religious participant in a dominant cultural framework. Paradoxically, they also actively sought to be as American as possible. With the passing of generations, many of the culturalisms ensconced behind the boundaries came to be altered, lost, and/or replaced by content of a more American nature.[258] Yet, in order to maintain their ethno-religious identity, the original boundaries had to be maintained, leading to a most challenging social situation: Americans seeking refuge behind Russian or Greek Orthodox ethno-religious boundaries.[259]

While this strategy did maximize the preservation of ecclesial tradition,[260] it has had several less than positive effects on being

256 Some research has suggested that the retention/assimilation strategies and their outcomes depend on the relative strength of the religion in the home and host geographies, i.e., the shift in majority/minority status caused by geographic transplantation. Cf. Yang, Fengg and Helen Rose Ebaugh. "Transformations In New Immigrant Religions And Their Global Implications." *American Sociological Review* 66(2) (2001): 269-88. and "Religion And Ethnicity Among New Immigrants: The Impact Of Majority/Minority Status In Home And Host Countries." *Journal For The Scientific Study Of Religion.* 40(3) (2001), 367-378.

257 Similar to the idea of an imagined community. Cf. Benedict Anderson. *Imagined Communities.* "It is imagined because the members of even the smallest nation will never know most of their fellow-members, meet them, or even hear of them, yet in the minds of each lives the image of their communion. Imagined as limited because even the largest of them… has finite, if elastic boundaries, beyond which lie other nations…do not dream, e.g., of a wholly Christian planet. Imagined as sovereign because the concept was born in an age in which Enlightenment and Revolution were destroying the legitimacy of divinely-ordained, hierarchical dynastic realm. Imagined because regardless of the actual inequality and exploitation that may prevail in each, the nation is always conceived as deep, horizontal comradeship." (6-7)

258 One example was the introduction of pews, which were rarely, if ever used in the countries from which the immigrants came. Another example, was the introduction of a club like mentality/structure replete with elected officials, Robert's Rules of Order, and dues (instead of traditional tithing).

259 Vigen Guroian. "The Americanization Of Orthodox: Crisis And Challenge." *Greek Orthodox Theological Review* 29(03) (2001), 255-267.

260 It should be noted that much of Orthodox practice was in fact preserved in this way.

Orthodox. For one thing, this led the Church into a reversal of roles whereby it became the guardian of a particular culture rather than the faith.[261] Since its undisputed role depended on the hegemony of the cultural enclave established by its constituents, the Church now had a vested interest in actively maintaining that cultural context. For this reason, its educational efforts were shifted toward sustaining elements of that culture (language, traditions, foods, clothing, arts) rather than the specifically religious (biblical, theological) content of the faith. This was evident in the Russian and Greek language schools once operated by many parishes, as well as their annual ethnic festivals, and the persistent use of traditional languages (Greek and Slavonic).

As a result, being Orthodox came to be associated with certain aspects of the enclave's culture. It was almost as if being Orthodox was as much about the language you used and the foods you ate as it was about the content of the religion itself. While the specifics of doctrine and biblical knowledge were simply assumed or considered the domain of the clergy, the practice of the faith—the Church and its services—remained central to religious identity. Being was focused primarily on conformity to the traditions of the community rather than the specific theological or biblical content (dogma, canons) of the faith. What catechetical work there was focused on the Priest's vestments, liturgical colors, and the specifics of the rites such as baptism.[262]

Speaking of tradition in this context is not meant to say anything about the Orthodox doctrine of Tradition, which is used to express the idea that that which was handed down by Christ to His apostles has been preserved and is still being practiced today. The tradition of which I speak here is rather a combination of basic rubrics[263] and regional expressions of those rules. These catalogues prescribed the exact implementation of various elements of the Church's practice—vestments, processions,

---

261   Kunkelman. *The Religion Of Ethicity*, 91-105.

262   Typical of this approach is the Church School workbook *Our Life in the Church* (Yonkers: OCEC, 1971).

263   As one example, consider the English translation of the Russian Typica, which is widely used in North America. *Abridged Typicon* Feodor A. Kovalchuk, ed. (South Canaan: St. Tikhon's Seminary Press, 1985).

readings, blessings, etc. While there are ancient instructions that should be followed and that have stayed essentially the same, each regional Church developed localized adaptations of these rules.[264] To the degree that the life of the Church was rooted in the culture of the immigrant's enclave, doing things the Russian or the Greek way became extremely important to one's sense of belonging—being Orthodox.

Limiting Orthodoxy to the cultural confines of the immigrant enclave effectively prevented its application to the larger social context. On the one hand, becoming Orthodox by deliberate, individual choice out of a non-orthodox context was, within Orthodox circles, practically inconceivable. It wasn't that one had to become Russian or Greek in order to become Orthodox, but simply that, if one was not Russian or Greek, one would not become Orthodox. Why would any American want to become Orthodox? This attitude was illustrated by the Orthodox member who asked Protestant visitors if they didn't "have a church of their own to go to." As a result, converts were not expected and were not generally well received.

On the other hand, this approach led to marked resistance to contact with or encroachment by other groups/religions. This made it nearly impossible to propagate the faith outside the ethnic sub-communities, limiting prospective members to the children of immigrants or new waves of immigrants.[265]

(2) Belonging by Subscription

In spite of the intentional isolation, Orthodoxy was eventually discovered by Americans, many of them Protestants, whose ethnic origins did not lie in any of the geographies dominated by the Orthodox

---

264 For example there are distinct differences between the Slavic and the Greek implementation of certain services. See how, for example, the day on which the feasts fall affects the order and sequence of the services leading up to Christmas. Mother Mary and Archimandrite Kallisos Ware. *The Festal Menaion* (South Canaan: St. Tikhon's Seminary Press, 1996), 252-253.

265 This would have disastrous results when the rate of immigrations slowed and the Church began to lose its own children. In spite of these difficulties, there are still some Orthodox groups (jurisdictions) in the United States that deliberately maintain the use of traditional languages during their services, and project a deliberately ethnic image. This is particularly true of the Russian Orthodox Church Outside Russia and the Greek Churches which still use Greek during their services.

Church. These individuals were generally seeking more liturgical forms of worship, deeper spiritual practices, and an alternative theological context. Thinking that they had found those things in the Orthodox Church, they actively sought membership. Their reception into the Church opened up another path to membership[266]—*belonging-by-subscription*—membership chosen freely, which generally leads to a mode of being shaped by a sense of privilege and deliberate participation.

Because the converts were on a quest for specific content and practice the process of becoming took on an educational character. Since these individuals had not been privileged with the gradual enculturation enjoyed by those born into the Church, the only path to knowledge was reading, instruction,[267] and direct involvement. Once adequately informed, the seekers were able to make a decision—a free choice—to become Orthodox.

However, in the Orthodox Church that does not automatically lead to membership. Rather, it initiates the Catechumenate, a set period of time (several months to several years) during which instruction is continued and the candidates are evaluated. Once the Church is convinced that the Catechumen is ready, membership is conferred, i.e., they are received into the Church. Thus, it might be more accurate to say that the path to belonging was only initiated by a free choice and that membership was actually awarded as a result of study. Yet, the component of choice is retained, even emphasized. At the service during which the catechumen is received into the church the very first question asked is, "Do you desire to join the Holy Orthodox Church?"[268]

In any case, this path to belonging obviously affects the resultant mode of being Orthodox. Rooted in free choice, this mode of being tends to emphasize its voluntary nature. Participation in the life of the Church is itself an act of choosing. But, it is a choice based on the things the

---

266   Institutionalized in the *Service for the Reception of Converts* (Syosset: Orthodox Church in Aamerica, 1989).

267   Especially in the context of classes offered for the Catechumens.

268   "Do you desire to enter into and abide in the unity of the holy orthodox Faith?" *Service for the Reception of Converts*, 1.

converts hope to gain by becoming Orthodox. If they are looking for a more formalized liturgical setting, they tend to love the services and are, in many places, the most frequent and consistent participants. If they are looking for a deeper spiritual life, they tend to immerse themselves in Orthodox piety and learn more about the breadth of Orthodox spirituality and prayer than do those born into the Church. If they are looking for an alternative frame of theological reference, they continue reading and studying, often amassing considerably more knowledge, at least "head" knowledge, than those who have become Orthodox by default or ascription. Being Orthodox is seen as a continuation of the adventure of becoming Orthodox and one's sense of belonging depends on being allowed to actively participate. Indeed, it is often these converts who are the most regular attendees, who aggressively aspire to reading (chanting) and serving, who practice tithing,[269] and who quickly rise into leadership positions.[270]

This typically American approach has been adopted by recent émigrés (post-Soviet Union), as well as converts to Orthodoxy and represents a challenge to the earlier immigrants' initial resistance to translating Orthodoxy, i.e., it directly exposes Orthodox tradition (as defined above) to the homogenizing forces of multiculturalism—the possible loss of that tradition—robbing its discourse of cultural and religious distinctiveness.

(3) Belonging by Ascription

What then of the contemporary descendants of those early 20th century immigrants?[271] With the passing of time the definition and strength of the sub-cultural enclave was eroded by the gradual assimilation of its members into American culture. By the 4th quarter

---

269 Until recently tithing was not the primary form of giving in the North American Orthodox Churches. The assimilation of converts coming from a Protestant background where they may already have been involved in tithing, has led to some changes.

270 I base these statements on observations made during my 10 years of serving in 5 different parishes.

271 Basically those who have been born since WWII and grew up in the church of the 50's and 60's.

of the century the ethno-religious enclaves had all but disappeared.[272] The bulk of the original cultural content had been replaced with Americanisms—language, education, socialization, and employment. Yet, a religious identity of sorts could still be defined, bounded by the fact that many[273] of these 2nd and 3rd generation Russians, Serbians, Greeks continued to consider themselves Orthodox Christians. But rather than circumscribing the whole culture of an ethnic enclave (it was now mostly American), these boundaries defined only their religious identity, but did so in terms of the remembrance of a minimal set of ethno-religious markers (traditions). Since that identity was no longer mediated by direct participation in (conformity to) a well-defined ethno-religious enclave (it no longer existed), it depended on a kind of mimesis[274]—the imitation of traditions remembered.[275] And, since those memories were of a time when members of the community became Orthodox by default, these contemporary descendants tended to ascribe belonging to themselves in a similar manner. As a result, being Orthodox was simply taken for granted, with all of its attendant disinterest in religious content, but with the unassailable conviction that they belonged to the Church.

This *belonging-by-ascription* is then chained to the memories of the culturalisms of the once vibrant enclaves. Being Orthodox is no longer experienced via immediate conformity to living traditions of the community, but rather through the occasional capture of disconnected fragments of those traditions—recreations of past (childhood) experience. In the case of the traditional languages, for example, these contemporary Orthodox seem to validate their religious being by singing (or having sung) hymns in, let us say, Slavonic, even though they do not

---

272   There were, of course, new immigrants, some of whom were already Orthodox and fell into the first group described above, and others who were not Christian at all, putting them into the second group.

273   This might be an exaggeration, since relatively few remained actively Orthodox after the dissolution of the entho-religious enclave.

274   Charles Taylor's social imaginary *Modern Social Imaginaries* and Michael Taussig's *Mimesis and Alterity. A Particular History of the Senses* (London: Routledge, 1993).

275   Their love of Slavonic hymns, the text of which they do not (no longer) understand.

understand the language. They are Orthodox because they have grown up in it, because they are able to parrot certain practices, not because they understand the teachings of the Church or the content of the Holy Scriptures. But they are Orthodox.

On the other hand, these individuals are thoroughly immersed in the freedoms of American culture—in particular the right to choose. With no ethnic community to encourage participation, they are free to choose which aspects of the faith to participate in. For example, many of them do not attend the services of the Church regularly, yet still consider themselves Orthodox.[276] Others avoid the sacraments (confession & communion), taking communion no more than once a year. Still others avoid all instruction by refusing to attend classes or discussion groups. For them it is enough to know that there is an Orthodox Church in town doing the services. Whether they attend or not seems irrelevant to the question of their being Orthodox. It is as if the fact of their membership were shielded from all the forces of the late modern world, a conviction that, in its isolation, cannot be unseated.

So the advantage these members have lies in the strength of their affiliation. They may neglect the Church, but they will never leave it. They also voluntarily attend the church and for that reason are, at least theoretically, open to instruction and growth. One member recently said, "We have always had icons, but do we know what to do with them? Couldn't you teach us how to use them?" As such, these people represent one of the most promising segments of the contemporary church. If they could be re-converted,[277] their commitment and sense of belonging would be strong indeed.

✕ ✕ ✕ ✕ ✕

---

276 Alexei D. Krindatch. *The Orthodox Church Today. A National Study of Parishioners and the Realities of Orthodox Parish Life in the USA.* (Berkeley: Patriarch Athenagoras Orthodox Institute, 2008), 156-165. Available on line at http://www.orthodoxinstitute.org/orthodoxchurchtoday.html This survey of Orthodox parishioners indicates that 35% of cradle Orthodox and 35% of those under 45 believe that they can be good Orthodox Christians without going to Church every Sunday.

277 We have seen a number of examples of just this phenomenon. So called "cradle Orthodox" rediscovering their faith.

As stated at the outset, today Orthodox Churches in America are comprised of members who have come to Orthodoxy through each of the paths to belonging described above. Each group reveals a discernible mode of being Orthodox, and each group establishes a more or less robust religious identity by tapping into those registers of Orthodoxy that are most comfortable/familiar to them. Thus, those who are Orthodox by *default* tend to have a strong, stable identity rooted in their vigilant preservation of the Traditions of the Church, especially its liturgical components. Those who have come to the Church by *subscription* have a dynamic, evolving identity shaped by their efforts to assimilate new doctrine and practice. And those who are Orthodox by *ascription* often reveal a static and vulnerable identity fixed on mimetic appropriation of memories and traditions.[278] The presence of all three patterns represents a significant challenge to the life of the local parish, as well as its witness, since each brings both strengths and weaknesses.

C. REFLECTIONS ON BELONGING IN THE LATE MODERN SOCIAL CONTEXT

The contemporary North American religioscape is extremely fluid. According to the Pew Forum on Religion & Public Life[279] 44 percent of adults have either switched religious affiliation, moved from being unaffiliated with any religion to being affiliated with a particular faith, or dropped any connection to a specific religious tradition altogether. The survey also finds that constant movement characterizes the American religious marketplace, as every major religious group is simultaneously gaining and loosing adherents.

This situation has come about, at least in part, because belonging has become such a difficult proposition in the late modern context. The self-authenticating reflexivity of late modern identity and the boundless proliferation of choice, in the name of freedom of expression,

---

278 Here it might be useful to distinguish between Traditions and traditions (customs) See Mary Paloumpis Hallick. *The Treasured Traditions and Customs of the Orthodox Churches* (Minneapolis: Light and Life, 2001).

279 Pew Forum on Religion & Public Life, 2008. http://religions.pewforum.org/ Accessed 06/23/2008.

has undermined the very nature of and possibility of true belonging. Obviously, faith groups have not succeeded in nurturing a strong sense of allegiance and belonging. How, then, are we to belong in the late modern context? How can the radically reflexive self learn the art of discourse? What has been learned from the Orthodox struggle, and in what way does it offer concepts and alternatives helpful to others?

First, a strong sense of belonging is closely tied to the concept of Tradition or historical continuity.[280] Each of the above mentioned paths to membership includes some sense of being part of the stream of history, belonging to that great cloud of witnesses (Heb. 12:1). In other words, the notion that we are not alone, that the institution to which we belong has a stable existence over the course of time, that the beliefs and practices are shared by a large portion of the population and have not been constructed for the immediate context, but have been passed down from generation to generation. I realize that this runs counter to late modern conceptions of relevance, newness, and the celebrated absence of unifying narratives. Yet, the security of belonging sought as a refuge from the anxieties of a pluralistic society is not found in an unattached, expeditious grouping of individuals hovering around some temporally localized interest. Nor is it to be found in the ever-changing context of individual histories. At each stage of its encounter with its pluralistic surroundings, North American Orthodoxy has sought stability in the larger flow of history, in the grand narrative of the Christian faith.

Second, the Orthodox experience shows that the sense of belonging has something to do with the degree to which the individual member has owned the teachings and content of belief and practice. Each in their own way, the three groups mentioned above internalized either the external practices of the Church, the biblical, theological teachings of the Church, or both. As a result, they gained a level of familiarity with the ecclesial setting that put them at ease, helping them to feel like they belonged. There is also a negative lesson in all of this. To the extent that biblical content was neglected, the practices were emptied of meaning

---

280 It is interesting to note that some credit card companies show how long a person has been a member on the card itself, as in "member since xxxx."

and became rote ritual with little ability to facilitate communion with Christ or the larger community. This failure to teach more than the rudiments of religious practice has, at times, led to large scale exodus from the Church,[281] since not knowing what or why one believes will inevitably undermine the sense of belonging.

Third, there is the matter of trust. Becoming a member by default, subscription, or ascription implies a great deal of trust in the people of the Church. The most immediate object of this trust is going to be the person of Christ our Savior. But belonging to Christ means belonging to His Body, the Church. For that reason, the Church itself has to present a context of trustworthiness that includes its clergy and its members, both past and present. The trust that leads to belonging is a multilayered attitude, which, on the one hand, is willing to be identified with contemporary members of the group and, on the other hand, accepts the link to those who have gone on before. The objects of this trust are not expert systems of religious knowledge, nor abstract catalogues of teachings, but real people made one in their faith around the Eucharist. In the Orthodox experience, an environment of stability and trust is established during the weekly celebration of the Divine Liturgy. They refuse to give up this time honored form of worship, sung by the Saints before them, as it unites *all* the faithful around the Lord's table. This communion of the saints is the very ground of trust being offered to all.

Fourth, the Orthodox experience indicates that active participation in the life of the Church increases one's sense of belonging. Stark and Finke[282] suggest that a sense of belonging is a function of what they call religious capital. The more people do together, the more they will want to do things together, that is, the more religious capital they generate. Here again we note the differences between the three paths to belonging. Membership by default tends to generate a solid sense of belonging

---

281   Statistics on the Orthodox Church in America. http://www.oca.org/QA.asp?ID=44&SID=3 Accessed 8/21/2008.

282   Rodney Stark and Roger Finke. *Acts of Faith. Explaining the Human Side of Religion* (Berkeley: University of California Press, 2000).

based on regular participation in the services of the Church, in particular the Sunday Liturgy. Membership by subscription, develops the strongest sense of belonging, since it enthusiastically participates in the widest possible range of ecclesial activities. Membership by ascription generates a rather weak sense of belonging, since these individuals often choose not to participate.

These patterns indicate the possibility of a new model of belonging, a path to belonging by invitation and being by obedience. In this case, we, who have gotten to know our contemporaries, invite them to put their trust in Christ, to become his followers, to participate in the Church and to join that great historical movement we know as the Church.

— 2 —
Diversity: Identity in a Multicultural Society

Earlier, in Chapter 3, I argued that the identity of the late modern self was seriously damaged, and that, in the absence of a unifying ontic core, the self has to make due with a series of loosely connected identity fragments. At that point I proposed that unbracketing the question of human being and recognizing its iconic center, the image of God, would allow the individual to chain the fragments around a stable core and develop a coherent identity. Now I would like to suggest that this fragmentation carries over into the realm of collective identities and that our group identities, such as nationality, ethnicity, and religion suffer a similar disintegration because we cannot decided on, or simply don't have, a domain which is central or unifying.

The problem is adequately illustrated by the host of hyphenated monikers used to describe national and/or ethnic identity. I, for example, am a Norwegian-American. So, which realm is dominant? Which unifies my identity? Similarly, our religious identities could and are hyphenated into American-Baptist, German-Lutheran, Polish-Catholic, Greek-Orthodox. So, am I Greek or Orthodox or some combination of the two? Which one regulates identity? Are we not left with fragments of cultural and religious identity: cultures, as it were, in between?[283]

Obviously, part of the difficulty here has to do with what is known as multiculturalism.[284] The term emerged in the 1970's as the name for government policies designed to deal with ethnic pluralism. Based on the "values of equality, tolerance, and inclusiveness toward migrants of ethnically different background" its intention was to ensure "that all citizens can keep their identities, can take pride in their ancestry and have a sense of belonging."[285] For all the good that this doctrine has achieved, it does require the individual to negotiate the proximity[286] of the several ethnic or religious domains she occupies, and it provides no real help for doing so.

If multiculturalism involves an energetic interplay between multiple religions and a multiplicity of cultures all within the bounds of one nation state, how, then, are the competing claims of the various cultures and religions to be managed? Do the members of each group have the right to transplant, propagate, and maintain their own cultures and religions? This is particularly difficult in the case of religions, many of which claim absolute, supra-cultural truth. Christians, for example, would insist that the Gospel is not just another religious message and that the Church is not just another social institution. Moreover, this is not just a matter of rights, but of a perceived responsibility to defend and maintain. The third player in this context is the state and, obviously, it has the power to affect and regulate the interaction of the religions and cultures. Several roles have been suggested:

---

283 See Homi Bhabha's discussion on cultures in-between. *The Location of Culture* (London: Routledge, 199). 1-9.

284 See Charles Taylor, et al *Multiculturalism*. Amy Gutman ed. (Princeton: Princeton University Press, 1994).

285 http://www.blackwellpublishing.com/newkeywords/PDFs%20Sample%20Entries%20-%20New%20 Keywords/Multiculturalism.pdf Accessed 6/25/2008 As an alternative to the natural process of assimilation.

286 Timothy Rommen. *Mek Some Noise: Gospel Music and the Ethics of Style in Trinidad* (Berkeley: University of California Press, 2007).

State Neutrality. One possibility is to allow the state to take no position and undertake no action that would privilege one culture/religion over another. This amounts to leaving the interrogation and dialectic of social discourse to purely social dynamics. But this is not possible, it is an illusion, since the dominant elements of cultures will prevail as can be seen in the desecration of Native American burial grounds by developers.

Assimilation. Another option is to ensure that the state take no overt action against particular groups, but expect and support the idea that each will be assimilated into the common culture, language, etc., shared by the citizens of the state. This, for example, would assume that everyone who comes to the United States would eventually learn English, and that English would be the only language taught at our schools. The effect of this approach is to privilege the composite (dominant) culture and condemn all others. It is like the Orthodox person who abandoned her own heritage and took her children to the Baptist church because that was the predominant religion.

Proceduralism is an option that sees the state accepting the idea of equal rights for all cultural/religious groups and actively seeking to legislate protections for each. This, of course, is unrealistic and will inevitably be undermined by the dominant forces.

Hybridization/Fusion. In this case, we accept the value of some elements of each culture and the state seeks to promote a situation in which the horizons are fused, i.e., join to create a new (third) entity. In a global environment, this option seems to be unavoidable. The best that the state can do is establish a context in which each group has a fair chance at discourse.

One wonders, then, if there might be some way of establishing an existential core of collective identity that would help us relate and integrate the various fragments. I believe that for Christians that core lies in the Church itself, that is, the individual's *ecclesial being.*[287] It is the center around which we can chain the elements of our identities.

---

287 Title of a book by Constantine B. Scouteris. *Ecclesial Being* (South Caanan Mt Tabor Publishing, 2005).

Moreover, I suggest that the process of "*minding*" the Church[288] can help us navigate the spaces between those identifiers and take full advantage of the diversity offered.

A. Ecclesial Being: On the Possibility of a Stable Collective Identity

As stated above, individual identity is centered on the image of God around which each human being is hypostasized. This act of creation has to be explored in terms of its directedness. On the one hand, human being is directed at the Creator; that is, our being is a contingent and relational being in the tri-hypostatic God. This being in God, which reflects His image, is the ontic core of individuality and gives order and meaning to human existence. On the other hand, human being is directed at creation itself, in particular at other human beings. Having been made of the "dust of the earth" we share a certain connectedness with all of creation.[289] Having been made relational in the image of God we are also identified with all other hypostasized creatures, in what might be called a hypostatic multi-unity.[290] For that reason, we should not look at humanity simply as a collection of individuals who are bound by certain similarities,[291] but, rather, as a whole unified by one and the very same nature. Thus, each person exists not only in and for him or herself, but together with all human beings. Each individual integrates, is all-humanity. Moreover, being thus attached, sharing the same nature and the same divine image, we are bound to respect both the being and the individuality of every other human being. Diversity, that which established individuality, is not simply the right of an individual, but it is the life of humanity, the general foundation of our collective identity.

---

288 Cf. St. Paul's reference to the mind of Christ (Phil 2:5).

289 As Gregory of Nazianzus put it, "In my quality of earth, I am attached to life here below, but being also a divine particle, I bear in my breast the desire for a future life" as quoted by Vladimir Lossky. *Orthodox Theology* (Crestwood: St. Vladimir's Seminary Press, 1989), 71.

290 Sergius Bulgakov. *The Bride of the Lamb.* (Grand Rapids: Eerdmans, 2002), 109.

291 Ibid., 110. Which would amount to an unorthodox homoiousianism rather than the orthodox homoousianism.

But this has to be taken a step further, for as Christians we "live and move and have our being" (Acts 17:28) in Christ, that is, in our communion with Christ. The context for our collective identity is the Church, the Body of Christ. In this Body the multiplicity of contingent beings is gathered into a whole, around a common faith and the celebration of the Eucharist, in such a way as to preserve the individuality of each member. Each with a specific set of gifts that contribute to the building up of that common life. At the same time, there is the hypostatic multi-unity of the Body itself, an ecclesial being, established and fulfilled in Christ. The one spiritual reality (temple) built up of many living stones (1 Pt 2:5). This supra-individualistic ecclesial being is the unifying center of our collective identity. Each member, then, is not only a part of the Body but is the Body, has ecclesial being. So it becomes possible to speak of a collective consciousness that, superintended by the Holy Spirit, governs the life of the Church.

On the one hand, the Church demands and offers the Christian a positive unity, by demanding an allegiance that transcends all cultural concerns. The Church's claim on the life of the faithful is absolute. There is no area of life that does not fall under its influence. Every phase of life, from conception, to birth, to baptism, to marriage, to death is covered by some aspect of ritual. There is almost no occurrence for which there are no prayers.[292] We plan our giving by first offering the tithe to the Church and then living off the rest. We plan our time, by noting the feast days of the Church and then setting up our vacations. We regularly attend the services and participate in the Eucharist. It is this intense context of belonging that characterises the relationship between the believer and the Church. As believers, we are above all else ecclesial beings. Unfortunately, there are many Christians who are only dimly aware of this being, mainly because they do not submit to the collective consciousness and do not participate in the life of the Church.

---

292   The Orthodox Church in America has a four volume set of books that contains prayers for the entire liturgical cycle as well as almost every event likely in the life of a believer. *The Great Book of Needs* (South Canaan: St. Tikhon's Seminary Press, 2000).

On the other hand, ecclesial being helps establish my relationship to others, both inside and outside the Church. According to this ontology, we are one, because we share in the one bread and wine of the Eucharist. This, then, is the very centre of our collective identity. I am, first and foremost, one of the faithful and then an American, a Greek, Eastern, or whatever. Thus, the Church "in its essence has the potential, to a far greater extent than any narrow nationalist message, to show us the real meaning of history—and of all cultures, not just one."[293] It is this transcultural nature of the Church that was celebrated at Pentecost. The Church is not itself a culture and, because it stands above all culture, it can retain its core identity while incorporating any other culturally based identity. In the Church there are no hyphenated identities. Eastern-Christian, Brazilian-Christian, and the like make no sense. At the same time any Asian or Brazilian can be a Christian without sacrificing the unique characteristics of that individuation. Around this core all other elements are subdued and arranged.

B. Minding the Church: A Christian Approach
    to Diversity

With a core established, the Christian can then start the process of chaining the various identity fragments that come at him from the larger context. The difficulty with this process is that some of these fragments are more acceptable than others. In fact, some of them stand at odds with the core of Christian identity and are potentially destructive. So, imagine the advantage if we had a lens or a filter that would allow us to celebrate diversity without running the risk of destroying ourselves in the process. Fortunately, just such a filter exists. St. Paul refers to it as the "mind" which is in Christ (Phil 2:5) a pattern of thinking that conforms to His understanding and love of the world, of the risks and the opportunities. Some Christians have extended this idea to include this pattern of thinking as it had dynamically, under the guidance of the Holy Spirit, developed in the Church. It is sometimes referred to as

---

293   Mihail Neamtu. "Revisiting Orthodoxy and Nationalism" *Pro Ecclesia* (Spring 2006, Vol XV, No 2), pp 153-160.

the catholic consciousness of the Church and at other times simply as the Mind of the Church.[294] So if the mind of Christ were in us, or if we were actively minding[295] the Church, we would sustain ecclesial being while we safely navigated the spaces between the various cultures that make up our society.

What is being referenced here is what many Christians call Holy Tradition. Unfortunately, this idea has generated a great deal of misunderstanding and mistrust among Christians. I say unfortunate, because much of the discord stems from misinformation and caricature. So, in light of the potential benefits, let me take another look at the idea of Tradition.

In its most general form Tradition has two components: a) the totality of the various ways by which everything *given* in Christ passes over into the reality of human life (first to the Apostles, then through them to others) and b) the actual process of transmitting these ways— this life in Christ—from generation to generation under the guidance of the Holy Spirit.

In the overall context of biblical and patristic theology Tradition is not a mere doctrine about God, not a set of commandments and moral rules, not a collection of customs, not an authority structure, but it is that which has been given to us—life in Christ, the life of the whole Trinity as revealed by Christ and validated by the Holy Spirit.[296] These good and perfect gifts come down from the Father of lights (James 1:17-18), and have been given to us by Christ through His Apostles and their successors and this life composes the totality of the Christian revelation and Tradition. It is "a dynamic and active reality, which is lived by the people of God in the Church."[297]

---

294   George S. Bebis. *The Mind of the Fathers* (Brookline: Holy Cross Orthodox Press, 1994). 1-29

295   I like the linguistic play this word minding allows with its dual meaning of attending to (as in listening to or being guided by) and tending to (as in taking care of).

296   Metropolitan Athenagoras. "Tradition and Traditions" *St. Vladimir's Seminary Quarterly* 7 (1963), 103.

297   St. Irenaeus. *Letter to the Ephesians* Chap. 17 as quoted by Bebis. *The Mind of the Fathers*, 10.

The convergence of the two elements of Tradition (Apostles and Holy Spirit at Pentecost) generates the context of the Church—the context within which the fullness of the revelation in Christ passes over into the lives of individual believers. It thus seems reasonable to suggest that a primary mission of the Church is the preservation and advancement of that which has been received from the Apostles and activated in the lives of the faithful (2 Th. 2:5). Indeed, to that end the Church has been given and/or developed what I would like to call mechanisms of preservation and advancement. First and most important are the Holy Scriptures, which were developed within the context of the Church in order to assure that the Word of Christ and his Apostles was faithfully preserved. We can also include Apostolic Succession, Liturgical Structures (Services and Sacraments), Councils (Creeds, Canons), Iconography, Hagiography, Missions, and Dogma.[298]

Note that these various mechanisms constitute neither a hierarchy nor an authority structure, but rather an organic synergy of separate and unique processes, each designed to facilitate the safeguarding of some aspect of the Church's life—each contributing in a different way to that fullness which is life in Christ, i.e., Tradition. The truths transmitted by each instrument are harmoniously fused together into a unified whole, which defines the "catholic consciousness" or "mind" of the Church, a consciousness that is guided by the Holy Spirit. Thus, if we *were* to speak of authority, it would have to be in connection with the Holy Spirit, who superintends the dynamic advance of the Church and/or with reference to the overall consciousness of the Church (Acts 15:28 "…it seemed good to the Holy Spirit and to us…").

In other words, the service performed by Scripture, cannot be accomplished by any of the other instruments. Similarly, the benefits

---

298 That various means were used to transmit the Church's teachings and practices was clearly stated by St. Basil *On the Holy Spirit* Chap. 27 "Of the dogmas and sermons preserved in the Church, certain ones we have from written instruction, and certain ones we have received from the Apostolic Tradition, handed down in secret. Both the one and the other have one and the same authority for piety, and no one who is even the least informed in the decrees of the Church will contradict this. For if we dare to overthrow the unwritten customs as if they did not have great importance, we shall thereby imperceptibly do harm to the Gospel in its most important points. And even more, we shall be left with the empty name of the Apostolic preaching without content."

of Apostolic succession cannot be achieved through Liturgical structures or iconography. Yet, taken together under the guidance of the Holy Spirit, they constitute a unity—the fullness of Life in Christ. Thus, there are no dogma that are not supported by Scripture, preserved by Apostolic succession, reflected in icons, lived out by the Saints, facilitated by Liturgical structures, defended by the Councils, and proclaimed by missionaries.

From this it can be seen that Tradition has nothing to do with the local adaptations of culture that characterize the Church throughout the world. It is rather the mechanism that is used to process that diversity. The differences in hymnography, architecture, and iconography, are evidence of the Church being able to incorporate local cultures while protecting itself against injury. In fact, it is a "minding" of Church Tradition (life in Christ) that has consistently allowed this dynamic interchange, it has removed fear and distrust and has led to a celebration of human diversity. This has been practiced everywhere the Church has spread. Consider the work done on language and catechesis by Ss. Cyril and Methodius,[299] the work of the monastics who evangelized central Russia,[300] and of course the adaptation of the Orthodox faith to the Alaskan native populations by the North American Saints.[301]

So, on the one hand, there is no reason to deny an individual's national, ethnic, or linguistic heritage. In fact, the Church becomes the defender of *all* peoples. Each one will be considered equi-valuable and equi-legitimate for potential use in the Church. In some cases, this will require us to adjust the way we do things, in order to accommodate the differences. This could involve a multiplicity of language snippets during the Liturgy and the incorporation of a wide range of practices. For example, some Serbian Christians leave cash on the icons they venerate in the Church. While it is not common among the other Orthodox, a

---

299   Cf. Franz Grivec. *Konstantin und Method* Lehrer *Der Sklaven* (Wiesbaden: Otto Harrassowitz, 1960).

300   James H. Billington. *The Icon and the Axe: An Interpretive History of Russian Culture* (NY: Vintage Books, 1966), 52.

301   Michael Oleska. *Alaskan Spirituality and Orthodox Alaska.* (Crestwood: St. Vladimir's Seminary Press, 1992).

grateful and gentle acknowledgement of the practice, which is in keeping with Tradition,[302] goes a long way to make those people feel at home. By keeping the Traditions of the Church in mind, we are able to accept, accommodate, and help every worshiper develop a sound and stable collective (Christian) identity.

On the other hand, minding the Church will also allow us to evaluate and possibly use various aspects of the late modern social imaginary. Here there is a range of usefulness and our minding has to be careful and deliberate. Take the idea of freedom, in particular freedom of choice. According to Tradition, our life in Christ is to be based on our having freely chosen to put our faith in Christ. That individual freedom is then carried over into our participation in the life of the Church. We have choices to make concerning our daily prayer rule, our attendance at services, our participation in the sacraments, following the instructions of a spiritual mentor, and so on. Here there is to be no coercion. Faith is to be exercised freely. So the late modern emphasis on individual freedom should, to the degree that it conforms with Tradition, be promoted within the Church since it easily translates into responsibility, active participation, and thus growth.

However, freedom can also violate Tradition and thereby injure the Church. This could occur if we were to imitate the late modern desire for a proliferation of choice in the area of worship. The idea that we have unlimited options could easily lead to the introduction of practices that are inappropriate and even harmful. For example, Tradition places a great deal of emphasis on the celebration of the Eucharist. In fact, the instructions[303] that have been handed down to us view it as the very centerpiece of ecclesial being. If the pressures for more choice and variety were to lead to a neglect of the Eucharist, that would damage the Church. The same thing could be said for a number of other liturgical elements, such as the reading of scripture, the homily, and the recitation

---

302 There are many occasions when bread, fruit, wine, etc. is brought to the Church and left at the icons.

303 In the form of various Liturgies. In spite of the differences, the centrality of the Eucharist characterizes them all.

of the Creed. So, it would seem that in the case of worship, we do not have the freedom to simply do as we please.

What we see, then, is that minding the Church can help us incorporate and, in some cases, transform elements of our culture. Thus, the use of reason is to be welcomed and promoted within the limitations set for us by Tradition, namely, that we will not fall into a hyper rationalism knowing that we will not be able to understand everything about God, ourselves, or our world. The idea of progress can be welcomed if governed by the Church's concern that each member make progress in the spiritual life.[304] And processing these disparate elements of our lives within the context of the Church, centered on ecclesial being, enables us to develop a stable collective identity in the midst of diversity.

---

304 The second prayer of the Faithful from St. Chrysostom's Liturgy. "Again and ofttimes we fall down before thee and pray thee, O Good One who lovest man, that thou, regarding our supplication, mayest cleanse our souls and bodies from all pollution of flesh and spirit and mayest grant us to stand guiltless and uncondemned before thy holy altar. Grant also, O God, to those that pray with us progress in life and faith and spiritual understanding. Grant them always to adore thee with fear and love, and guiltless and uncondemned to partake of thy holy Mysteries and to be made worthy of thy heavenly kingdom."

Chapter 6

ETHICS AND RELIGION

*A still young, avowedly Christian man, never married, becomes
engaged and is jilted just before the wedding. Grieving, he develops an
on-again-off-again relationship with a recently divorced mother—
plying a precarious route between episodes of promiscuity and regret.
When challenged as to the "goodness" of such a life, all appeals to
absolute truth are relativized either on the basis of his own need (grief
relief) or of the changing character of the pool of potential mates
(since almost all women known to him have already been married,
the statistical likelihood of being able to comply with the teaching of
his faith is close to zero).*

In this chapter I will dig into the social domains of ethics and religion.
As I see it, two conflicting features of the late modern socioscape—the
loss of metanarrative and the rise of spirituality—are reshaping the
ways in which we deal with questions of morality and faith. The self-
referencing mode of late modern being, together with the fragmentation
of identity, effectively prevent the individual from appealing to any
kind of metadiscourse when seeking to legitimize the various beliefs
and actions of everyday life. At the same time, secularization and the
depersonalization of social institutions are turning people away from
the traditional setting of religious practice, the Church. This, however,
has not led to a demise of religion. Quite to the contrary, interest in the
spiritual realm seems to be thriving. That is why I say that these two

features of the social bond appear to be in conflict. One might expect the loss of, let us say, the metaphysical horizon to lead to a lack of faith, yet spirituality, whatever that might mean today, abounds. How, then, are ethical and religious discriminations to be made? On what basis do we say that something is good or right? What can be the role of religion if metanarratives and their institutions alike are abandoned?

The loss of metanarrative is a much discussed feature of our social context. Jean-François Loytard uses the idea to set a sharp divide between the modern and the post modern in his book *The Postmodern Condition*.[305] For him knowledge, science, or art are modern if they legitimize themselves "with reference to a metadiscourse... making explicit appeal to some grand narrative, such as the dialectics of Spirit, the hermeneutics of meaning, the emancipation of the rational or working subject, or the creation of wealth."[306] This he claims is the Enlightenment narrative in which the legitimacy of knowledge itself, questions of institutions, justice and truth are all "consigned to the grand narrative."[307] By way of contrast, he defines "postmodern as incredulity toward metanarratives."[308]

> This incredulity is undoubtedly a product of progress in the sciences: but that progress in turn presupposes it. To the obsolescence of the metanarrative apparatus of legitimation corresponds, most notably, the crisis of metaphysical philosophy... The narrative function is losing its functors, its great heroes, its great dangers, its great voyages, its great goals. It is being dispersed in clouds of narrative language elements—narrative, but also denotative prescriptive, descriptive, and so on. Conveyed within each cloud are pragmatic valencies specific to its kind. Each of us lives at the intersection of many of these. However, we do not necessarily establish stable lan-

---

305   Jean-François Loytard. *The Postmodern Condition: A Report on Knowledge*. Trans. Geoff Bennington and Brian Massumi. (Minneapolis: University of Minnesota Press, 1984).

306   Ibid., xxiii.

307   Ibid., xxiv.

308   Ibid.

guage combinations, and the properties of the ones we do establish are not necessarily communicable.[309]

But where does that leave us, if all we have are subnarratives at the intersections between disparate clouds of language fragments? As Loytard himself asks, "where, after metanarratives, can legitimacy reside?[310] We don't have to look far for the reasons of this development. As mentioned above, once we bracket the question of human being, we have excluded the practical significance of a transcendental horizon. With that gone, one has to posit the self as the source of legitimacy. But, the lack of an ontic core has shattered the unity of the self and, here too, we are left to relate, where possible, the various fragments (clouds?) of our identities. It is as if we have become the objects of our own science.

It is precisely this point that Michal Foucault takes up in his book, *The Order of Things*.[311] In order to show how human beings became the object of knowledge he traces the path of knowledge through three periods of history; Renaissance, Classical, and Modern. His basic assumption is that the scientific discourse of each age is organized by a latent grid of knowledge, what he calls an *episteme* or a paradigm. According to this scheme each age has its own order, a set of fundamental rules governing knowledge; its own signs (semiology), a mode of representation; its own language, a medium of representation; and its own knowledge (epistemology), the experience of the signs and language of a given period.[312]

When Foucault comes to the Modern Episteme (19th Century onward) he describes its order in terms of organic structures of history related by analogies of function rather than concretized stable instances of actual identities. Those identities are now seen as ever-changing and

---

309 Ibid.

310 Ibid., xxv.

311 Michal Foucault. *The Order of Things. An Archaeology of the Human Sciences.* (New York: Vintage Books, 1994).

312 Ibid., xxi-xxiii.

only temporarily stabilized products of history. Representation loses its power to define the mode of being common to things and knowledge. The link between one organic structure and another is the identity of relation between the elements and the functions they perform. Language is no longer a means of transparently representing knowledge, but an object of knowledge to be studied. Finally, knowledge breaks down into three realms—formal (mathematics, physics), empirical (biology, economics, philology), and philosophical (analysis of finitude). Human sciences are now possible, since human being can be viewed as both the subject and the object.[313]

Again I ask, "Where does that leave us?" The dilemma of late modernity intensifies. If human beings are now the objects of their own study, and if their identities are reduced to ever-changing historical subplots, related by analogies of function, and only occasionally stabilized in history, then the futility of referencing the self becomes obvious.[314] In that case, who is to act as the subject of right action, and who would be its object? If representation can no longer describe that which things and knowledge have in common, and if language can no longer represent knowledge, then the ethical and religious uselessness of narrative, whether meta- or sub-narrative, seems apparent. How, in this environment, will it even be possible to speak of truth, good, and right?

Let me turn now to the second feature of the late modern socioscape that is affecting the way we deal with questions of morality and faith, namely spirituality. During the last few decades we have witnessed a widespread resurgence of interest in the spiritual. One can easily make the case just by taking note of just a few recent publications such as the series *Traditions of Christian Spirituality* 12 vols. (Maryknoll: Orbis Press), *Classics of Western Spirituality* 25 vols. (Mahwah: Paulist Press),

---

313 Foucault. *Order of Things*, 217-221.

314 No wonder then that Foucault predicts that man could "be erased, like a face drawn in sand at the edge of the sea. *The Order of Things*, 387.

and *World Spirituality. An Encyclopedic History of the Religious Quest* 25 vols. (New York: Cross Roads).[315]

But there is more to this than just a tidal wave of publications, for the renewed interest is more inclusive, more far-flung than ever before, a staggering proliferation of meanings and manifestations, fanning out into almost every realm of human existence.[316] Spirituality is often associated with New Age (just about anything new). Michael Downey notes that New Age Spirituality has room for everything from Transcendental meditation, to Zen prayer disciplines, T'ai Chi, acupuncture, dream-work, enneagrams, star gazing, channeling, Wicca cults, and even a fascination with the demonic.[317] Some of this includes a new appreciation of the importance of psychological insights in the spiritual quest—personal experience as such.[318] With the self as focal point, the idea of healing, i.e., the therapeutic, takes over as a governing category in spirituality. Others have turned to Eastern religions and Native American peoples for inspiration and practical guidance. Note the wide spread interest in the meditative practices of Hinduism, and Buddhism (esp. Zen), as well as techniques for the control of mind and body, such as Yoga. All of this supports the proliferation of self-help movements, twelve-step programs of healing and wellness (divorce, alcoholism, various forms of abuse, stress, etc.). In some cases contemporary spirituality is focused on the sacredness of the earth, nature, non-human life—drawing on various sources as diverse as native American spirituality and the Gaia hypothesis.[319] This has also spawned an ever-widening range of specific spiritualities: feminist, masculine,

---

315 To this could be added any number of Journals including *Spirituality Today, Spiritual Formation, Spirituality and Health, Journal of Experimental Spirituality, International Journal of Children's Spirituality, Journal of Gay Men's Spirituality,* and *Spirituality Journal.*

316 "Spirituality in America" *Newsweek* Aug 29, 2005.

317 Michael Downey. *Understanding Christian Spirituality* (New York: Paulist Press, 1997),

318 Harvey Cox. *Fire from Heaven* (Cambridge: Da Capo Press, 1995).

319 The Gaia Hypothesis proposes that our planet functions as a single organism that maintains conditions necessary for its survival. Formulated by James Lovelock in the mid-1960s. Cf. *Gaia: A New Look at Life on Earth.* (Oxford: Oxford University Press, 1979).

sexual, etc.,[320] raising the possibility of associating just about anything with the concept of spirituality.

While it may be easy enough to demonstrate this rise in interest, understanding the reasons for these developments is a far greater challenge. As I see it, this recent rise in popular interest in spirituality is one of the most intriguing enigmas of the late modern context. This increased interest in the spiritual dimension of human existence comes at the same time that secularism and the after effects of the Enlightenment project seem to have all but eliminated the supernatural from vast domains of our collective enterprise—natural sciences, social sciences, social services, etc. Yet we still speak of spirituality, but in the absence of the divine, the supernatural. What, then, can spirituality mean, if we have lost the supernatural horizon? What is one to meditate upon, draw strength, peace, and virtue from? Just what is the spirit of this new spirituality? This increased interest is also accompanied by a gradual, general decline in appeal of institutionalized forms of religion—the very institutions, the business of which it is or has been to promote and articulate the spiritual. As Michael Downey states,

> There is a sharp line drawn between spirituality and religion. Together with this is an implicit or explicit conviction that spirituality is what really matters. Religion and adherence to the beliefs of a religious tradition may be helpful, but are certainly not essential in cultivating a spiritual life.[321]

Consider the words of Martin Marty,

> …millions speak of their being spiritual but not religious. They shun the disorganized fronts of what they call 'organized religion,' and go their own way, sometimes finding new company. You will find them at retreats or book signings where the Tibetan Dalai

---

320   Downey. *Understanding*, 6-11

321   Ibid., 7.

Lama is almost as recognized a figure as the pope or Billy Graham. Devotees of alternative medicine speak of their disciplines as spiritual.[322]

The concept itself has been divorced from its traditional moorings and is now being used to describe an ever-widening array of ideas and activities. But, if an idea can mean just about anything, then it generally means nothing—it loses its specificity, it is generalized into meaninglessness. That being the case, you might expect interest in the idea to fade. Yet, that is not happening. With one best seller after the other, one author after the next finds yet another aspect of the human experience to which to apply the term spiritual. From New Age practices to all manner of self-help programs, from the spirituality of Native American Peoples and oriental meditation to prayer groups and retreats in the desert, the trend shows no signs of abating.

One reason why the supernatural has been eliminated from major domains of life has to do with the radically reflexive and self-referencing nature of the late modern ontological project. One of the sources of the contemporary understanding of human existence is the extreme inwardness [323] fostered by the Enlightenment (modernity). This turn inward is sometimes expressed as an extreme confidence in human ability to define itself (rational capabilities). That idea is rooted, in part, in the assumption that existence precedes essence. As noted earlier, the human subject just exists, turns up, appears on the scene, and it is only after this thrust toward existence that definition can take place. Accordingly, there is no universal human nature, there is no God who conceives and concretizes it. There are only human beings conceiving themselves.[324]

The reason that religious institutions have fallen out of favor has to do with the ways in which social discourse and its attendant institutions have been transformed by an absolutizing of inwardness.

---

322   "The Long and Winding Road" *Newsweek* Aug 29, 2005.

323   Cf. Charles Taylor. *Sources of the Self*, 111.

324   Sartre, Jean-Paul. *Essays in Existentialism* (New York: Citadel Press, 1988), 35-36.

Inwardness seems to have left us with no one and nothing to trust but ourselves. Yet the complexity of late modern life requires some form of trust. Traditionally, that has been developed and expressed within the context of a network of stable and persistent relationships. But under the influence of social complexity and extreme inwardness many have opted for transitory commitments in which what is important is the utility of some shared interest, choosing and managing select associations only as need requires. This leads to a transformation of the institutions involved, including religious institutions. Whereas these institutions were once used to help manage risks and opportunities based on ongoing relationships of trust, they had now taken on the character of abstract systems of knowledge or expertise, to which one turns for temporary assistance. Where there is no perceived need for expert assistance in a particular area, the institutions, systems associated with those domains, are simply ignored.

So, exaggerated inwardness prevents individuals from actually trusting (depending upon) others. That, in turn, transforms the way we interact with institutions, preventing us from admitting to our anxieties and trusting institutions, unless, of course, they are deemed necessary for day-to-day survival. If the supernatural has been removed from vast swaths of modern life, then there is no need for the "expertise" provided by a religious institution. If any need for assistance is perceived, it is pursued in the context of self-help, expeditious associations, and/or expert systems, and not in the network of trust traditionally associated with religious institutions.[325]

But I would like to suggest that, in spite of this reflexive dishonesty, people begin to suspect that personal existence is not simply the individualized product of choices made and that there are levels of reality not immediately apparent—even some ultimate, uncreated reality. In spite of all attempts to shrug off the transcendent horizon, the inescapable presence of the supernatural remains perceptible.

---

325 Stark and Finke. *Acts of Religion.* 160-162. The only religious institutions growing are the ones that are rooted in dense social networks of interpersonal trust relationships within the group. One might ask "where are your friends?"

In spite of all attempts to deny the anguish, the isolation of the absolutized self invades the very fabric of honest self-reflection. In the midst of these unnerving discontinuities the fragmented individual recognizes an inner dimension, some aspect of human existence, human nature, the human spirit, the core, the deepest center of the self crying out for integration—for resolution, for integration with that of which it is an image. And it is this desire, rooted in the very nature of human being, that leads to the phenomena we have been describing, this churning, swirling, endless attempt to name, to manage, to experience, to control those unseen dimensions of human existence.

How then do these two conflicting features of late modern life affect the ways in which we seek to make moral and religious discriminations? In what follows I would like to give a few examples of the approaches to ethics and religion that have been taken by thinkers who have largely freed themselves from the metanarratives of the past, especially the metaphysical, but who, at the same time, want to hold on to moral and/or religious thought.

— I —

Ethics in the Absence of Subject, Object, and Horizon

Part of the challenge for late modern ethics is that it is often attempted in the absence of either a stable subject, a clearly defined object, and/or a totalizing horizon. As indicated above, if the self is an ever-changing, rarely stabilized entity, how can it be the subject or for that matter the object of moral thought or action. Of course, one can be so focused on the other that the subject becomes practically irrelevant to moral action. And if all metanarratives, especially the metaphysical, are abandoned, then what standard or authority can be used to evaluate moral discriminations?

After all of our talk about the dissolution of the self, one has to wonder if moral action is even possible. What would ethics look like if the subject were to recede into the background? Emmanuel Levinas gives us an instructive example. According to him the only context for ethics is that of interpersonal relationships. Ethics involves understanding the meanings involved in person-to-person interaction. The correlation between knowledge, understood as disinterested contemplation, and being is the very site of intelligibility, the place where meaning occurs. The comprehension of being would thus be the very possibility of or occasion for wisdom and, as such, is first philosophy.[326]

However, if knowledge is taken to be the real other, then I have, in fact, cut off discourse with that person, by denying the other's alterity, but seeking to co-opt it, make it the same. This is what Levinas calls the violence of totalization, something which makes ethics impossible—there is, then, no other, no person.[327] For this reason, Levinas turns his attention to a relationship with the other person that cannot be reduced to comprehension. Being is inseparable from the comprehension of being, yet how can a relation with a being be other than comprehension? It cannot unless we are able to move back to a pre-comprehensional, pre-ontological point, to a precognitive moment to what he calls passive sensibility. Subjectivity on the plane of sensibility is the site of the face-to-face meeting of the real other, for sensations are discovered, not invented. It is in this sensible meeting of the other that the self first encounters the ethical moment—the refusal of the other to be known, consumed, enjoyed. The resistance from the other side of being is evident in the face of the other—thou shalt not kill. There is in this experience an astonishment, a moment of surprise which is captured in the idea of proximity.

> The proximity of the Other is not simply close to me in space, or close like a parent, but he approaches me essentially insofar as I feel myself—insofar as I am—responsible for him. It is a structure that in nowise resembles the intentional relation, which in knowledge

---

326   Sean Hand, ed. *The Levinas Reader* (Oxford: Blackwell, 1989). 78.

327   Emmanuel Levinas. *Totality and Infinity* (Pittsburg: Duquesne Univ. Press, 1969), 42.

attaches us to the object—no matter what object, be it a human object. Proximity does not revert to this intentionality, in particular it does not revert to the fact that the Other is known to me.[328]

Proximity is responsibility, the ability to respond,[329] held hostage by the other. Thus, the self becomes a projection toward the other in responsibility, a being for-the-other. This leads to the notion of substitution, the means by which the self can respond before knowing, transcending sameness. "In substitution my being that belongs to me and not to another *is undone*, and it is through substitution that I am not 'another' but me."[330] The subject, it seems, has been effectively decentered.

This emphasis on the other has drawn its share of criticism and has led to ethical models that downplay or even eliminate the other. For example, Alain Badiou[331] has proposed an ethical reconstruction that he calls an ethics of truths. In response to Levinas he asks, "Does the Other Exist?[332] According to Levinas, ethical responsibility arises out of the encounter with the other, who is not merely a mirror image of the subject (Sameness), nor something comprehended (owned) by the subject. The other comes unmediated[333] and with radical alterity from a point anterior to cognition. According to Badiou

> This means that in order to be intelligible, ethics requires that the Other be in some sense carried by a principle of alterity which transcends mere finite experience. Levinas calls this principle the 'Altogether-Other', and it is quite obviously the ethical name for God. There can be no Other if he is not the immediate phenome-

---

328 Emmanuel Levinas. *Ethics and Infinity* (Pittsburg: Duquesne Univ. Press, 1985). 97.

329 Emmanuel Levinas. *Otherwise Than Being: Or Beyond Essence* (Pittsburgh: Duquesne Univ. Press, 1998) 139.

330 Ibid., 127. See also Alenka Zupan i . *Ethics of the Real* (London: Verso, 2000).

331 Alain Badiou. *Ethics. An Essay on the Understanding of Evil* (London: Verso, 2001).

332 Ibid., 18.

333 Peter Hallward. "Translator's Introduction" In Badiou. *Ethics*, xxii.

non of the Altogether-Other. There can be no finite devotion to the non-identical if it is not sustained by the infinite devotion of the principle to that which subsists outside it. There can be no ethics without God the ineffable.[334]

But if, as Badiou insists, there is no God, then an ethical system will have to be a-religious. That, in turn, means "the whole ethical predication based upon recognition of the Other should be purely and simply abandoned. For the real question—and it is an extraordinarily difficult one—is much more that of recognizing the Same."[335] The Same is not a multiplicity of differences, but rather, that which comes to be, it is truth. Since only truth is indifferent to differences, the only ethics "is of processes of truth, of the labour that brings some truths into the world."[336] That labor involves some-one—an animal of the human species—a spectator whose thinking has been set in motion, caught up in the process of the truth of a situation, to which he remains faithful, and through and of which he becomes a subject. The general maxim of this ethic is "'Keep going!' Continue to be this 'some-one,' a human animal among others, who nevertheless finds him or herself seized and displaced by the eventual process of a truth. Continue to be the active part of that subject of a truth that you have happened to become."[337]

What then of the problem of evil? According to Badiou it is one of the paradoxes provoked by his maxim. Evil is possible only through an encounter with the Good, or with truths. It is the dark underside of those very truths. Evil has three basic forms: simulacrum (to be the terrorized follower of a false event); betrayal (to give up on a truth in the name of one's interest); disaster (to believe in the total power of a truth). So an ethic of truths does not seek to struggle with an external or radical Evil, but seeks rather to ward it off by means of discernment (do

---

334 Ibid., 22.

335 Ibid., 25.

336 Ibid., 28.

337 Badiou. *Ethics*, 91.

not fall for simulacra), of courage (do not give up), and of moderation (do not get carried away to the extremes of Totality).[338]

Finally, here is an example of an ethical approach in the absence of metanarrative. In contrast to those who seek to link reason to theoretical insights into the world as a totality, Jürgen Habermas[339] takes a post-metaphysical, procedural approach to the grounding of moral authority. With the loss of meta-narratives, post-metaphysical thought views the rationality of a given proposition purely as a matter of the procedures used in deciding its truth.[340] Habermas develops his system in the context of what he calls communicative action. According to him, interactions are communicative "when the participants coordinate their plans of action consensually, with the agreement reached at any point being evaluated in terms of the intersubjective recognition of validity claims."[341]

There are, of course, several types of validity claims: Truth deals with the totality of existing states of affairs; Rightness, the totality of the legitimately regulated interpersonal relationships of a social group; Truthfulness, the totality of experiences to which one has privileged access. These claims can be promoted by means of several types of action: strategic action, through which one actor seeks to influence the behavior of another by means of the threat of sanctions or the prospect of gratification in order to cause the interaction to continue as the first actor desires; and communicative action, by which one actor seeks rationally to motivate another by relying on the illocutionary binding/bonding effect of the offer contained in his speech act. If one is to focus on discourse, then one has to ask which claims to validity can be discursively redeemed. We could speak of propositional truth in the case of an unambiguous relationship of language to the objective world. We might also speak of normative rightness. But these claims

---

338   Ibid., 91.

339   Habermas, Jürgen. *Moral Consciousness and Communicative Action* (Cambridge: MIT Press, 1999).

340   Steven Hendly. *From Communicative Action to the Face of the Other* (Lanham: Lexington Books, 2000), p 53.

341   Habermas. *Moral Consciousness*, 58.

to validity mediate a mutual dependence of language and the social world that does not exist for the relation of language to the objective world. They are ambiguous and require criterion for generalizing maxims of moral action, that is, every valid norm would have to fulfill the condition of universalism, i.e., all affected by the norm can accept the consequences and the side effects its general observance can be anticipated to have for the satisfaction of everyone's interests. This is a rule of argumentation that makes agreement in discourse a possibility and leads to the fundamental principle of discourse ethics: only those norms can claim to be valid that meet (or could meet) with the approval of all affected in their capacity as participants in a practical discourse. This amounts to a reformulation of the categorical imperative: Rather than ascribing as valid to all others any maxim that I can will to be universal law, I must submit my maxim to all others for purposes of discursively testing its claim to universality. It is in this sense that the individual is the last court of appeal for judging what is in his best interest.

> Discourse ethics, then, stands or falls with two assumptions: a) that normative claims to validity have cognitive meaning and can be treated like claims to truth and b) that the justification of norms and commands requires that a real discourse be carried out and thus cannot occur in a strictly monological form, i.e., in the form of a hypothetical process of argumentation occurring in the individual mind.[342]

✕ ✕ ✕ ✕ ✕

As these examples show, developing a coherent system of ethical thought is far from trivial in the late modern context. The realities of individual dissimulation and social simulation seem to compel one to either decenter the subject, over emphasize the other, or seek validation of

---

342 Habermas. *Moral Consciousness*, 68.

truth in something other than a metanarrative. This, of course, creates a host of questions. How, for example, can we speak of moral action if the subject is "undone?" What is the good of moral action if its object is the "truth of a situation" rather than another human being? How are those truths to be established as truth, that is validated, if they are merely the products of individual recognition? How is Evil to be recognized, distinguished from the Good? Whatever weaknesses these models might show, there is one aspect, shared by all of them, that I find intriguing. Each, in its own way, emphasizes the inherent value of the individual. In what amounts to an antidissimulational move to the other, the some-one, the participants all play a crucial role in the development and application of moral thinking. They are said to be capable of recognizing truth, seeing the face of the other, and forming a consensus. As such, they are themselves worthy of respect, justice, and love. But, how do we know what is respectful, just, and loving? In spite of the apparent rejection of grand narratives, each one of these models hints at a totalizing horizon. In one case, it is the totality of the Good and the Evil. Or it is the overarching narrative of consensus, the reason(s) for communicative action. And in another case, it is the transcendent horizon of the Absolute-Other. Is a totalizing narrative necessary after all? I think so and suggest that the work of ethics will have to be based on an integration of human existence and the transcendent life in which it has its being. But, before I come to that, let me take a brief look at the place of religion in the late modern context.

— 2 —

Religion in the Absence of Subject, Object, and Horizon

Unfortunately, religion has not fared any better than ethics in the late modern context. Religious communities, in particular Christianity, have become active participants in the hyper real simulation (spectacle) by condoning the lie of selflessness, by adopting the intellectual underpinnings of dissimulation, by withholding counter-dissimulational truth, and by simply ceding large tracts of the socioscape. For this reason religion, at least in its institutional form, cannot stand "over-against," cannot, to use Levinas' term, responsibly "face" the ever changing world and is gradually losing its influence in society. Indeed, churches are emptying and, to use the words of the philosopher Mauizio Ferraris

> Christianity as we have known it in history is disappearing. That is, the Christian religion as a faith whose defenses include that of being the most rational, the most true, of a truth that has an essential relation with the truth of history and science, is in the process of dissolving. Nothing will be able to make it rise again.[343]

But, then, what else was to be expected? Why complain about the irrelevance of religion when its diminishing significance was an obvious and predictable result of the Enlightenment, of Cartesian egocentricity? Why lament its demise, when it was the Christians' own attempt to prove that Christianity was reasonable, to play the game on Enlightenment terms, that caused it to give way to rationalism?[344] Shouldn't we expect, even acknowledge that the self-referencing, de-totalizing achievements of the late modern self have effectively superseded the very need for religion? For many today that is true. But, then, how are we to account for the fact that those whose thought has shaped the current intellectual climate constantly speak of religion, the religious, even of faith. What are we to do with Derrida's prophetic announcement of the "return of religion."[345] And how are we to explain the resurgence of popular interest in religion and spirituality? Wasn't modernity supposed to have been the end of religion? Indeed! But, perhaps we have actually progressed beyond the modern. Is there, after all is said and done, something truly post modern afoot—the return of religion?

---

343 Ferraris as quoted by David J. Tracey. *The Spirituality Revolution. The Emergence of Contemporary Spirituality* (New York: Routledge, 2004), 132.

344 Gay. *The Enlightenment*, 326

345 Jaques Derrida. *Acts of Religion*, Gil Anidjar ed. (New York: Routledge, 2002), 75.

But what can religion look like in the absence of the self, the other, and a transcendent horizon? Let me briefly explore three ways in which religion is affected by the late modern context. In some cases, religion is simply lifted above the fray, put into another realm, a kind of hyper-realization of religion. In some cases, religion is generalized using the categories of human spirituality. And in other cases, religion is simply overwhelmed by culture, leading to a reversal of roles.

In 1994 a group of philosophers met on Capri to discuss the condition of 'religion' in society and culture today. According to Derrida the participants were "not priests bound by a ministry, nor theologians, nor qualified, competent representatives of religion, nor enemies of religion as such, in the sense that certain so-called Enlightenment philosophers are thought to have been."[346]

No! These were philosophers who recognized the return of religion and were intent on discussing what religion might mean today and how one might go about speaking of it. To begin with, they identified two sources of religion, both outside the restrictions of dogma or doctrine, and always within the realm of human experience and social reality. One is messianicity, the trust in the other that is the inevitable result of discourse—the opening of the future, the coming of the other. This is only possible when no anticipation sees it coming, since anticipation closes the future. This an anticipation with no concrete, determinative Messiah. The other is what they called chora, that which defies the law of non-contradiction, no being, nothing present, but not the Nothing.

Another way they looked at this was to speak of the experience of faith, that is, trusting the coming of the other, acquiescing to the testimony of the other—the utterly other who is inaccessible in its absolute source. Moreover, there is the experience of the unscathed sacred, that is experiencing the Nothingness of the sacred—"that which carries beyond the presence of what would offer itself to be seen, touched, proved…"[347] "That which is separated from the human

---

346 Derrida. *Acts of Religion*, 47.

347 Ibid., 70.

by a veil of its own devising... God being the name of that which gives the order to give the (impenetrable) veil."[348]

The Capri participants also determined that neither faith nor the sacred are necessarily correlated, although they might be. It is possible to maintain oneself in the presence of the sacrosanct without bringing into play an act of trust or faith. Conversely, trust in that which is beyond seeing, touching, and knowing does not necessarily involve the sacred. This is the case because neither can be deconstructed—they exist rather outside of that which can be deconstructed—religion (language and nation as the historical body for all religious passion).

All of this amounts to a hyper-realized religion, a religion without religion, messiah without messiah, faith without specific content, faith in a God who cannot be known, i.e., who is dead. In other words, this is religion beyond, or at the limits of reason alone. So what the delegates accomplished was simply a way of talking religiously without admitting to its reality—or, as I have been saying, a dissimulation of the person, and religion as pure simulation.

The religious can also be sought as a transcendent aspect of human nature itself, a God deep within the self[349]—a spiritualized religion. As Harold Bloom indicates, transcendence, that climbing beyond the material universe and ourselves, is often rejected as an illusion by materialists. Nevertheless, it has an uneasy existence in many of us and has had a more secure hold in a scattering of individuals through the ages: mystics, visionaries, sages, men and women who have a direct experience of the divine, of the angelic world and are able to convey something crucial of that encounter to us. It is this knowledge, this gnosis, which sets us free, allowing us to transcend the limits of our existence.[350] In truly late modern fashion the actual source of insight is not considered important. This mediated knowledge can be pagan,

---

348   Ibid., 317.

349   Harold Bloom. *Omens of Millennium. The Gnosis of Angels, Dreams, and Resurrection* (New York: Riverhead Books, 1996), 30.

350   Ibid., 20.

Jewish, Christian, or Muslim or can even take on the outer forms of more Eastern spiritualities.[351]

Ultimately, the reflexive project of modernity seeks to transform religion into a form of self-knowledge—knowing the self's potential—knowing the spark that is the inmost Self as evidenced in dreams, near-death experiences, and the obsession with angels. While Bloom's approach is an acknowledgement of human transcendence/spirituality, it is coupled with a refusal to ground faith in anything other than the human perception of the transcendent. This amounts to a faith without content, without frameworks, and without form. It has the feel of a designer religion keyed to the momentary state of an individual. Once again, we see the effects of the self-referencing aspect of late modern life.

Finally, religions are sometimes overwhelmed by culture. In the absence of totalizing horizons culture has often overtaken, transformed and even replaced religion. In the multicultural environment of North America this can take place within the specific confines of one of the sub-cultures or on the more generalized plane of the prevailing (homogenized) culture.

The former phenomenon has been the experience of many immigrant communities. For example, even as the members of the Greek immigrant community sought to navigate a path of assimilation they vigorously struggled to retain something of their Greekness.[352] In this struggle they turned to the traditional Greek Orthodox church for help in perpetuating and reinforcing their ethnicity. Since many of these people had become members of the Church by default, they did not have, at least spiritually speaking, high levels of commitment. They rarely "express strong personal faith... or look to Orthodoxy for a charter of beliefs and practices that can be applied to the business of daily life."[353] This did not diminish their attachment to the Church or their sense of belonging. However, "there is a fundamental de-emphasis of religion

---

351   Ibid., 248.

352   Kunkelman. *The Religion of Ethnicity*, 172-180.

353   Ibid., 177.

as a belief system or as a provider of a system of conduct: the priest is effectively relegated to a cultural icon and teacher of Greek ethnicity, whose function is to perpetuate Greek distinctiveness."[354] In effect, there was a reversal of roles. The Church was no longer seen as a provider of truth, spirituality, and the sacraments, but as the chief defender of ethnicity. "The church has been largely shaped into an ethnic identity that provides a badge of identification, perpetuates Greek distinctiveness and serves a belonging-providing function."[355]

On a more generalized plane, Alan Wolfe[356] points out that, "In the United States culture has transformed Christ, as well as all other religions found within these shores. In every aspect of religious life, American faith has met American culture—and American culture has triumphed."[357] Attempting to attract or to keep congregations whose members have been so strongly influenced by a common American culture, all of America's religions face the same imperative: personalize or die.[358] American religion survives and even flourishes, not so much because it instructs people in the right ways to honor God, but because people have taken so many aspects of religion into their own hands.[359] Evangelicalism's popularity is due as much to its populist and democratic urges—its determination to find out exactly what believers want and offer it to them—as it is to certainties of the faith.[360] So, religion involves telling Americans what they already want to hear. It would seem, then, that a part of the North American Church has aided and abetted the cultural forces that assured its own demise—they have effectively become an instrument of the culture.

✕ ✕ ✕ ✕ ✕

---

354   Ibid.

355   Ibid.

356   Alan Wolfe. *The Transformation of American Religion. How We Actually Life our Faith* (New York: Free Press, 2003).

357   Ibid., 3.

358   Ibid., 35.

359   Ibid., 36.

360   Ibid.

These, then, are some of the ways in which religion is affected by the late modern context. What remains remarkable is that in spite of the secularizing trends inherited from the Enlightenment, religion is still with us, or perhaps with us again. And this is all the more remarkable since it is spoken of even by those who posit God in the Nothing, beyond all knowing. It is still called religion even when practiced in institutions that have become the gatekeepers of culture rather than the supernatural. I wonder why, in the absence of religious essentials—knowing God, belief in the transcendent—religious thought and practice can still flourish. Perhaps Bloom is right in suggesting that people are intuitively aware of another dimension, that in spite of external appearances, they sense something of their own spirituality and of the transcendent plane. That might help explain the indefatigable interest in spirituality and it might point us to a more fruitful understanding of the place of religion in society.

− 3 −
Religion as Spiritual Integration

In its most general sense the term spirituality can be used to identify the deep desire of the human being for "personal integration—for a reconciliation between the unseen dimensions of reality and the every day markers of the sacred—a movement via self-transcendence toward the horizon of some ultimate concern."[361] In the language of our deliberations this will have to involve a re-centering of the real as the horizon against which to articulate human ontology, develop moral frameworks, make value discriminations, and practice religion. I am speaking of a personal encounter with God incarnate, the person of Jesus Christ, within the context of the Christian community and, as such, the quest for integration is a process that involves the self, the Church, and God.

---

361   Downey. *Understanding*, 14.

I have already stated that when we speak of the self we are generally referring to an individual's awareness of who and what they are. The self is a composite whole, which takes shape at the confluence of the three overlapping registers of self-hood: being, identity, and self-awareness. This, then, is the active subject of the quest for integration which involves a conscious effort to overcome the isolation and self-absorption of reflexivity and transcend the self by reaching out to the divine horizon. This activity takes place within the institutional context of the Christian community. The idea of self-transcendence implies that there is no such thing as a generic spirituality. It always involves some coherent and articulate understanding of a specific framework within which experience is mediated, facilitated, and evaluated, in which the individual is held accountable. So, the ultimate horizon toward which integration strives is God as revealed in Jesus Christ and as experienced through the gift of the Holy Spirit within the life of the Church. For this reason the articulation of the ultimate horizon and the process of integration will take shape in the form of theology—a basic theological context.

As I see it, spiritual integration of the individual rests on a willingness to acknowledge human existence as contingent and relational. Fundamental to Christian teaching is the idea that God exists as three persons—Father, Son, and Spirit—each sharing one and the same essence. The tri-hypostatic nature of this unity also implies a relational character. This relational nature is passed on to human beings, who possess being only as it is granted by the creative will of God and who, because of that contingency, exist as beings in relation.[362] Thus, the ontological potential of created being can only be realized if it participates in the life of communion with God—the first axis of spiritual integration.

Having been created in the image of God the relational aspect of created being also extends to communion with beings of like substance. In general terms this involves participation in the multi-hypostatic union of humanity—a kind of inner-creational communion analogous to inner-Trinitarian communion. But, authentic spirituality will

---

362   Zizioulas. *Being as Communion*, 88.

require some way of integrating both aspects of human spirituality, the inter-creational and the divine-human relationships. This, I believe, is provided by the ecclesial being that is offered by the community of Christians centered on the Eucharist. In Christian thought, the incarnation of Christ is seen as the ultimate integration of the divine and the human. The created and uncreated aspects of reality that have been torn apart by Bad Faith are reunited. In the Eucharist we celebrate and participate in both the reality of and possibility of that reunification. By mystically participating in Christ, the individual acknowledges (by faith) and experiences spiritual integration with the divine and, at the same time, with other participants, an integration that reestablishes the dignity of human existence, overcomes depersonalizing isolation and fragmentation, and restores trust, both in other individuals and in the institutions of spirituality—the second axis of spiritual integration.

If, as I am suggesting, a Christian spirituality is possible in this late modern context, where do we go from here? What will this quest for integration involve? Karl Rahner summed it up nicely when he spoke of the shape of contemporary spirituality. He begins with the past. Despite all the change, Christian spirituality will remain the old spirituality of the Church's tradition and history. We will have to continue to learn from the Church's past.[363] However, contemporary Christian spirituality will also have to concentrate on rediscovering and re-articulating the most essential features of Christian piety,[364] since many of these things are no longer widely believed in our culture. The spirituality of the future will be concentrated on the ultimate data of revelation: that God is, that we can speak to him, that his ineffable incomprehensibility is itself the very heart of our existence and consequently our spirituality...[365] Furthermore, because it will not be supported by a sociologically Christian homogeneity of its situation, "it will have to love much more clearly than hitherto out of a solitary, immediate experience of God

---

363   Karl Rahner. *The Practice of Faith*, 18-19.

364   Ibid., 19.

365   Ibid., 20.

and His Spirit in the individual."[366] This will require a more radical, lonely responsibility in the decisions of faith. "That is why the modern spirituality of the Christian involves courage for solitary decision contrary to public opinion.[367] This underscores the need for a renewed ecclesial aspect, a kind of attachment to the Church.[368] Spirituality, then, will grow out of a genuine experience of God in Christ emerging from the very heart of our existence, within the context of the Church. This is the real, basic phenomenon of Christian spirituality.

---

366   Ibid., 21.

367   Ibid., 22.

368   Ibid., 25.

Part IV.

Evangelism in the
Late Modern Context.

Now that I have surveyed the trajectory and socioscape of the late modern self, I would like to turn to the question of evangelism. As a backdrop to suggestions on how it can be done, let me first describe what I will call a topography of conflict, the landscape of discontinuity between the Gospel-as-Person and the late modern mind. On that score, I will suggest that the conflict arises because a realistic presentation and acceptance of the Gospel will require a kind of self-affirmation that is at odds with the current loss of self restraint of our assumed freedoms, an abandoning of the self to trust, both in individuals and institutions, as well as a transcendence of the self, that is, an apprehension of the supernatural. Having recognized the obstacles I will then propose that we revitalize evangelistic efforts by re-personalizing the witnessing community, re-socializing the process of witness, and re-integrating the direct experience of sacred reality.

Chapter 7

THE TOPOGRAPHY OF CONFLICT

*But certainly for the present age, which prefers the sign to the thing
signified, the copy to the original, representation to reality, the appearance to the essence...illusion only is sacred, truth profane. Nay,
sacredness is held to be enhanced in proportion as truth decreases and
illusion increases, so that the highest degree of illusion comes to be the
highest degree of sacredness.*[369]

As already indicated, I believe that evangelism in the late modern era
has become extremely difficult because there is essential conflict between
the nature of the Gospel and the contemporary mind. Another way to
look at this is to consider the topography and dynamics of the social
matrix that develops as individuals interact with others in an attempt
to live out, present, and receive the Gospel-as-Person. In other words,
to examine the field of play created by intentional evangelism.

The field itself is strewn with obstacles, key Enlightenment principles
captured in the late modern social imaginary. Ideas such as rationality,
reductionism, freedom, consilience, and progress have combined to
undermine the plausibility of the Gospel. Moreover, the process of
secularization has effectively removed the sacred from much of daily
life. And so the late modern conditions of faith render unbelief the
default position[370] and there appear to be very few late modern people

---

369 Ludwig Feuerbach, Preface to the second edition of *The Essence of Christianity*, as quoted by Guy
Dubord in *the Society of the Spectacle* (New York: Zone Books, 1994), 11.

370 Taylor. *A Secular Age*, 12-13.

interested in the Gospel. Its not that they are consciously against it, it is simply not an issue for them.

As for the participants, I have described the trajectory of the late modern self as being characterized by: a loss of self (due to a refusal to interrogate the sources of being itself), a loss of a unified identity (due to the absence of an ontic core of identity), an illusion of freedom (fueled by a demand for unlimited choice), a loss of coherence (due to the many forms of disembodiment), and a loss of value (due to the abandonment of metanarratives). I went on to describe the socioscape created by the interaction of these individuals as having difficulties with belonging and diversity (due to the multi-cultural nature of our populous) as well as ethics and religion (due to the loss of self, the Other, and horizons). I should point out that Christians too have been affected by the late modern context and have developed their own forms of depersonalizing indifference, which make it difficult to participate in the life of Christ and His community and share what they are supposed to be experiencing with individuals outside their own community. The Gospel, then, is met with a degree of skepticism, incredulity on both sides of the evangelistic playing field.

Of course, this tension could be eased by presenting[371] the Gospel in such a way as to mask or distort its life-altering implications. In an effort to make it more attractive it might be offered as an aid to achieving the most cherished late modern desires. Indeed, some have even offered it as a guarantee of health and wealth. Others make it out to be an "easy" path devoid of effort, sacrifice, and suffering. These and other alterations of the Gospel have had some success by pandering to what the listeners already believe and want. There is no doubt that this feel-good approach to the faith has attracted a following. However, the question is, what is the message that has been offered and accepted? In what ways have these other gospels (Gal. 1:6-9) changed the lives of their adherents? If all that is offered are the spiritualized fantasies of

---

371 We are under great pressure to adapt the Gospel to its cultural surroundings. While there is a legitimate concern for contextualization, what most often happens in these cases is an outright capitulation of the Gospel to the principles of that culture.

the late modern mind cloaked in Christian terms,[372] then there is really nothing to accept, since it is already part of the listener's imaginary. Moreover, no change is required, since the recipient agrees with the message even before it is presented.

Where, then, is the incredulity of which I speak? It inevitably arises when the Gospel-as-Person, presented in all the radicality of a life changing, personal relationship of trust and belonging, collides with the late modern mind. The Gospel-as-Person is the invitation to a restorative relationship with the eternal, uncreated, and personal being of Jesus Christ: who reunited the created and uncreated by being incarnate (Gal. 4:4); who, by dying without dying[373] released human nature from the bond of mortality (1 Cor. 15:12ff); who, by sacrificing his own life and rising again, released humanity from the curse of their own sinfulness (Rom. 8:1); and who offers to actualize these freedoms within the context of a personal relationship of trust with Himself (Rom. 10:13) and those of like trust (1 Cor. 10:17). Given the personal nature of the Gospel, evangelism is essentially the issuing of an invitation to participate in the restoration offered by Christ. Conversion[374] is agreeing to fully participate in that relationship. So why has this become so difficult? Basically, because issuing, understanding, and participating in the invitation requires self-affirmation, self-restraint, self-abandon, and self-transcendence—the very things that the late modern mind has the most difficulty with.

---

372 For example Joel Osteen's *Become a Better You: 7 Keys to Improving Your Life Every Day* (New York: Faith Words, 2004). Every one of the seven steps have already been discussed in previously published secular books. So it seems that this is simply a superficially Christian remake of those popular self-help manuals. It should also be pointed out that Osteen's definition of success has to do with things like becoming Miss America, getting the expensive house you desire, and having God favor you by providing parking spaces and open check out registers in the face of long lines. It is obvious that the prescriptions of this book are nothing more than the general expectations of the late modern age. It is devoid of the Gospel. There is no mention of sin, of transformation in Christ, of a personal relationship with Christ, and, for that reason, it offers no alternative to the current cultural expectations.

373 Eastern Easter Hymn "Christ is risen from the dead, trampling down death by death, and upon those in the tombs bestowing life."

374 Talking about conversation instead of conversion misses the point, since the end result of evangelism is an acceptance of the invitation and a radical transformation of the recipients life.

— I —

Self-Affirmation

Any involvement with the Gospel will require an affirmation of the full reality of human personhood. This may sound a bit odd in light of the reflexive nature of the late modern project. Surely individuals who define their lives by referencing, monitoring, and authenticating themselves don't need to be encouraged to affirm themselves. Yet, it is actually the denial of the self that has caused this self-centeredness. Taking human existence (being-in-the-world) as the point of departure, late modern individuals refuse to engage the question of human essence (being-as-such), and seek to define life by their own actions. So life is lived without much interest in the nature and meaning of human being and, for that reason, it loses something of the fullness of its reality. Without the stability of that central reality, identity becomes the disjointed accumulation of those life defining activities. This leads to further depersonalization at the hands of late modern institutions and technologies, which de-emphasize personhood and often limit the individual to prescribed scripts (customer, client, patient, etc.) in social simulation. Finally, under the overwhelming weight of these institutions and with little to counter it, the individual capitulates and dissimulates, denying the importance of personhood.

It is this truncated and unrealistic understanding of human being that is directly challenged by the Gospel. It invites the individual into a relationship that defines being as contingent upon God (Acts 17:28). It does not allow the bracketing of the question of being, since what it means to be fully human depends on understanding its contingent and relational nature. Being an instance of hypostasized human nature and having the divine breath of life breathed into him, the human being is a divine-human person, containing something, the image, of divinity. As such, some of what it means to be human precedes existence, that is, it is given and not definable by human action, and it can only be fully realized by participating in, relating to its source. This is the core around which a stable identity can be built. It is this understanding of human essence that firmly establishes the importance of personhood. It disallows the depersonalizing of the individual by affirming the self. It allows for the intensely personal sacrifice made by Christ in order to overcome human sinfulness and finitude, to reestablish their participation in the divine nature (2 Pet 1:4).

So one obstacle to the Gospel arises out of the role that the self plays in the context of social discourse. Prerequisite to any inter-personal relationship is the ability to affirm the self and the other, that is, to interact with or participate in the existence of another personal being. To do so I have to allow for the being of the other on the same basis, with the same degree of legitimacy, that I accord my own existence.[375] This is essential both for the presentation and the reception of the Gospel's invitation. But, it is extremely difficult for the late modern mind.

On the one hand, it is difficult to affirm something which I myself have lost. As mentioned above, the late modern mind tends to bracket the question of its own being and reference it by means of its own actions. However, the mind of a self-referenced being is not likely to range beyond that which it defines. Unable or unwilling to interrogate its own being, it cannot and does not care to authenticate the existence of others; they too are bracketed. Moreover, because the ontic significance of one's own phenomenology is uncertain, the self-referencing actions of other beings are either discounted as largely unintelligible or appropriated as external affirmations of the self. Either way there is no basis for a relationship, there is no other, since this amounts to little more than interaction with a projection of the self (John 4:9-10).

On the other hand, it is difficult for the late modern mind to acknowledge the nature of the subject of the Gospel's invitation, Christ. It invites us into a relationship which goes way beyond an exchange between beings of like nature. It involves a relationship with a being upon whose will our existence is said to depend. For an individual to participate in the Gospel, self-affirmation would have

---

375   Cf. Emmanuel Levinas' concept of the Face of the Other. *Totality and Infinity*, 187-219.

to take on the added, almost paradoxical quality of self-surrender, an acknowledgement of contingency. To accept the invitation would be to abandon the idea of referencing one's own being and to accept the idea that one's being is established externally, defined by something other than its own actions. But, since a degree of ontological security has been brought by bracketing being, the idea of abandoning it will be quite threatening and will take incredible trust, faith.

Another obstacle grows out of the fragmentation of individual identity. In the absence of a stable ontic core, identities are tied to the activities used to define life. As a result, I am what I do, where I go, and who I am associated with. While this occasionalist approach might appear to satisfy the needs of the self-defining life, it cannot accommodate the Gospel.

On the one hand, the Gospel demands one unified center through which the individual relates to God. To Christ I am not just a consumer, a patient, a client, but a whole person. The sacrifice of Christ is applied to the totality of my person and not to various time-slices of identity. By faith, the work of Christ removes mortality from my entire being and grants forgiveness of all my sins. So the Gospel offers and requires the reestablishment of a totalizing, pan-personal identity core around which all other fragments can be arrayed. Once we are in Christ, he lives in us (Gal. 2:20) and we are filled with the fullness of God (Eph. 3:19).

On the other hand, the Gospel requires an affirmation of the true identity of all other believers. In light of our being ecclesial, we relate to other members of the body on the basis of their identity in Christ and not according to any of the fragments that might otherwise mark our relationships. So other Christians are not to be engaged merely as executives, lawyers, doctors, and the like, but as children of the light (Eph. 5:8); forgiven, grace endowed, co-participants in the life of the living God (Col. 3:13).

There is, then, a fundamental discrepancy between the late modern, dissimulational denial of the self and the affirmation of the full reality of the self implied by the Gospel.

— 2 —
Self-Restraint

Accepting the Gospel also implies a willingness to limit one's own freedom. As I have sought to show, freedom, in particular freedom of choice, is one of the primary characteristics of late modern thought. The desire for freedom is so strong that it often transmutes into a demand for choice. And, as if to convince ourselves that we are free, we pursue an almost unlimited proliferation of choice, as if more choices actually secured more freedom. This, in turn, leads to the chaos of unrestrained expression, the notion that we always have a right to a personal opinion (no matter the topic) and always have the right to express that opinion (no matter the setting). This is, then, carried over into the physical, bodily realm. I have a body and I can do anything I choose to it and with it. The disembodiment that this occasions is thought to be a small price to pay for personal freedom. The right to choose also extends to moral thinking, the value of the self, others, and our actions, in which the individual becomes the primary arbiter of what is right.

This preoccupation with freedom conflicts with the Gospel at several levels. First of all, the Gospel offers a remedy to the human situation that has only one option, complete surrender to Christ. Obviously, that puts an end to the idea of unlimited choice. While there are certainly many who believe that there are multiple ways to Christ, to God, to salvation, it remains an undeniable truth that the Gospel-as-Person provides only one alternative. The relationship being offered cannot be earned, won in a spiritual lottery, or mediated by any other practice or person. It cannot be demanded as a right, and our opinion about this lack of choice is utterly irrelevant. The terms cannot be negotiated. It is an invitation that is either rejected or accepted by an act of total submission to the Person of Christ.

The Gospel-as-Person eliminates the idea of unlimited choice in the believers' life as the Church. As ecclesial beings we are bound to live according to his precepts alone (1 John 2:3), to commune with him through the one Eucharist (1 Cor. 10:16-17), and to build up the one Church (1 Cor. 3:9). But this runs counter to the contemporary notion of freedom that has convinced us that we even have the right to freely choose our church. And, as if striving to secure that freedom, the proliferation of jurisdictions, denominations, and sub-denominations continues unabated. There is something very late modern and anti-Gospel about the idea that we have a right to be in a Church that suits our tastes, and that, if we can't find one, we can start a new one. The same thing applies to various aspects of life within the Church. For example, in the area of worship, our likes and dislikes are not the issue. As the Body of Christ, our actions are limited by that which is pleasing and honoring to Christ. As St. Paul admonished the Colossians, "...let the peace of God rule in your hearts, to which also you are called in one body... Let the word of Christ dwell in you richly in all wisdom; teaching and admonishing one another in psalms and hymns and spiritual songs, singing with grace in your hearts to the Lord." (Col. 3: 15-16). Being a follower of Christ, then, puts an end to the idea that we have rights, especially the right to choose. In Romans 12:1 St. Paul speaks of being a living sacrifice, that is, one who has abandoned all claims and rights. Following Christ is not about the right to choose, but about being in Him.

The Gospel-as-Person limits our freedom of expression. In Christ we are no longer free to formulate personal opinions on every doctrine, every passage of Scripture, every pronouncement of the Church. Instead, we are to be of one mind with Christ. Rather than expressing our own opinions, we should be tapping into the collective consciousness of the Church for the interpretations, explanations, and directions we need. This also applies to the witness of the Church. We are not free to use any technique to communicate and persuade, just because it happens to be effective in the secular world. Anything that is manipulative, designed to gain power over the listener, anything that is depersonalizing must be rejected, since they do violence to the recipient. We are, after all, inviting others to a relationship, not selling a product. So, rather than putting ourselves in the foreground, we should be highlighting the

Fathers and the Saints of the Church, those whom God has "graced" with his presence, learning from what they taught and from the way they presented Christ. The idea that in some instances our opinions are unimportant, our likes and dislikes are irrelevant, is very difficult for the late modern mind to accept. Yet, self-restraint, not unrestrained self-expression is what the Gospel calls us to.

The Gospel-as-Person challenges the notion that we have bodies that are no more than instruments with which we express our freedom. Once we are in Christ we are his Body (1 Cor. 12:27). We are temples, filled by the living God, for that reason holy and not to be defiled (1 Cor. 3:16-17). We, in our totality, body and soul, belong to God and are to submit to Him. Therefore, we do not have the right, the freedom, to do with the body what we please. For whatever purposes the body is used, it is to glorify and honor God. This may even include restraining the body through ascetic activities such as fasting, prayer vigils, and serving others.

Finally, the Gospel and not our whims determines what is good and valuable. Christ himself has given the Church a set of precepts to follow. The Holy Scriptures contain instructions for our lives and throughout the centuries the Church has taught the faithful how to live. These are the precepts to which we are to hold. These are the standards by which to measure the flourishing of ordinary life. While we have many choices, as followers of Christ we are not free to do as we please. To present and accept the Gospel involves a self-restraint that will be, to say the least, difficult for the freedom intoxicated inhabitants of the late modern age.

– 3 –

Self-Abandon

Another complex of difficulties has to do with the relationship between trust and social discourse.[376] In order for the Gospel invitation to be

---

376   I am assuming that evangelism is a form of social discourse.

heard and accepted, the listener will have to abandon all skepticism and trust those who issue the invitation, as well as trust unconditionally the actual subject of the proposed relationship. There appear to be three distinct fields of trust required: witness, Christ, and Church. The kind of trust we are speaking of is a function of identity and belonging—we tend to trust those who can be or have been identified and those to whom we belong. Once again we notice how difficult this has become for the radically self-referencing mind.

One way to look at identity is to view it in terms of a dynamic interplay between a core identity around which chained identities are arrayed. According to this scheme the human subject is, on the one hand, determined by the nature of human being (ontic identity) and, on the other hand, by the manifold roles required by the complexity of life. In the context of Christian teaching this is viewed in terms of human beings having been created in the image of God. That image, human nature, is a central and stable core, which integrates the various identity fragments that arise in the course of being-in-the-world. This should enable us to identify with every other human being, since we share the same core identity—image of God—and therefore the same dignity (worth) and basic trustworthiness.

However, late modern discussion denies the presence of a stable human subject. Having rejected the notion of a totalizing human essence/nature, the whole decentering project would have us believe that the self, and thereby identity, are altered by every act of discourse, by every movement of self-monitoring. In other words, both being and identity are defined with reference to the independent actions of the self, who I am is what I do, giving rise to identity fragments or roles. So, rather than actually identifying the other person, we simply label them according to a given action or role. Notice, for example, that in John 4 Jesus and the woman are initially identified by their respective roles: man, woman; Jew, Samaritan; drawer of water, giver of living water.

Even when those actions involve other human beings that can be identified, one cannot necessarily speak of a relationship of trust, but rather expeditious associations tolerated for the purpose and duration of specific needs. These provide for nothing more than a fleeting fragment of identity. We "trust" the other person (or some depersonalized expert system) only to the extent that some need requires it—which is not to trust a person at all. We see something of this in John 4:15, when the woman asks for living water so that she does not have to draw water herself. But, is this really trust? It seems that we have actually redefined the idea of trust. We "trust" the other person only to the extent that some need requires it, or to the extent that we can preclude a violation of trust, which is not to trust a person at all.

The other dimension of trust is belonging. Unlike individual identity, belonging would seem to be a more inclusive or integrating phenomenon, an entire context of trust. It is a kind of identity that is based, not on some functional fragment, but on the degree to which we belong, are like (or unlike) some larger grouping of individuals. It might be assumed that membership in such a group would facilitate a certain amount of trust. Unfortunately, that is not always the case, in part because of the ways in which membership is achieved and perceived in the late modern context.

As noted above, individuals acquire membership in three basic ways. First, there is belonging by ascription: membership ascribed or attributed without any particular action on the part of the individual, as is the case, for example, with citizenship. Second, there is belonging by achievement: Membership acquired or earned through some form of effort, a purchase, or the fulfillment of requirements, for example, sports teams, hobby groups, and business associations. Third, there is belonging by association: In this case membership is the result of having been related to (kinship) or invited by current members, e.g., country clubs, business clubs, and churches.

What is interesting about each one of these paths to membership is that the limited sense of belonging that results does not engender much more actual trust than do the afore-mentioned modes of individual identity (expeditious associations). If membership is ascribed, we tend to think of belonging in terms of entitlement or rights, that is, it is about what we can get out of it, and we only trust other members to the extent that they provide or facilitate those privileges, something like expeditious association (citizenship). If we somehow achieve membership, the sense of belonging will be dominated by the idea of voluntary choice, in which case we choose to trust others, again, only to the extent that they help us achieve our own goals, similar to one's relationship to an expert system, such as a buyers' cooperative. Finally, if membership is a result of some association, then belonging translates into a sense of privilege or status that allows us to distinguish ourselves from non-members, as is often done by members of denominations that are intentionally aware of the ways in which they differ from other groups. In each case, whatever trust can be spoken of remains limited to the utilitarian, voluntary actions of the self and, at worst, is a hedge against the need to trust at all, a kind of trust substitute.

The point of departure for contemporary social discourse is characterized by a trust-deficit. We tend to trust individuals only to the extent to which they can be identified, which is, in turn, a function of their playing a role in an expeditious association. We trust groups (institutions) and their members only to the degree that they help us identify others or ourselves, that is, define belonging. It is this prevailing trust-deficit that makes both the presentation and the reception of the Gospel-as-Person difficult.

In the case of the witness, we face the problem that we simply do not trust individuals. This is obviously the case if we cannot identify the person we are dealing with. However, even if that identity is established, the discourse is likely to be understood within the context of an expeditious association or in relation to some expert system. But this would presuppose some particular need (and here is the problem) either on the part of the messenger—which would be seen as some kind of ulterior motive[377]—or on the part of the recipient, which might be hard to identify. After all, what would motivate the late modern individual to seek out and put trust in the Christian message, messenger, and or institution?

---

377 Which is why we tend to avoid people distributing flyers, etc.

Accepting the Gospel obviously requires that the recipient trust the Savior. The problem here is that standard criterion of ontological reference, physical presence, is missing. Christ, the subject of the invitation, exists on a different plane, is of a fundamentally different mode of being. How, then, being limited to the phenomenology of being-in-the-world, can the individual know, or even acknowledge the existence of such a radically different being?

As for the Church, evangelism is hindered by the general suspicion of institutions. It goes without saying that we will rarely trust a group or institution to which we do not belong. Yet, even if we are somehow members of a group, the sense of belonging may not necessarily translate into trust. If belonging is a form of entitlement, then we want to know what we get out of it? If belonging relates to some expert system, then we ask what aspect of late modern complexity requires its use? What area of life does the supposed expertise cover? If the institution were being used to establish identity by belonging, then how and why would the average late modern belong to a Christian group? The only way this can be imagined is if the individual is willing to abandon all doubt and trust both Christ and his Church.

— 4 —

Self-Transcendence

Finally, in order for the Gospel-as-Person to be presented and received the individuals involved will at some point have to transcend themselves and experience the presence of the supernatural subject (Christ) of the Gospel message, to apprehend Him with the senses and or the mind. In other words, there has to be some kind of direct encounter with the sacred, experience of the supernatural.[378] Since the word experience is used in so many ways, we do well to define it and perhaps pick another

---

378 Rudolf Otto's idea of *tremendum* in his famous book *The Idea of the Holy* (London: Oxford University Press, 1923).

term.[379] This experience is not necessarily some kind of spectacular, miraculous happening. Nor is it an ecstatic state that we work our way into. It is not an emotional episode, although there might be strong feelings. And it is not necessarily a sensory event, although it may well involve hearing, seeing, or smelling. What I am talking about is an awareness, a perception of God's presence; God making Himself known to us and our apprehension of that movement. Since the object of this encounter is both personal and supernatural, self-transcendence will have to occur on two separate planes, the personal and the metaphysical or mystical.

To begin with, the only way to apprehend another person is to unconditionally acknowledge the full scope of their reality. This would have to include affirming the nature and the identity of the other because bracketing the question of being or disallowing its definition by its essence rather than its action would hinder the apprehension of the object or person's reality. To the extent that we deny or distort this reality we are either unable to experience anything at all or (and this is more likely and more damaging to evangelism) we experience some distortion, some simulacrum of the thing itself. The Gospel, then, requires its presenters and recipients to acknowledge the divine-human nature of Christ, as well as his identity as the Son of God, the risen Messiah. Any deviation from this, such as the suggestion that Christ was only human or that he was merely a good teacher, results in a distortion and prevents apprehension.

Notice how these elements come together in the story of Jesus' encounter with the Samaritan woman. Through the course of their exchange the woman gradually comes to recognize both his nature and his identity. First she sees only the human elements, a man, a Jew, then she transitions to the supernatural, prophet, and finally she gains a full understanding of him as the Messiah, the Christ. It is only after she has transcended herself and apprehended his nature and identity

---

379　It is difficult to find an appropriate word for this. One possibility is "contuition" a term used by contemplatives to express the perception of the sacred within the context of every day life. Cf. Ronald Rolheiser. *The Shattered Lantern* (New York: Crossroad Publishing, 2001), 26, note 9.

that she fully enters into a relationship with him and proclaims that fact among her fellow villagers (John 4: 19, 29).

Unfortunately, all of this has become even more difficult because the late modern lie of bad faith robs the individual of a real context for such an experience. If we lie about the importance of the self and then lie about lying, we are twice removed from personal reality— be that the self, the other, or the Ultimate Other—and are therefore deprived of the conditions and the context for an experience of that reality. Yet, contemporary interest in things spiritual would seem to offer an opening. At the very least, there are people who do not deny the transcendent aspects of life and seek some kind of integration between themselves and the sacred that they perceive.

In addition to the personal plane, the self will have to ascend to a metaphysical plane. This will require some effort. Like the Psalmist, we will have to actively look for God in order to see his power and his glory." (Ps 63:2) "Without God and me being aware of each other in a way, that on my side, is properly called perception, there could be no intimate relationship of love, devotion, and dialogue..."[380] We will have to do our part and create the conditions of the heart that enable us to become aware of God's presence. This work includes quiet (enough peaceful moments so that we can actually hear the voice of God over the roar of everyday life), repentance (continual turning to God), keeping the commandments, and above all, vigilance in prayer, for it is in prayer that we experience the hidden energy of God's holiness and inner union with it. So as St. Symeon the New enthusiastically reminds us

> ...he who is continent in every respect and has trained his soul
> not to wander in disorderly manner, nor to follow its own will in
> any of the ways which are displeasing to God, but instead ardently
> compels it.... To keep all of God's ordinances, this man will shortly
> find Him Who is hidden within His divine commandments...[he]

---

380   William Alston. *Perceiving God*, 12

enters the bridal chamber,... sees the Bridegroom,...is filled by the mystical cup,...by the Lamb without spot.[381]

These, then, are some of the obstacles strewn across evangelism's field of play. There is a fundamental conflict between the nature of the Gospel and certain elements of the late modern mind. Some of these are unique to our age, especially those centered on individual freedom. Others have always been with us, such as the need to transcend the self and apprehend the sacred. All of them are difficult, but none of them are insurmountable. Any presentation of the Gospel-as-Person that avoids capitulations of convenience will face the impediments that grow out of dissimulation and simulation. Only a Gospel that yields a relationship implemented in all of its radicality will have a chance of effectively issuing the invitation to the late modern mind.

---

381   St. Symeon. *On the Mystical Life* 6th Ethical Discourse, 68.

Chapter 8

A Horizon of Hope

In what I have presented above, I have sought to isolate four areas of difficulty, four aspects of the late modern mind that make it difficult (sometimes nearly impossible) to present and receive the Gospel-as-Person, Christ himself. I have spoken of a process of dissimulation, the loss of self, that has led to widespread existential anxiety and an inability to affirm the self. I have described the exaggerated demand for freedom and the resultant resistance to self-restraint. I have also suggested that social discourse engaged in by those who have lost the self can be no more than a simulation, something in which we are not likely to place any real trust. Finally, I have pondered the dilemma of bad faith, which robs us of the conditions and the context needed for an experience of the real nature of both human and divine being.

What, then, is to be done? Are there any practical ways in which we might address, perhaps even overcome these impediments to evangelism? As I think this book has shown, we cannot hope for any kind of "how-to" instructions, no new and improved techniques or methodologies. However, we can map a way forward by bringing together the practical and theological observations explored thus far. It might be best to start with the general idea that evangelism is a form of social discourse. In order for it to be effective (leading people to accept the invitation), it must under no circumstances be a simulation. That, however, can only be achieved if, on the one hand, the individuals involved are truly personalized and, on the other hand, if self and society can be reintegrated with that which is real. Given the nature of the Gospel-as-Person and the challenges of the late modern era, I think we will have to consider ways in which we might re-personalize the evangelistic context, rediscover real freedom, re-authenticate the witness and the Church, and reintegrate the experience of sacred reality. Along the way I will reference the encounter between St. Peter and Cornelius described in Acts 10.

— I —

Re-personalize the Evangelistic Context

As mentioned in the previous chapter, the presentation and acceptance of the Gospel requires an unqualified affirmation of the full reality of both human and divine personhood. That being the case, the depersonalization of late modern life has created formidable obstacles to evangelism. The only way of overcoming those obstacles is what I would like to call the re-personalization of the entire communicative context, including the messenger, the recipient, the message, and the mode of presentation.

I believe that a large part of our evangelistic difficulty grows out of the late modernization of the Christian community. I fear that we have become active (or should I say anxious) participants in the hyper real simulation by condoning the lie of selflessness, by adopting the intellectual underpinnings of dissimulation, by withholding counter-dissimulational truth, and by simply ceding large tracts of the socioscape. As such, we actually forfeit our position and simply cannot stand over-against, cannot face the ever changing late modern world, cannot offer any real alternative. Note the way in which St. Peter's narrow, ethno-religious frame of reference prevents active witness (Acts 10:13-15).

The way forward is, on the one hand, to replace this self-referencing approach to being with the stability of human being viewed as contingent communion and, on the other hand, to replace the self-monitoring horizon with an identity centered on a divinely given ontic core. The advantages of this are that a) it leads to precisely the kind of ontological security that marks an alternative to what we find in the late modern mind, b) it is the basis for the confidence we should have in presenting the Gospel, and c) it facilitates self-affirmation that will allow us to see the face of the other—avoid treating them as objects. In St. Peter's case this re-personalization is achieved by means of a God-given vision (Acts 10:9-16).

As a first step toward re-personalizing our witness we will have to collectively un-bracket the issue of our own being-as such. Christians are going to have to have serious discussions about the fact that our being is dependent on God's will and that that (not our activities) pre-defines our identity. We need to rediscover what it means to live in Christ, to participate in the divine nature (2 Pet 1:4), to be filled with and animated by the Spirit. But, more than that, we will have to learn to take full advantage of the ontological security provided in a restorative relationship with Christ, be/become whole and complete persons, made new and alive in Christ. Notice St. Peter's affirmation of the person of Cornelius. (Acts 10:26 "stand up; I myself am also a man," 10:28 "it is not lawful… but God has shown me").

The questions of contingent being and ecclesial identity will have to have been settled before any kind of witness takes place. This stage of evangelism must not be neglected or underestimated, for it is only in the context of communion with Christ that we will overcome our own existential anxiety and will be able to offer the world a living alternative. Unless the faithful rediscover the self, in communion with and contingent upon God, defined by a God-given nature, our invitation remains hypothetical at best and hypocritical at worst. Unless we rediscover the security of an integrated identity anchored in a God-given image, there will be no evidence of the transforming nature of a relationship with Christ and our invitation devolves into mere simulation. The first step in evangelism, then, is for the members of the witnessing community to become fully and visibly human in Christ. Until Christ transforms us there can be no evangelism.

Another benefit of being-in-communion is that we learn to rely on the validating, verifying power of the Holy Spirit. Throughout the history of the Church successful mediation of the Gospel has always been based upon and driven by a spiritual base of power. This power was variously centered in: monasteries, the residents of which devoted themselves to ascetic labor of prayer for the salvation of those around them; Mother Churches that developed a vision for evangelization and the willingness to share of their own resources in order to fulfill that vision; family units, who willingly turned their backs on the world, devoting themselves to the spiritual work of missions; and individuals, lay people, clergy, and monastics who through prayer and holy living attracted those around them to faith in Christ. In every case there seems to have been recognition of the fact that "the most effective means of proclaiming the gospel came through living Christ-centered lives,"[382] for it is in such lives that the *testimonium Spiritus Sancti* is most evident—a presence of God's Spirit.

Speaking of the 14th century revival of (hesychast) spirituality in Russian monasteries one author likened their spiritual power not to some sophisticated strategy, but to "...a magnetic field ...spiritual energy [which] attracted loose elements and filled the surrounding area with invisible powers"[383] and triggered "one of the most remarkable missionary movements in Christian history."[384]

There is no reason why our local churches cannot become centers of spiritual power. But for that to happen, our members will have to become what Morris Berman calls "New Monastic Individuals."[385] Speaking of the decline of American culture Berman asks if there is anything we can do to arrest the onset of what he calls the corporate

---

382   Luke Veronis. *Missionaries, Monks, and Martyrs.* (Minneapolis: Light and Life, 1994), 34.

383   James H. Billington. *The Icon and the Axe: An Interpretive History of Russian Culture* (NY: Vintage Books, 1966), 52-53.

384   Ibid., 52. Every time a monastery was moved it attracted a new flock of inquirers who settled around the monastery, prompting yet another move.

385   Morris Berman. *The Twilight of American Culture.* (New York: W. W. Norton, 2000), 135.

Mass Mind culture.[386] Reflecting on the way in which monasteries have preserved culture and civilization in the past,[387] he suggests that we consider a modern version of the monastic option. He is not suggesting that we form new monasteries, but that we raise up a new kind of people—new monastic individuals—who are willing to live against the grain, reject the corporate consumer culture and work to preserve the historical treasures of our civilization.

Applied to the evangelistic task, we might say that we need a new kind of Christian, willing to withdraw from the lies of the late modern context and quietly[388] exemplify the new life in Christ. These would be people who realize that we cannot simply organize, market, manage, or resource evangelism into being. These are individuals who, having overcome existential anxiety, who, having recovered their being and identity in communion with Christ, reflect that being like the "living books" of Ray Bradbury's *Fahrenheit 451*. The new monastic individuals will devote themselves to living the faith and confidently rely on the Spirit to draw and attract[389] others, to establish the evangelistic contact with those already prepared by God himself. Consider St. Peter's confidence, "I came without objection." (Acts 10:29) and "the Spirit told me to go with them, doubting nothing" (Acts 11:12).

True dependence on God not only re-establishes true human being, it also frees us from the narcissistic preoccupation with the self. No longer in need of self-definition, the re-personalized self is able to put the needs and desires of the other above his or her own (Phil 2:4)

---

386   For Berman this market driven Mass Mind culture involves things like the corruption of modern politics, the "Rambofication" of entertainment, and the collapse of the educational system.

387   Berman. *Twilight*, 69-70, 87-90.

388   Berman states that "those genuinely committed to the monastic option need to stay out of the public eye; to do their work quietly, and deliberately avoid media attention." Ibid., 131.

389   Although, I think it might be best to abandon as manipulative anything that might imply using the power and/or control a speaker might exert over the listener, I am still convinced that the idea of presenting a credible and attractive communicator has merit. However, given the ways in which late modern culture has undermined the very notion of credibility, and given the proliferation of vendors competing for attention, I have wondered, of late, what chance we have of appearing either credible or attractive. There is simply no way for the Church to compete with CNN, the NFL, and the like. What could possibly draw people to the Gospel and render it believable except the Holy Spirit?

and live in anticipation of whatever occasions for witness God chooses to give—with a heightened sensitivity, ability to recognize those opportunities (Acts 10). Being genuinely concerned for the other would transform our witness. Rejection, imposition, and sacrifice would become non-issues. Having gotten over ourselves, we would be able to enter into the lives of those to whom we hope to issue the invitation of Christ (Acts 10:23). Having fully embraced the person of Christ, we would no longer feel the need to define the witnessing situation ourselves. We would, as already noted, confidently wait for and readily act upon those opportunities provided by the Holy Spirit. It would be the Spirit and not our strategies, materials, selves that defines the context of invitation.

Reliance on the Holy Spirit would also transform our view of the recipient of the Gospel message. Having fully accepted our own personhood in Christ, we would be inclined to extend that evaluation to those we hoped to introduce to Christ. They would cease to be objects of our activity, but would be viewed as other in the sense of Levinas—another personal entity worthy of our attention. In the language of this book, we would not engage them in the context of expeditious associations, but on the basis of interpersonal engagement.

In order for this to happen the identity of the witness will have to be tied obviously and observably to Christ and not some aspect of the evangelistic process. To the extent that we give the impression that who we are is a function of what we are *doing*—handing out a tract or invitation, conducting an interview—the encounter is cast in the light of utilitarian expedience and forfeits trust. Evangelism cannot be seen in terms of a) an announcement divorced from life, b) a conversion as opposed to invitation, c) an assignment as opposed to an expression of life. Consider the difference between St. Paul's activity before and after his conversion (Gal. 1:11-24).

Modern game theory might be very instructive here. First, we learn that a game is an activity in which one does not have to participate. Any form of coercion effectively undermines trust and eliminates the game. Second, we learn that a game is an activity, which can be either finite or infinite. In a finite game the idea is to end the game as quickly as possible, but in any case, with a winner(s). In an infinite game the idea is to maintain, indefinitely, a state of play—no winners or losers, just players. So we might do well to think of evangelism as an infinite game a) in which we participate by virtue of our new life in Christ and not some set of rules or obligations—we have to live to do it, and b) which has no end, no specific objective other than its own continuation. As such, it may not be necessary to distinguish evangelism as an activity distinct from living in Christ.[390]

Along this line, there is some merit in ideas such as friendship and life-style evangelism. However, the problem is that even these seemingly non-coercive approaches tend to be practiced as programs and/or strategies. As a result, our identities are tied to what we do and trust will be limited to the narrow range of that activity. What I am proposing is an identity that is tied to what I am. I don't want to be identified as doing a specific thing, but rather as being-something-as-such—not doing friendly things, but being a friend, not doing Christian things, but being in Christ.

In any case, the recipient of our invitation to Christ is not an object, but a person, not some one we wish to score, but rather someone as in need of God's love as we are. It is of particular importance that we emphasize that we share a common image of God with those we seek to invite. If we can learn to see them as fellow travelers and not as the condemned, the sinners, the evil ones, we may be able to approach them with the love of Christ and his forgiving revitalization.

In light of the fact that the presentation of the Gospel-as-Person involves an invitation, as opposed to the simple transmission of information, our message will have to be crafted as a personal profile rather than a typical sales pitch. We are not selling or marketing some product or service. If that were the case, we would spend a great deal

---

390   I am not suggesting that we do not have a specifically evangelistic responsibility. But, I am saying that to the extent that we divorce evangelism from being in Christ by setting it up as a specific and definable activity, we run the risk of reducing it to a program, thus coercive and trust inhibiting. Perhaps we will need to apply Heidegger's methodology and ask what ontic significance our evangelistic activities have—what do they say about what we are?

of our time relaying specifications, expectations, and capabilities. And we are not promoting a particular world view or system of belief. If that were the case, we would have to expend our energy defending (apologetics) or presenting (marketing) our teaching in contrast to others.

But what we are trying to do is introduce a person. Consider the ways in which we do that today. As just one example, one of the candidates in this year's presidential election has a web site. One of the sections of the site has to do with the person of the candidate, entitled "meet the candidate." Under that link we find information on his family, birth, upbringing, education, professional career and no facts and figures on his physical status, financial dealings, and holdings. We seem to have a clear idea of how to introduce a person as opposed to simply identifying her. So, in the case of Christ, we don't want to simply identify him. In that case we would just provide a driver's license and social security number. No, what we really want to do is engage his person, meaning that we will have to relate aspects of his own story, his narrative. In order to introduce Christ we are going to have to know his life like the back of our hands. Gospel literacy[391] will be the key. We are not identifying him, but telling his story. We will have to show what kind of person he was, how he treated others, what personal qualities he had. It will include his own stories and parables. The things he thought important. So it will not be "God loves you and has a great plan for you," but rather, let me introduce you to someone who has genuinely loved others. This is a person who took the children under his wing, who healed the paralytics and the demon possessed, who let the suffering woman touch him for healing, who selflessly gave himself for us. Our message is a person, not just information.

All of this indicates that our mode of presentation is going to have to be a form of engagement or encounter rather than a simple presentation of information. It also means that our methods of communication will have to avoid the depersonalizing effects of many late modern

---

391 What I mean by this is familiarity with the Gospel accounts of Jesus' life and teaching as opposed to a few memorized fragments from the Epistles.

modes of communication. As useful as email might be, it is not an adequate medium for communicating the Person of Christ. As helpful as Power Point presentations might be, they simply cannot capture the personal reality of the Christ we seek to introduce. As efficient as automated dialing programs might be, they are too impersonal to relate the person of Christ. As impressive as mass gatherings might be, they do not contain the simply personal one-on-one encounter required by the Gospel. Similarly, mass mailings remove the person of Christ from the transaction. The only medium that will be effective is the face to face meeting. There is simply no substitute for a person to person encounter, a believer introducing a non-believer to the person of Christ. I can imagine several effective discussion topics. We could ask who Christ is and relay the story of Christ stilling the storm and the disciples asking that very question "What manner of man is this, that even the winds and the sea obey him?" (Mt. 8:27). The same question could be asked of the encounter between Jesus and the paralytic: Who is this man who claims to forgive sins? (Mk. 2:1-12). Likewise, the story of Jesus meeting with Zacchaeus: Who is this man who loves even the outcasts of society? (Lk. 19:2-10)

— 2 —
Re-discover Real Freedom

The late modern demand for freedom, unlimited choice, and unrestrained expression, has created significant obstacles for evangelism. The Gospel seems to severely restrict that freedom. This, of course, is not meant to imply that human beings have no freedom. All created beings have a kind of natural freedom, an ability for spontaneous movement. Human beings also have a personal freedom which enables creativity and self-determination. However, this freedom is a paradox.[392] Unlike divine freedom which is absolute,[393] human beings are caught in the interplay

---

392 "Creaturely freedom is necessarily a play of light and shadow: The rays of freedom must be reflected from a wall which is its boundary..." Bulgakov. *The Bride of the Lamb*, 127.

393 In fact, it might be better to say that God was beyond freedom.

between freedom and its limits, that is, the givens of human existence. When these boundaries are respected, human freedom, although limited, functions at its best, is real freedom. The fall into sin involves a rejection of those limits and disrupts the way in which freedom works. In this case, freedom, although relative, is seen as an unlimited badge of existence. It is demanded as a right almost as if we could validate our being in terms of the perceived level of freedom. In addition, the late modern Self refuses to interrogate its own being and, as a result, remains unaware of, or sinfully rejects those givens. Detached from that which defines its being, freedom turns chaotic, unwieldy and demanding. The passions take over and dominate life. Freedom is turned on itself and Scripture even speaks of us being the "slaves of sin" (Rom. 6:17, John 8:34). But we also learn that real freedom can be restored within the confines of a relationship with God. It is in the recognition of the limits of our contingency that we experience real freedom. It is in the context of truth that we can be set free (John 8:32). It is the Son of God who makes us truly free (John 8:36).

The potential of real freedom in Christ is the best way to overcome this set of obstacles. On the one hand, it enables the faithful to exemplify that which the Gospel-as-Person offers. On the other hand, it answers one of the most deeply felt needs of the late modern self. Once again the whole communicative context is affected.

Beginning with the messenger, let me observe that the strongest witness to the truth of the Gospel is the transformation that takes place in the life of a Christian. Life in Christ is the ultimate in observable freedom. The believer is released from the tyranny of having to demand freedom as a right, since freedom is provided for and safeguarded by the context of her relationship with Christ. Loved, forgiven, made new, there is no need to demand anything. In fact, the whole notion of individual rights melts away in the warmth of mutual affirmation. The believer is also liberated from the chaos of unlimited choice. Freedom and its limits are brought back into harmony. In Christ there is only one choice, Him, and everything else follows suit. We choose to keep his commandments because we love Him. That certainly does limit our options on many issues, but knowing that these are offered by God for our own well being gives us the freedom to follow. Moreover, the faithful are relieved of the burden of unrestrained expression. Embedded in the Scriptures, the teaching and tradition of the Church, they no longer have to pontificate on every subject, but can join in with that great cloud of witnesses to the truth handed down throughout the ages.

Another way in which a Christian can demonstrate real freedom is in his dealing with the body. We know that the effects of sin are particularly pronounced in this area. For that reason, freedom from the passions is a powerful witness to the transformed life. This raises the possibility of an ascetic aspect of evangelism. The believer, who acquires freedom from lust through chastity, from gluttony by means of fasting, not only prepares herself for witness, but also establishes an example of the freedom offered by the Gospel. We know that those who overcome the passions create in the heart a context for pure prayer. "When the soul has become purified through the keeping of all the commandments, it makes the intellect steadfast and able to receive the state needed for prayer."[394]It is that victory over sin combined with the intimate relationship with the Lord through prayer that enables the Christian for witness. The same thing could be said for other ascetic labors such as times of solitude, of intense prayer, and almsgiving.

Now I realize that what I have just described is the ideal case and that many Christians do not live this way. That is a big part of the problem we face. Christians are so much like those around them that they offer no alternative. Sometimes God intervenes and reintroduces us to the freedom we have in Him. Think of St. Peter's vision. Repeatedly God reaffirms the freedom that Peter has in Christ and, secure in that freedom, he crosses the ethno-religious divide and reaches out to Cornelius (Acts 10: 10-17). Wherever and whenever the faithful allow themselves to be wholly transformed by Christ and observably live in the real freedom He offers, our freedom-demanding contemporaries will recognize an answer to one of their deepest longings.

---

394   Ibid., #2 57.

Now, if part of the evangelistic goal is to introduce others to real freedom in Christ, then that freedom is going to have to characterize not only the life of the witness, but also the encounter with the recipient. What can it mean to approach someone in real freedom? First of all, it means that I will make an effort to move beyond identification and get to know that person; to get involved in their life, to hear their story, to listen to their dreams. This will take more time than we are used to spending on evangelistic contacts and it means that the average Christian will only be able to maintain a few such relationships at a time. Nevertheless, real freedom takes shape within the context of interpersonal relationships. Being known by someone who is truly free will resonate with the non-believer's own longings. It is there that she may get her first inkling of the nature of real freedom and the one who can set her free.

Of course, this knowing of the other should not lead to the kind of co-opting of alterity that Levinas was so afraid of. To know someone is not to own or possess them. It does not mean imposing opinions, setting schedules, requiring attendance. In spite of sin, all human beings have some level of freedom and self-determination. They don't have to listen. They can reject the message. To know someone, then, is to accept that and affirm them in that relative freedom, for, as limited as it might be, that freedom may eventually give birth to a willingness to follow Christ into real freedom.

This also means that the listener must, under no circumstances, be reduced to an object of our evangelistic efforts. If that occurs, freedom dissipates and the other disappears in sameness. I once heard of students who were taking a class on evangelism being required to "witness" to a certain number of people during the course of the semester. They were even graded on their encounters. This, it seems to me, effectively reduced those listeners to components of a course, that is, objects of selfish academic concern. Rather than being approached in freedom, they were limited by, defined by the requirements of a syllabus. I want to believe that there are Christians who even under those circumstances could truly love and engage the non-believer. However, I fear that, given the way we are, the secondary, in this case academic motivations would effectively dispel the real freedom that should characterize Christian witness. We face the same danger with every programmatic evangelistic effort. As soon as our programs become the primary focus, the listener becomes an object.

Finally, approaching the other in freedom means refusing to manipulate. Unfortunately, we have been deeply affected by the market mentality of North America. The basic idea seems to be that we can sell anything we choose to sell, or persuade anyone of anything. One communications expert boldly proclaimed that if given enough time he could convince any Christian to deny Christ and any pagan to accept him.[395] This confidence is based on the idea that if we learn enough about our listeners we can use that knowledge to persuade them of just about anything. Indeed there are myriad text books and articles[396] that offer guidance on the subject. Sadly, many evangelistic efforts are tainted with this manipulative spirit. Some suggest that certain personality types are more open to persuasion than others and that we can even gain a certain power over such individuals. Some offer tips on how to enhance one's credibility with the listener. Others show how the presentation of the Gospel can be cast as an argument with specific components aimed at certain individuals and opinions.[397] The problem with all these techniques is that they do violence to the recipient by interfering with their freedom to choose. If we are going to introduce real freedom, we cannot go about it by further restricting the limited freedom the listener already has.

---

395 "The time has come when, if your give me any normal human being and a couple of weeks... I can change his behavior from what it is now to whatever you want it to be, if it's physically possible. I can't make him fly by flapping his arms, but I can turn him from a Christian into a communist and visa versa." James McConnel quoted in Marvin Karlins and Herbert Abelson, *Persuasion: How Opinions and Attitudes are Changed*, (New York: Springer Pub., 1970), 1.

396 For example, Emory A. Griffin. *The Mind Changers: The Art of Christian Persuasion* (Wheaton: Tyndale House, 1976), 28.

397 Years ago I was very much caught up in the idea that one could craft a persuasive presentation in such a way as to more or less guarantee a positive response. Cf. *Namenschristentum*, 114-138.

— 3 —
Re-authenticate the Witness

The third set of obstacles created by the late modern environment has to do with the question of trust. The Gospel requires that the recipient trust both the witness and Christ, as well as the Church. But in a context of dissimulation and simulation trust is extremely hard to come by. Sure we trust some individuals to the extent that we are dependent on them for help. And yes, we trust institutions, again, to the extent that they provide some service or information we need. But in general we tend to trust only ourselves, at least when it comes to unqualified trust or self-abandon. For this reason, we will have to re-authenticate all three components of Christian witness, that is, we will have to establish or confirm that the claims we are making about life in Christ are true. But, how is that to be done?

In today's technological environment, authentication is generally a procedure used to verify an individual's identity. This identification is made on the basis of what are called authentication factors of which there are three types: Something the individual has, such as an identity card; something the individual knows, such as a pass word; and something the individual is, such as a fingerprint. We have gotten very used to (satisfied with) these types of procedures since we use them every time we logon to a computer, do our banking, or gain access to secured areas of buildings. Once you have established that you are who you claim to be, you are afforded a certain level of "trust," although I'm not sure you can speak of trust between a user and a computer.

In any case, it should be obvious that the authentication needed for Christian witness goes way beyond the simple verification of identity. It is not only a question of being who I say I am, but being what I say I am in Christ. What we are talking about is establishing a web of interpersonal trust that binds two (or more) people together, a context of intimacy in which one person believes in the integrity, goodness, and competence of another person. Accordingly, a non-believer will come to trust the believer's ability to adequately relate and discuss the details of his faith (competence). She will come to trust the believer's intentions, that is, recognize the absence of coercion, the use of power, or any kind of ulterior motive (goodness). And this relationship of trust will play itself out on the entire breadth of each participant's person (integrity). If this trusting state of mind is achieved, trusting behavior will follow; spending time together, sharing resources, freely exchanging ideas. It is in this kind of context that the invitation to follow Christ develops traction, makes sense. But, as mentioned above, this web of trust can only be established over the course of time, with a few people, and only if we have freed ourselves from the narrow confines of programmatic efforts, depersonalizing technologies, and engage others in the wholeness of their persons. What is required here is true human intimacy.[398] It cannot be achieved by identifying ourselves to some list server. It will not happen even if we are authenticated by someone's blog. Email just won't do. Not even Facebook.[399] User-machine-user "trust" is no trust at all and is a completely inadequate context for the Gospel-as-Person.

---

398 There is, of course, some talk of online intimacy. Often it is associated with virtual sex or with possess
ing intimate knowledge of another in the absence of that person. But this amounts to a redefinition
of the concept of intimacy. One interesting example comes from the world of Twitter. In a piece
entitled "17 Ways you can use Twitter" Leisa Reichelt concept of "ambient intimacy" is referenced.
"... it is about being able to keep in touch with people with a level of regularity and intimacy that you
wouldn't usually have access to, because time and space conspire to make it impossible... It makes
us feel closer to people we care for but in whose lives we're not able to participate as closely as we'd
like. Knowing details creates intimacy." But is having knowledge, even intimate detailed knowledge,
of a person in who's life we do not otherwise participate the same thing as personal, face-to-face
intimacy? http://www.doshdosh.com/ways-you-can-use-twitter/

399 While recognizing the desire for friendship the Pope has warned against the unreality of so-called
social networking. " The concept of *friendship* has enjoyed a renewed prominence in the vocabulary
of the new digital social networks that have emerged in the last few years. The concept is one of
the noblest achievements of human culture. It is in and through our friendships that we grow and
develop as humans. For this reason, true friendship has always been seen as one of the greatest
goods any human person can experience. We should be careful, therefore, never to trivialize the
concept or the experience of friendship. It would be sad if our desire to sustain and develop *on-line*
friendships were to be at the cost of our availability to engage with our families, our neighbors and
those we meet in the daily reality of our places of work, education and recreation. If the desire for
virtual connectedness becomes obsessive, it may in fact function to isolate individuals from real
social interaction while also disrupting the patterns of rest, silence and reflection that are necessary
for healthy human development." http://www.vatican.va/holy_father/benedict_xvi/messages/com-
munications/documents/hf_ben-xvi_mes_20090124_43rd-world-communications-day_en.html
(accessed March 17, 2009).

That requires the unmediated face-to-face encounter with the other, at a restaurant over coffee, during a hike. I remember a bumper sticker on the back of a big truck. It said, "if you can't see my mirror, I can't see you." Well, if I can't see the face of the other, he will not see the face of my Savior in me.

So far I have focused mainly on individual encounters and very small groups. What then of the Church? How, given today's generally negative view of institutions, can we re-authenticate the Body of Christ as an environment of trust and belonging? Interestingly, in addition to the above mentioned authentication factors, some researchers mention the need for a social network as a means of identity verification. In this case, one's identity is validated (determined) by the members of a group to which he or she belongs. Being ecclesially, the Christian is secure in her identity as part of the body of Christ, unified with other believers through the Eucharist. This stability helps the witnesses in their encounter with the world, to which they only partially belong, by providing an established center. But what of the non-believer, the spiritual pilgrim?

Fortunately, a re-personalized witnessing community is capable of several layers of trust engendering authentication. At the social level, if the seeker is brought to the Church by the personal invitation of someone they know and trust and then sees that that person belongs to a network of people he or she trusts, an authentication of the trustworthiness of the context is established and the seeker begins to trust the Church itself. At a liturgical level, if that person can verify that the Church is what it claims to be, the willingness to trust grows. If worship, for example, turns out to be a God centered living offering of those gathered, rather than the execution of some kind of program (as might take place in an empty ritualistic context) or the entertainment of the assembled, the trust continues to grow. At a didactic level, if the message of the Church is consistent with the invitation to Christ, that verification leads to a deepening of trust. However, if the teaching of the Church is nothing more than a Christianized restatement of late modern self-help, feel-good philosophy, then suspicion and waning trust is inevitable.

That is not to say that a message devoid of the radical content of the Gospel cannot command a following, it just means that it is not and will not be authenticated as the trustworthy teaching of Christ. We should not underestimate the seeker's ability to distinguish between the Gospel-as-Person in all its radicality and the diluted substitutes that are sometimes offered in His name (Gal. 1:6-8).

All too often the Church (witnessing community) presents itself as an expert system designed to help the hapless pagan deal with the complexities of the Christian faith. When that happens, the spiritual traveler is, on the one hand, kept at a distance, not included in the evangelistic process, just has answers imposed, and is, on the other hand, depersonalized, as if his or her previous knowledge, questions, needs are all irrelevant in the face of the answers and knowledge the system provides.[400] While the late modern mind may have become accustomed to using (being used by) expert systems, the very nature of the Gospel-as-Person renders the concept inappropriate. The Gospel is not a complex body of information[401] but an invitation to a personal relationship. So what is needed is not some network of expertise but a context of belonging and trust. Notice St. Peter's approach to Cornelius, an open exchange, give and take, an inclusion in the process, not the simple imposition of information (Acts 10:27, 29, 47).

This raises the much discussed question of whether 'becoming' comes before 'belonging'—as in becoming a Christian before one can belong to a Christian community. In the strictest sense, one cannot be a member of Christ's body without having first become one through faith. However, we might speak in terms of layers of belonging. Some Churches have an interesting institution—the catechumenate—which invites and inaugurates seekers into the Christian community while recognizing that they have not yet fully entered the Church. Pilgrims will have to be allowed increasing levels of access to the community—not

---

400   I sometimes think that we treat the Church like an airplane—the experts maintain, fly, navigate, and serve. The passenger just cooperates and has done to her.

401   Obviously, information is involved. But, as previously stated, the information references a person.

by ascription, achievement or mere association,[402] but by an invitation to participate in the life of Christ (2 Pet. 1:3-4) They will have to be made to feel like they belong even before they have fully embraced the invitation (1 Cor. 14:24-25 "God is truly among you.") otherwise they will not trust those who issue the invitation.

− 4 −
Re-integrate the Experience of the Real

Obviously, inviting someone to enter a relationship with another person presupposes an awareness of that other. The experience of that awareness is usually mediated through physical proximity and a social context. Talking about experience is, of course, a very tricky business since it can and often is nothing more than an expression of the individual's own desires and position. For example, the listener might "experience" God as a charismatic preacher or as some aspect of the ecclesial context, such as the music. But these are false perceptions and can only derail the witnessing process, prevent the listener from encountering Christ himself. How, then, is it even possible for a human being to experience the person of the risen Lord?

One way of dealing with this is to think in terms of a personal encounter and its interpretations. Denis Edwards asks "What do we mean when we say that we have some experience of this person? Usually we mean (1) that we have had one or more encounters with the person, and (2) that we have formed some kind of interpretation or understanding of this person as a result of these encounters."[403]

Another possibility is to use the term perception, as in sense perception. After exploring a series of case studies, Alston concludes that there is

---

402 See above, my discussion on paths to membership.

403 Denis Edwards. *Human Experience of God* (New York: Paulist Press, 1993), 6.

...substantial support for the claim that mystical experience can be construed as perception in the same generic sense of the term as sense perception. If mystical experience is a mode of experience that is perceptual, so far as its phenomenological character is concerned, and if it is in principle possible that the other requirements should be satisfied for mystical experience to be the experiential side of a genuine perception of God, then the question of whether mystical experience does count as genuine perception of God is just a question of whether it is what it seems to its subject to be. And this question arises for mystical perception in just the same way as for sense perception... [404]

In addition, we can distinguish between indirect and direct perception of divinity. An indirect experience is mediated through some other aspect of creation. For example, the Psalmist speaks of the heavens declaring the glory of God (Psalm 19). In that case, something of God is known by engaging the created order. Another indirect channel is human being itself. Created in the image of God, each one of us displays something of the beauty and character of God which can be seen by others.

This divine-human characteristic of human existence also provides the foundation for the direct perception of divinity. There is something in human beings that corresponds to divinity, a link, a compatibility that allows for the human-divine/divine encounter. More specifically, the early Church Fathers spoke of the human *nous* as the instrument by which we perceive the divine. This was based on a tripartite description that divides human being into *soma* (body), *psyche* (soul), and *nous* (mind, intellect). Accordingly, Clement of Alexandria divides the soul into three parts; the intellectual (*noeron*), the irascible (*thymikon*), and the appetitive (*epiyhumetikon*)[405] In this case, the soul represents

---

404 William Alston. *Perceiving God. The Epistemology of Religious Experience* (Ithica: Cornell University Press, 1991), 66.

405 Clement of Alexandria. *Stromata* V.80.9 cited by Tomas Spidlik. *The Spirituality of the Christian East* (Kalamazoo: Cistercian Publications, 1986), 92.

the spiritual aspect of human beings, and the *nous/noeron* the point of contact between the divine and the human. Evagrius also spoke of prayer as the ascent of the mind (*nous*) to God.[406]

This raises a question related to the absolute transcendence of God. How can we maintain the absolute sovereignty and transcendence of God and at the same time speak of his active presence in the world? How can we insist on the immaterial nature of God and yet speak of his presence and activity in the material world? How are we to know Him whose essence is inaccessible?

When addressing these issues, the Fathers developed the concept of the energies of God. St. John Damascene, for example, begins with the fact that God, who is without form, immaterial and uncircumscribed, has no spatial dimension, "For He is His own place, filling all things and being above all things, and Himself maintaining all things."[407] Yet, we can speak of God being or acting in this or that place, if by that we mean those places where God's energy becomes manifest. "For He penetrates everything without mixing with it, and imparts to all His energy…"[408]

What are these energies? According to St. Gregory Palamas they are "nothing other than the deifying powers which proceed from God and come down to us, creating substance, giving life, and granting wisdom."[409] Thus does God descend and make Himself known to us while remaining absolutely transcendent. Although "God is entirely present in each of the divine energies, … He transcends them all."[410]

---

406 Evagrius *On Prayer: One Hundred and Fifty-Three Texts.* In *The Philokalia* Vol. I. (London: Faber and Faber, 1983), 55-71. According to Evagrius "Prayer is communion of the intellect with God." (#3 57) or "… the ascent of the intellect to God."(#36 60) It is the intellect reaching "…out to its Lord without deflection and communing with Him without intermediary?" (#3 57) As he envisioned it, it could only take place when the intellect had achieved a certain state: When the soul has become purified through the keeping of all the commandments, it makes the intellect steadfast and able to receive the state needed for prayer.(#2 57)

407 St. John Damascene's "Exposition of the Orthodox Faith." I, 13. *Nicene and Post-Nicene Fathers* Vol 9. Philip Schaff and Henry Wace, eds. (Peabody: Hendrickson Publishers, 1994), 15.

408 Ibid.

409 St. Gregory Palamas. *The Triads* (Mahwah: Paulist Press, 1983), 94.

410 Ibid., 95-96.

Even though we are not able to penetrate the essence of God, we are able to perceive and participate in the energies. This is because "[t]he divine intelligences move in a circular movement, united to the unoriginate and endless rays of the Beautiful and Good."[411] Since these "rays" are not the very essence of God, we are able to participate in them. But because they are fully God we, illumined by the Holy Spirit, are able to contemplate the eternal glory of God and know God. In any case, Christian teaching has always considered it possible for human beings to directly perceive or commune with the divine person of God.

Although an experience of God is possible, the contemporary context of disbelief and the general business or noisiness of life make the perception of God difficult at best. There seems to be a matrix-like[412] denial of the very realities we need to comprehend if we are going to experience the transcendent power of God. The "awareness or non-awareness of God within ordinary experience depends on the quality and depth of our ordinary experience in general."[413] It is here that late modern life works against us, since we are inclined to hide our refusal to ask the most important questions behind a veil of noisy, selfish activity. As Ronald Rolheiser puts it, "…narcissism, pragmatism and unbridled restlessness…severely limit what we are aware of in ordinary experience."[414] So how can we mediate or facilitate this experience within the framework of Christian witness?

First, this perception of the divine must become a regular part of the witness's own experience. I am convinced that until we as Christians regularly experience the presence of God as person we will have little chance of mediating the Gospel. How can we credibly invite others to a relationship we ourselves seldom if ever experience? How can we introduce a person, Christ, that we ourselves have not encountered? And this encounter has to take place in the personal, as well as the

---

411   Pseudo Dionysius as quoted by St. Gregory. *The Triads*, 99.

412   Here I am thinking of the film "The Matrix."

413   Rolheiser. *The Shattered Lantern*, 23-24.

414   Ibid., 22.

ecclesial realms. The words of St. Symeon the New Theologian[415] are instructive in this regard.

He insists these mysteries of divine being cannot be acquired by means of human reason, especially the exterior wisdom and book-learning of the theologians.

> We think we will receive the full knowledge of God's truth by means of worldly vision, and fancy that this mere reading of the God-inspired writings of the saints is to comprehend Orthodoxy, and that this is an exact and certain knowledge of the Holy Trinity.[416]

> He therefore shuts up the shameless and flapping mouths of those people who say and think that by exterior wisdom and book-learning they know the whole truth, know God Himself and possess knowledge of the mysteries hidden in God's Spirit.[417]

Yet, knowledge of God is possible, but as a gift of God to those who are worthy, who have purified themselves from the passions

> Master how could I describe the vision of your face?
> How could I ever speak of the ineffable contemplation of your beauty?
> How could mere words contain One whom the world could never contain?
> How could anyone ever express your love for mankind?
> I was sitting in the light of a lamp that was shining down on me,
> lighting up the darkness and shadows of the night,
> where I was sitting to all appearances busy in reading,

---

415 Symeon the New Theologian (949–1022) is one of three fathers with the title of Theologian (the others are St. John the Apostle and St. Gregory Nasianzen). Born in Galatia and educated at Constantinople, he became abbot of the monastery of St. Mamas.

416 St. Symeon the New Theologian. *On the Mystical Life. Ethical Discourses* Vol. 2 Translated by Alexander Golitzin. (Crestwood: St. Vladimir's Seminary Press, 1996), 113.

417 Ibid., 114.

but more engaged in meditating on the ideas and concepts.
While I was meditating on such things, master, suddenly you
   yourself appeared from on high,
far greater than the Sun itself,
What intoxication of the Light! What swirlings of fire!
What dancing of the flame of you and your glory within me,
wretched man that I am.[418]

St. Symeon goes on to emphasize the conscious, personal awareness of Christ and the Spirit. Faith involves more than a formal dogmatic orthodoxy, more than an observance of rules. It has to be experienced by each one of us, felt in a palpable and conscious way

Do not say, It is impossible to receive the Holy Spirit;
Do not say, It is impossible to be saved without him.
Do not say, then, that one can possess him without knowing it.
Do not say, God does not appear to men,
Do not say, Men do not see the divine light,
Or else, It is impossible in these present times.
This is a thing never impossible my friends,
But on the contrary altogether possible for those who so wish[419]

So it is possible to have an explicit awareness of the divine presence. Not just something of the past, as if the Holy Spirit had been withdrawn from the Church. If we do not experience God, it is because of the weakness of our faith, because we choose not to do the hard work of personal purification.

This direct personal experience of God is not "reserved for the elite and the holy, but is rather a grace which God gives to those who repent with genuine passion. The mystic, in his understanding, is thus the

---

418   St. Symeon "A Hymn of Divine Eros" quoted by John Anthony McGuckin. *Standing in God's Holy Fire* (Maryknoll: Orbis Books, 2001), 113-114.

419   St. Symeon *Hymn XXVII*, 125-132 quoted by Kallistos Ware in *The Study of Spirituality*. Cheslyn Jones, Geoffrey Wainwright, Edward Yarnold, eds. (New York: Oxford University Press, 1986), 238.

ordinary Christian who has supreme confidence to stand in God's presence… The mystic is not a stage of perfection distinct from the ordinary run of Christian life, but a full realization of the grace of God given to the broken of heart."[420]

Without this direct experience the individual is not in a position to instruct and or guide others.

> Do not try to be a mediator on behalf of others until you have yourself been filled with the Holy Spirit, until you have come to know and to win the friendship of the King of all with conscious awareness in your soul[421]

> Anyone who lacks this conscious awareness—even though he may be a bishop or patriarch—should not, and indeed cannot, exercise the ministry of confession.[422]

This vision of the spiritual path is deeply sacramental. For St. Symeon the reception of the Eucharist was the primary example of a direct, personal experience of God's sensible presence. It is a holistic absorption into the presence of Christ and a primary form of the divinization of the creature by the reception of the Godhead's own presence[423]

> My blood has been mingled with your blood,
>   And I come to the understanding
> Of how I have also been made one with your own Godhead.
> I have become your own most pure body;
> A member of that body scintillating and truly sanctified,
> Radiant, transparent, and light-emitting…
> What was I once? And what have I now become?
> How awesome to think of it.

---

420   McGunkin. *Standing*, 114.

421   Ware. *The Study*, 239.

422   Ibid.

423   McGunkin. *Standing*, 116-117.

Where shall I sit? What shall I touch?
Where shall I rest these limbs that have become your very own?
These members that are now so terrible and so mighty,
How shall I use them, to what work shall I now set them?[424]

While St. Symeon's idiom is rather mystical, his teaching is quit applicable to the late modern world. If we are going to proclaim the Gospel-as-Person, we are going to have to have an intimate knowledge of that person. What is needed, then, is a context of meditative abandon and of quiet contemplation. It is time for the witnessing community to reduce its level of activity, to concentrate on purifying the self, and on listening to God.

Second, in our personal encounter with the seeker we should actively anticipate and deliberately strive to provide opportunities for the experience of God as person. As we have seen, there has been a dramatic upsurge in interest in the spiritual in recent times. Many are reaching out to the transcendental horizon, aware of some unseen reality, seeking to integrate that into their lives. The witnessing community can tap into this wide spread interest and point the way. As the experience of Cornelius in Acts 10 shows, the seeker can experience God even before they put their faith in Christ. So part of the evangelistic task is to help the late modern individual move via self-transcendence toward an ultimate horizon of being.[425] There is no reason why we cannot begin to introduce spiritual pilgrims to spiritual realities even before they have fully accepted the invitation to life with Christ. If we create the proper context (quiet, purity of heart, spiritual disciplines), if we teach them to pray, to meditate, to contemplate Christ, we might well expect Him to make himself known to those who are honestly seeking him (Acts 10: 1-8).

---

424 St. Symeon. *Hymn* II, 13-29 quoted by McGunkin. *Standing*, 117.

425 In its most general sense, the term "spirituality" is used to identify the deep desire of the human being for personal integration of the unseen dimensions of reality and the every day markers of "sacred"—a movement via Self-transcendence toward the horizon of some ultimate concern. Downey, *Understanding*, 14.

The same thing can be said for the ecclesial context into which we seek to draw the inquirer. The activities of our churches, especially liturgy and worship, can be the quiet setting for a powerful encounter with Christ. Unfortunately, much of contemporary worship has become so noisy that it is difficult to hear the voice of God.[426] We seem to have imported the business of the world and have left ourselves scant possibilities for quiet, meditation, and contemplation. In some Churches the Sunday Liturgy is considered a spiritual event or happening. During the service ordinary time is suspended, the cares of the ordinary world are set aside, and one is said to be taken up into the divine realm, given a small foretaste of the Kingdom of Heaven. When the clergy and the faithful share this expectation, the environment is created in which the sacred becomes apparent, in which God makes himself known. Perhaps it was this collective ecclesial anticipation that caused the emissaries of Prince Vladimir of Kiev[427] worshiping at the great Cathedral in Constantinople to report, "we knew not whether we were in heaven or on earth. For on earth there is no such splendor or such beauty... We only know that God dwells there among men..."[428] This is what the Church has to offer those seeking God in Christ.

× × × × ×

When all is said and done, it is the great miracle of Pentecost that makes the witness of the Church possible and effective. Christ comes into the world as the Word sent and authenticated by the Father (Jn. 12:49, 14:10 14:24), but the application of that witness to the human situation is the work of the Holy Spirit.[429] The Spirit facilitates the mediation of the

---

426 For example, we seem to think that every aspect of worship, including silent prayer, has to be accompanied by background music. I'm not sure where this practice comes from, but it can be seen in a number of settings. For example, I have listened to a number of audio books and none of them have background music. However, I was unable to find an audio Bible that did not have that feature. In the end, the music just made it difficult to listen, to pray.

427 Vladimir the Great (958-1015) was the grand prince of Kiev who converted to Christianity in 988, and proceeded to baptize the whole Kievan population.

428 Sergei Bulgakov *Sophia. The Wisdom of God* (Hudson: Lindisfarne Press, 1993), xiii.

429 Otto Weber. *Grundlagen der Dogmatic* (Neukirchen-Vluyn: Neukirchener Verlag, 1962), 2: 276-279.

Word by validating the Word and the Christian witness thereof. We see this at the Baptism of Christ, where He is confirmed in His role by the descending Holy Spirit (Mt. 3:13, 4:1, Lk. 4:1). St. John tells us that the Spirit will remind us of everything Christ has taught (Jn. 14:26) and guide us into all truth (Jn. 16:13). St. Paul insists that it is the Spirit of God who validates that which has been received (tradition) as the true words of Christ Himself (1 Cor. 7:10).[430] It is this historical Word, which is given and, under the guidance of the Holy Spirit, passed on to and actualized in successive generations without alteration.

When the faithful, in obedience to Christ's command, proclaim the Gospel, what takes place is not simply a repetition, not just an application, but also a renewed stating of the Word, an actualization of that which is spoken, which, because of the Spirit's work, proves itself to be the word of God. Thus, it is the participation in the work of the Spirit of God, and not our linguistic skill, which enables us effectively to mediate what we ourselves have learned in our communion with the person of Christ.

---

430   Ibid., 2:278.

BIBLIOGRAPHY

Altshul, Paisius ed. *An Unbroken Circle. Linking Ancient African Christianity to the African*. St. Louis: Brotherhood of St. Moses the Black, 1997.

Alston, William. *Perceiving God. The Epistemology of Religious Experience*. Ithica: Cornell University Press, 1991.

Appadurai, Arjund. *Modernity at Large. Cultural Dimensions of Globalization*. Minneapolis: University of Minnesota Press, 1996.

Appiah, Kwame Anthony. *The Ethics of Individuality*. Princeton: Princeton University Press, 2005.

Asad, Talal. *Geneologies of Religion. Discipline and Reasons of Power in Christianity*. Baltimore: Johns Hopkins University Press, 1993.

Badiou, Alain. *Ethics. An Essay on the Understanding of Evil*. New York: Verso, 2001.

Barth, Fredrich. *Ethnic Group and Boundaries. The Social Organization of Culture Difference*. Prospect: H Waveland Press, 1969.

Barthes, Roland. *Mythology*. New York: Will and Wang, 1972.

Baudrillard, Jean. A. *Simulacra and Simulation*. Ann Arbor: University of Michigan Press, 1994.

Bebis, George S. *The Mind of the Fathers*. Brookline: Holy Cross Orthodox Press, 1994.

Berger, Peter. *The Homeless Mind*. New York: Vintage Books, 1974.

_____. *The Sacred Canopy*. New York: Anchor Books, 1969.

Berman, Morris. *The Twilight of American Culture*. New York: W. W. Norton, 2000.

Bhabha, Homi K. *The Location of Culture*. London: Routledge, 1994.

Billington, James H.. *The Icon and the Axe: An Interpretive History of Russian Culture*. NY: Vintage Books, 1966.

Blamires, Harry. *The Christian Mind*. London: S.C.K., 1966.

Bloom, Harold. *Omens of Millenium. The Gnosis of Angels, Dreams, and Resurrection*. New York: Riverhead, 1996.

Borradri, Giovanna. *Philosophy in a Time of Terror. Dialogues with Jurgen Habermans and Jacques Derrida*. Chicago: University of Chicago Press, 2003.

Bruce, Steve. *Religion in the Modern World*. Oxford: Oxford University Press, 1996.

Bulgakov, Sergius. *The Bride of the Lamb*. Grand Rapids: Eerdmans, 2002.

_____. *The Lamb of God*. Grand Rapids: Eerdmans, 2008.

_____. *Sophia. The Wisdom of God*. Hudson: Lindisfarne Press, 1993.

Chadwick, Owen. *The Secularization of the European Mind in the 19th Century*. Cambridge: Cambridge University Press, 1975.

Cohen, Anthony P. *Signifying Identities. Anthropological Perspectives on Boundaries and Contested Values*. New York: Routlege, 2000.

Cox, Harvey. *Fire from Heaven*. Cambridge: Da Capo Press, 1995.

Debord, Guy. *The Society of the Spectacle*. New York: Zone Books, 1995.

Derrida, Jacques. *Acts of Religion*. New York: Routlege, 2002.

_____. *Of Grammatology*. Baltimore: Johns Hopkins University Press, 1997.

_____. *The Gift of Death*. Chicago: University of Chicago Press, 1995.

_____. *Writing and Difference*. Chicago: University of Chicago Press, 1978.

Descartes, Rene. *Discourse on Method and Related Writings*. London: Penguin, 1999.

Donnan, Hastings and Thomas M. WilBorders. *Frontiers of Identity, Nation and State*. New York: Oxford, 1999.

Downey, Michael. *Understanding Christian Spirituality*. New York: Paulist Press, 1997.

Du Gay, Paul and Stuart Hall, ed. *Questions of Cultural Identity.* Thousand Oaks: Sage Publications, 1996.

Eagleton, Terry. *The Idea of Culture.* Oxford: Blackwell, 2000.

_____. *Ideology. An Introduction.* London: Verso, 1991.

_____. *The Illusions of Postmodernism.* Oxford: Blackwell, 1996.

Ebaugh, Helen Rose, and Janez Saltzman Chafetz. *Religion And The New Immigrants: Continuities And Adaptations In Immigrant Congregations.* Walnut Creek, CA: Altamira, 2000.

Ecco, Umberto. *Kant and the Platypus.* San Diego: Harcourt, 1999.

_____. *The Limits of Interpretation.* Bloomington: Indiana University Press, 1994.

Edwards, Denis. *Human Experience of God.* New York: Paulist Press, 1993.

Ellul, Jacques. *The Technological Society.* New York: Vintage Books, 1964.

Florensky, Pavel. *Pillar and Ground of Truth.* Princeton: Princeton University Press, 1997.

Foucault, Michel. *The Archeology of Knowledge.* New York: Pantheon Books, 1972.

_____. *The History of Sexuality.* New York: Vintage Books, 1990.

_____. *The Order of Things. An Archaeology of the Human Sciences.* New York: Vintage Books, 1994.

Fraser, Jill Andresky. *White Collar Sweatshop. The Deterioration of Work and Its Rewards in Corporate America.* New York: W. W. Norton, 2001.

Gay, Peter. *The Enlightenment. The Rise of Modern Paganism.* New York: Norton, 1966.

_____. *The Enlightenment. The Science of Freedom.* New York: Norton, 1967.

Giddens, Anthony. *The Consequences of Modernity.* Stanford: Stanford University Press, 1990.

_____. *Modernity and Self-Identity. Self and Society in the Late Modern Age.* Stanford: Stanford University Press, 1991.

Gillespie, Michael Allen. *The Theological Origins of Modernity.* Chicago : University of Chicago Press, 2008.

Gleick, James. *Faster. The Acceleration of Just about Everything.* New York : Pantheon Books, 1999.

Gutmann, Amy. *Multiculturalism.* Princeton: Princeton University Press, 1994.

Habermas, Jürgen. *Moral Consciousness and Communicative Action.* Cambridge: MIT Press, 1999.

_____. *The Structural Transformation of the Public Sphere.* Cambridge: MIT Press, 1991.

Hallick, Mary Paloumpis. *The Treasured Traditions and Customs of the Orthodox Churches.* Minneapolis: Light and Life, 2001.

Hannerz, Ulf ed. *Transnational Connections.* New York: Routledge, 1996.

Harpham, Geoffrey Galt. *Language Alone: The Critical Fetisch of Modernity.* New York: Routledge, 2002.

Hart, David Bently. *The Beauty of the Infinite. The Aesthetics of Christian Truth.* Grand Rapids: Eerdmans, 2003.

Harvey, David. *The Condition of Modernity.* Cambridge: Blackwell, 1990.

Hauerwas, Stanley. *Dispatches from the Front. Theological Engagements with the Secular.* Durham: Duke University Press, 1994.

Hebdige, Dick. *Subculture. The Meaning of Style.* New York: Routledge, 1979.

Heidegger, Martin. *Being and Time.* Albany: State University of New York, 1996.

Hendley, Stephen. *From Communicative Action to the Face of the Other.* Lanham: Lexington Books, 2000.

Henry, Paget. *Calliban's Reason.* New York: Routledge, 2000.

Herzfeld, Michael. *Cultural Intimacy. Social Poetics in the Nation-State.* New York: Routledge, 1997.

Hord, Fred Lee and J. S. Lee. *I Am Because We Are.* Amherst: University of Massachussets Press, 1995.

Hume, David. *Dialogues Concerning Natural Religion.* London: Penguin Books, 1990.

Jacobson, David. *Place and Belonging in America*. Baltimore: Johns Hopkins University Press, 2002.

Kant, Imanuel. *What is Enlightenment?* In *Perpetual Peace and Other Essays*. Trans. Ted Humphrey. Indianapolis: Hackett Publishing Company, 1983.

Kunkelman, Gary A. *The Religion Of Ethnicity. Belief And Belonging In A Greek-American Community*. New York: Garland Publishing, 1990.

Lacan, Jacques. *The Ethics of Psychoanalysis*. London: Routlege, 1992.

_____. *The Language of the Self. The Function of Language in Psychoanalysis*. Baltimore: The Johns Hopkins University Press, 1968.

Leach William. *Land of Desire. Merchants, Power, and the Rise of a New American Culture*. New York: Vintage Books, 1994.

Lee, Philip J. *The Protestant Gnostics*. New York: Oxford University Press, 1987.

Levinas, Emmanuel. *Otherwise Than Being: Or Beyond Essence*. Pittsburgh: Duquesne University Press, 1998.

_____. *Totality and Infinity*. Pittsburg: Duquesne University Press, 1969.

_____. *Ethics and Infinity: Conversations With Philippe Nemo*. Pittsburg: Duquesne University Press, 1985.

Lyotard, Jean-Francois. *The Postmodern Condition: A Report on Knowledge*. Minneapolis: University of Minnesota Press, 1984.

_____. *Postmodern Fables*. Minneapolis: University of Minnesota Press, 19 University of Minnesota Press, 1997.

MacIntyre, Alasdair. *After Virtue What. A Study in Moral Theory*. Notre Dame: University of Notre Dame Press: 1981.

Mantzaridis, Georgios, I. The Deification of Man. Crestwood: St. Vladimir's Seminary Press, 1984.

Marty, Martin E. *A Nation of Behavers*. Chicago: University of Chicago Press, 1976.

_____. *Three Paths to the Secular*. N.Y.: Harper and Row, 1969.

_____. *Pilgrims in Their Own Land. 500 Years of Religion in America*. New York: Penguin, 1984.

McGuckin, John Anthony. *Standing in God's Holy Fire*. Maryknoll: Orbis Books, 2001.

Merleau-Ponty, Maurice. *Phenomenology of Perception*. London: Routledge, 1945

Milbank, *Theology and Social Theory. Beyond Secular Reason*. Cambridge: Blackwell, 1993.

Miller, Stephen. *Conversation. A History of a Declining Art*. New Haven: Yale University Press, 2006.

Murdoch, Iris. *The Sovereignty of Good*. London: Routledge, 1970.

Nellas, Panayiotis. *Deification in Christ. The Nature of the Human Person*. Crestwood: St. Vladimir's Seminary Press, 1997.

Newbigin, Lesslie. *The Gospel in a Pluralist Society*. Grand Rapids: Eerdmans, 1989.

Nitzsche, Frederich. *On the Geneology of Morals. Ecce Homo*. New York: Vintage Books, 1989.

Oleska, Michael. *Alaskan Spirituality and Orthodox Alaska*. Crestwood: St. Vladimir's Seminary Press, 1992.

Otto, Rudolf. *The Idea of the Holy*. London: Oxford University Press, 1923.

Pannenberg, Wolfhardt. *Theology and the Philosophy of Science*. Philadelphia: Westminster Press, 1976.

Poole, Ross. *Nation and Identity*. New York: Routledge, 1999.

Putnam Robert D. *Bowling Alone. The Collapse and Revival of American Community*. New York: Simon and Schuster, 2000.

Rahner Karl. *The Practice of Faith*. New York: Crossroad, 1984.

Rolheiser Ronald. *The Shattered Lantern*. New York: Crossroad Publishing, 2001.

Rommen, Edward. *Namenschristentum*. Bad Liebenzell: Verlag der Liebenzeller Mission, 1982.

_____. *Die Notwendigkeit der Umkehr*. Giessen: Brunnen Verlag, 1994.

Rommen, Timothy. *Mek Some Noise: Gospel Music and the Ethics of Style in Trinidad*. Berkeley: University of California Press, 2007.

Rorty, Richard. *Contingency, Irony, and Solidarity.* Cambridge: Cambridge University Press, 1989.

_____. *Philosophy and the Mirror of Nature.* Princeton: Princeton University Press, 1979.

Seigel, Jerrold E. *The Idea of the Self.* Cambridge: Cambridge University Press, 2005.

Senge, Peter. *The Fifth Discipline.* New York: Doubleday, 1990.

Scouteris, Constantine B. *Ecclesial Being.* South Caanan Mt Tabor Publishing, 2005

St. Symeon the New Theologian. *On the Mystical Life. Ethical Discourses.* Vol. 2 Translated by Alexander Golitzin. Crestwood: St. Vladimir's Seminary Press, 1996.

St. Theophan the Recluse. *The Spiritual Life and How to be Attuned to It.* Forestville: St. Herman of Alaska Brotherhood, 2000.

Staniloae, Dumitru. *The Experience of God. Orthodox Dogmatic Theology. Vol. 2 The World: Creation and Deification.* Brookline: Holy Cross Orthodox Press, 2000.

Stark, Rodney and Roger Finke. *Acts of Faith. Explaining the Human Side of Religion.* Berkeley: University of California Press, 2000.

Stavropoulos, Archimandrite Christoforos. *Partakers of Divine Nature.* Minneapolis, MN: Light and Life Publishing Company, 1976

Taussig, Michael. *Mimesis and Alterity. A Particular History of the Senses.* London: Routledge, 1993.

Taylor, Charles. *A Secular Age.* Cambridge, MA: The Belknap Press of Harvard University Press, 2007.

_____. *Modern Social Imaginaries.* Durham: Duke University Press, 2004.

_____. *Sources of the Self. The Making of the Modern Identity.* Cambridge: Harvard University Press, 1989.

Thunberg, Lars. *Microcosm and Mediator: The Theological Anthropology of St. Maximus the Confessor.* Chicago: Open Court, 1995.

Weber, Max. *The Protestant Ethic and the Spirit of Capitalism.* N.Y.: Charles Scribner, 1958.

Weber, Otto. *Grundlagen der Dogmatic.* Neukirchen-Vluyn: Neukirchener Verlag, 1962.

Wilson, Edward O. *Concilience. The Unity of Knowledge.* New York: Vintage Books, 1999.

Wind, James P. and James W. Lewis. *American Congregations.* Chicago: University of Chicago Press, 1994.

Wolfe, Alan. *The Transformation of American Religion. How We Actully Live Our Faith.* New York: Free Press, 2003.

Yammoulatos, Archbishop Anastasios. *Facing the World. Orthodox Christian Essays on Global Concerns.* Crestwood: St. Vladimir's Seminary Press, 2003.

Zizek, Slavoj. *The Fragile Absolute or why is the Christian legacy worth fighting for?* New York: Verso, 2000.

_____. *Welcome to the Desert of the Real.* New York: Verso, 2002.

Zizioulas, John D. *Being as Communion.* Crestwood: St. Vladimir's Seminary Press, 1997.

Zupancic, Alenka. *Ethics of the Real.* London: Verso, 2000.

INDEX

Numbers

P